The Quick, the Dead
and the Revived

ALSO BY JOSEPH MADDREY
AND FROM MCFARLAND

*The Making of T.S. Eliot:
A Study of the Literary Influences* (2009)

*Nightmares in Red, White and Blue:
The Evolution of the American Horror Film* (2004)

The Quick, the Dead and the Revived
The Many Lives of the Western Film

JOSEPH MADDREY

McFarland & Company, Inc., Publishers
Jefferson, North Carolina

LIBRARY OF CONGRESS CATALOGUING-IN-PUBLICATION DATA

Names: Maddrey, Joseph, 1979– author.
Title: The quick, the dead and the revived : the many lives of the western film / Joseph Maddrey.
Description: Jefferson, North Carolina : McFarland & Company, Inc., Publishers, 2016 | Includes bibliographical references and index.
Identifiers: LCCN 2016021549 | ISBN 9781476665511 (softcover : acid free paper) ∞
Subjects: LCSH: Western films—United States—History and criticism. | West (U.S.)—In motion pictures.
Classification: LCC PN1995.9.W4 M23 2016 | DDC 791.43/65878—dc23
LC record available at https://lccn.loc.gov/2016021549

BRITISH LIBRARY CATALOGUING DATA ARE AVAILABLE

**ISBN (print) 978-1-4766-6551-1
ISBN (ebook) 978-1-4766-2549-2**

© 2016 Joseph Maddrey. All rights reserved

No part of this book may be reproduced or transmitted in any form or by any means, electronic or mechanical, including photocopying or recording, or by any information storage and retrieval system, without permission in writing from the publisher.

Front cover images © 2016 iStock

Printed in the United States of America

*McFarland & Company, Inc., Publishers
Box 611, Jefferson, North Carolina 28640*
www.mcfarlandpub.com

Table of Contents

Acknowledgments vi

Preface 1

Introduction: Oaters 4

    I. Year of the Gun (1939) 9

   II. Westerners at War (1940–1946) 21

  III. Blood on the Moon (1947–1949) 32

  IV. High Noon (1950–1956) 44

    V. The Masculine Mystique (1950–1959) 57

  VI. The Lost Cowboys (1955–1959) 71

 VII. The New Frontier (1960–1965) 82

VIII. Blood Money (1964–1968) 95

  IX. Mud and Rags (1967–1973) 107

    X. Death Wish (1971–1980) 121

  XI. Back to the Future (1977–1988) 133

 XII. Young Guns (1988–2001) 144

XIII. Fever Dream (2002–2010) 155

Afterword: Destiny or Dust? 167

Appendix: Filming Locations 169

Chapter Notes 185

Bibliography 188

Index 195

Acknowledgments

I am grateful to several friends and film enthusiasts who read this book in manuscript form and offered feedback. Tim Ferrante, Dennis Fischer, Robert F. Geary, Robert V. Hoskins, Tom Maddrey and James L. Ruff helped me avoid some embarrassing mistakes. Any remaining mistakes are mine alone.

Also, I owe endless thanks to my wife Liza—for exploring the American West with me, one filming location at a time.

Preface

Filmmaker John Ford once said, "The fathers enjoy westerns and the children give them an excuse to go."[1] That's as good a place to start as any. In 1992, my father took me to the theater to see Clint Eastwood's *Unforgiven*. I was a thirteen-year-old Virginia native who had never been on a horse and never traveled west of the Mississippi River. To be blunt: I had no interest in westerns. I was much more interested in contemporary action, science fiction and horror movies—and wholly ignorant of the fact that those genres were, in many ways, inheritors of the great western tradition. I went because my dad promised it would be a good movie. He was not wrong.

Eastwood's film, followed by the one-two punch of *Tombstone* (1993) and *Wyatt Earp* (1994), piqued my curiosity about the western genre, but what really changed the landscape for me was a film studies course I took in college with Shakespeare scholar Ralph A. Cohen. That class introduced me to the work of John Ford, beginning with *My Darling Clementine* (1946) and *The Searchers* (1956). I didn't expect to like these "classic" westerns, but I was instantly captivated by their humanism and majesty. After that I was hooked. I started programming my VCR to record old westerns on cable TV and, in due course, discovered the films of Howard Hawks, Anthony Mann, Budd Boetticher and Sergio Leone. I knew that I was still barely scratching the surface, but at that point my fascination with westerns was overwhelmed by a much bigger obsession with horror movies—an obsession that led to my first book, *Nightmares in Red, White and Blue* (McFarland, 2004).

I came back around to westerns a few years later, when my future wife and I moved to California. As we were driving across the country, I insisted that we take a detour through Monument Valley, the iconic setting of John Ford's most memorable westerns. It was on that trip that the Hollywood myths of the American West became real for me. During the following years, as my wife and I explored our new home in southern California, that world was constantly expanding. I wandered through Corriganville and the Iverson Ranch on the edge of L.A.'s Simi Valley—breeding grounds of countless TV westerns and B movies of the 1950s and 1960s. I went hiking at Vasquez Rocks and Red Rock Canyon, where many of the bigger budget westerns of the same era were shot. I fell in love with the Alabama Hills in Lone Pine, a cowboy movie Mecca, and the ghost town of Bodie, a snapshot of late 19th century frontier life in "arrested decay." I traveled further and further afield, into film-friendly landscapes in Utah, New Mexico, and Arizona. I also discovered Eddie Brandt's Saturday Matinee, a video store in North Hollywood with a staggeringly comprehensive collection of western films. As I obsessively made my way through a very long list of must-see titles, an idea of western films as a continuous historical narrative began to take shape in my mind.

I didn't go looking for 19th century U.S. history in Hollywood westerns. I don't think anyone does. Most viewers understand that filmmakers are generally more interested in dramatic storytelling than in historical accuracy; America's past is merely grist for the mill. That said, filmmakers often cannot help reflecting the times and places in which they make their films. All serious stories are, at least in part, products of time-bound worldviews. In much the way that Hollywood horror films reflect the dominant cultural anxieties of twentieth century America, westerns offer insight into the changing ideologies of the 20th and early 21st century America. By constantly rewriting history for successive generations of moviegoers, filmmakers have depicted the nation's ceaseless mental migration—not just into the West, but into the future.

Heroic cowboys have, of course, been with us since the early days of cinema. Hundreds of films produced in Hollywood during the silent era and throughout the 1930s created a popular misconception of westerns as simple-minded morality plays about Good and Evil. B westerns continued to carry on that tradition, but most film historians agree that things became more complicated in 1939, when a series of high-profile "outdoor dramas" effectively renovated the genre. From this point forward, there was no denying the cultural significance of westerns.

The major western films of the ensuing years reflect the changing values of twentieth century Americans, by presenting major political issues from a variety of perspectives. Building on philosophical and aesthetic innovations of postwar film noir, the genre reached the height of its popularity in the 1950s, when screen cowboys became a vital symbol of America itself. As such they carried the weight of the world on their shoulders, and were destined for a fall. The modern-day myth struggled mightily amidst forces of cultural change in the 1960s, then became nearly obsolete in the early 1970s. That's where most critical studies of the genre stop ... but not this one, because the western refused to die. Throughout the 1970s and 1980s, the familiar tropes and themes became subliminal forces in popular action, science fiction and horror films, setting the stage for a minor western revival in the 1990s, and a period of reconsideration and reinvention in the early 21st century.

Despite this long and persistent history, one question looms in every single analysis of the genre: *Is the western dead?* The question has dogged cinematic cowboys for almost as long as they've been around. It is a reasonable question, since the main subject of the genre is a bygone era of American history, but it raises another question: *What do we mean by "western"?* For me, the genre—or at least the appeal of the genre—can be summed up in one word: "Simplicity." I love the economical storytelling of great westerns ("long on action and short on dialogue," as Ford prescribed), and the chance to escape into an alternate reality where life has fewer distractions, and where every thought and deed counts for something. In such a simplified state of existence, human beings and their motivations become very clear and distinct. I don't mean that thoughts and actions necessarily become simple, only that we see everything more clearly—like riders on an open prairie.

The main reason westerns often seem passé is that they throw conflicts and characters into stark relief. At first glance, these are straightforward narratives about heroes and villains, Good and Evil. What I have noticed, however, is that the great westerns rarely offer a predetermined reality. The films express a longing for simple, timeless truths, but those truths become real only when the characters decide to *fight* for them. The great westerns thus pose significant questions about life in a culture that, more than one hundred years after the closing of the western frontier, continues to celebrate violence as a civilizing force. In westerns, one rugged individual must answer for all of us: *What's worth fighting for? How should we fight?* And, perhaps most importantly, *Where are we headed if the fighting continues indefinitely?* These questions are as relevant as ever, and so are the films that ask them.

Introduction: Oaters

> *To use the political terminology of the present day, the whole western movement of our people was simply the most vital part of that great movement of expansion which has been the central and all-important feature of our history—a feature far more important than any other since we became a nation, save only the preservation of the Union itself. It was expansion which made us a great power.*
>
> —Theodore Roosevelt, *The Winning of the West* (1900)

The dominant American ideology of the late 1800s—and the ideology behind most of the popular myths and legends of the Old West—was Manifest Destiny, a belief that settlers from the eastern United States had a sacred duty to expand the nation's borders all the way to the Pacific Ocean. In the aftermath of the Civil War, this belief helped to unite the country and renew the spirits of its people. As Manifest Destiny became the sustaining national myth, cowboys and gunslingers became national symbols. Popular western fiction, often masquerading as non-fiction, mined those symbols for everything they were worth, leading eventually to the creation of iconic screen cowboys like William S. Hart, Tom Mix, Gary Cooper and John Wayne.

The first story-driven western film was Edwin S. Porter's *The Great Train Robbery* (1903), which appeared at a time when the real American West was still relatively wild. Porter's film, however, was shot in West Orange, New Jersey, far from the action. D.W. Griffith became the first director to make a film in Hollywood, California; his short film *In Old California* (1910) helped to pave the way for Cecil B. DeMille's famous western *The Squaw Man* (1914), the first feature-length film made in Hollywood.

In the intervening years, G.M. "Broncho Billy" Anderson—a bit player in *The Great Train Robbery*—had made roughly four hundred one-reel westerns, and become America's reigning cowboy star. By 1914, his competitors were also producing westerns at such an overwhelming rate that when a middle-aged actor named William S. Hart arrived in Hollywood to ride the cinematic range, producer Thomas Ince turned him away, believing that the market was oversaturated. Hart, who had a deep and abiding love for the genre, persevered and made his first western for Ince the following year. The actor became an overnight sensation, and remained the most popular screen westerner for several years. So it was that the genre survived the first anticipations of its death.

Hart's overwhelming popularity was related to his perceived authenticity as a westerner. The actor had spent a significant part of his childhood in the Indian Territories, where he learned to speak the native dialects. During that time he witnessed at least one deadly shootout. In his 1929 biography, *My Life East and West*, Hart remembers:

> I saw two men killed at Sioux City. It was very early morning. My father was going to see about buying our horses. Some men half-rushed and half-stumbled out of a saloon, shooting. My father gripped my shoulder and said, "Stand still." It was a sheriff against two gambler gun-men and the sheriff got them both, although he himself was mortally wounded. My father had seen in a flash that they were all gunmen, so he told me to stand still, although we were right in a possible line of fire. If near a gun-fight and the weapons are wielded by amateurs, run for your life; if professionals are handling the trigger, *stand still*—they know where they are shooting.[1]

Later, at nearby Fort Randall in the Dakota territories during the Black Hills gold rush, the young man encountered a band of Indian raiders:

> Our visitors were in full war-paint. I had seen Indians in war-paint before, and I have seen many since, but I have never seen Indians in full war-paint but once in my life, and they were right in front of us right there on those Dakota prairies. [...] They were probably one of the marauding war-parties that had left their reservation and were on the way to attack any incoming white people trying to locate in the Black Hills. There is no question but what they would have stolen our stock and outfit and if we had resisted they would have killed us—they were out for that purpose.[2]

Hart asserts that he was unafraid, accepting the specter of violence as a natural part of life in the West, and claiming that he felt "at home" in his new surroundings in a way that many adults from back east could not. His family eventually returned to New York, where the young man attended school and took up acting, but he never forgot what he had seen, and he secretly yearned to return to the West. One day, after viewing a cheap western one-reeler starring an inept would-be cowboy, he saw his opportunity.

Between 1914 and 1925, movie-going audiences praised Hart's portrayal of a tough, no-nonsense Man of the West in films like *Hell's Hinges* (1916), *The Square Deal Man* (1917), *Square Deal Sanderson* (1919), *The Toll Gate* (1920), *Wild Bill Hickok* (1923) and *Tumbleweeds* (1925). Legendary Dodge City marshal Bat Masterson, who saw Hart perform in a Broadway adaptation of *The Barrier*, opined that "any one familiar with the character of the cool, calculating, and daring desperado, whose presence was a part of frontier life a generation ago, will instantly recognize in Mr. Hart a true type of that reckless nomad who flourished on the border when the six-shooter was the final arbiter of all disputes between man and man."[3] Hart himself explained the mythic persona of the westerner as follows: "The bigness of the West makes men quiet; they seldom talk unless they have something to say. The altitude clarifies their brains and gives them nerves of steel.... Once a man crossed the Missouri, the West got into his blood. All men were atoms in building an empire."[4]

With this passage, Hart depicts American pioneers as a hardy and determined lot, and also as members of a community, united by a shared vision. Hollywood appropriated the vision, and no doubt that's why movies got into Hart's blood in the same way as the West. His films expressed the hopes and dreams of a youthful nation; he was part of something bigger than one man's legacy. For Hollywood, these were the first steps in a commercial "winning of the West."

Hart's box-office reign only lasted a few years. In 1920, the much more animated Tom Mix assumed the mantle of America's "King of the Cowboys." According to *The West of Yesterday*, a pseudo-biography distributed by the Los Angeles Times-Mirror Press in 1923, Mix was an equally authentic westerner:

> His claim does not have its foundation in anything he may have done in the movies, daring and dangerous as his admirers know these to have been, but in something further back, more fundamental, nearer to the soil. It is founded in the fact that he himself is a native-born son of the great southwest; that he was raised among its horses and cattle and cowboys; that he lived their life and shared their difficulties and dangers, as

well as their mirth and their merrymaking; and that he too was a pioneer of the pioneers, an enforcement officer, a sheriff, a deputy U.S. marshal, a Texas Ranger, a soldier and a man.[5]

The truth is that Tom Mix was born and raised in Pennsylvania, and according to contemporary historians, his law enforcement career was grossly exaggerated.[6] A consummate actor, Mix nevertheless understood from a very young age what his destiny would be. When he was ten years old, he saw Buffalo Bill's Wild West Show at the Clearfield Fairgrounds in Pennsylvania, and he resolved to become a sheriff on the western frontier. By the 1920s, Mix's western persona was so popular that Fox studios built an elaborate western town set on the corner of Glendale Boulevard and Silver Lake Boulevard in Los Angeles and christened it "Mixville" in honor of their biggest star.

The popularity of the Hollywood western continued to grow. New screen cowboys like Harry Carey and Hoot Gibson emerged, and western films gradually became more elaborate and expansive. Historians cite *The Covered Wagon* (1923) as the first epic western, a grand-scale celebration of America's collective pioneer spirit, with John Ford's *The Iron Horse* (1924) following close behind. *In Old Arizona* (1929), a film that literally cost actor/director Raoul Walsh an eye, is usually recognized as the first sound western, followed by Victor Fleming's *The Virginian* (1929), which made a star of leading man Gary Cooper. Walsh went on to direct *The Big Trail* (1930), one of the first widescreen westerns and the first film to cast actor John Wayne in a starring role. Cooper and Wayne assumed the mantles of William S. Hart and Tom Mix for the 1930s and beyond.

Cooper, the son of a prominent frontier lawyer who grew up on a large ranch in Montana, arrived in Hollywood in 1925. Although he had aspirations to be a professional artist, he took odd jobs as a background extra and stunt performer in western serials. Within a year he was cast in the role of a heroic cowboy in *The Winning of Barbara Worth*, and his performance earned him a long-term contract at Paramount. After a few more supporting bits in high-profile projects, he landed the lead role in *The Virginian*, and his aw-shucks delivery of one memorable line ("If you want to call me that, *smile!*") cemented his future as a western star. The actor headlined three more oaters—*The Texan* (1930), *The Spoilers* (1930), and *Fighting Caravans* (1931)—before shifting his focus to romantic comedies and dramas for several years. When he returned to the genre, playing Wild Bill Hickok in Cecil B. DeMille's lavish production *The Plainsman* (1936), he was one of the most popular actors in Hollywood.

In his 1926 novel *Wild Bill Hickok: Prince of the Pistoleers*, Frank Jenners Wilstach presented the iconic western gunslinger as a hero beyond reproach, writing:

"Resting on the Rock of Gibraltar": Gary Cooper and Jean Arthur in *The Plainsman* (1936, Paramount).

> If greatness consists of an unswerving courage, an unquestioned honesty, a gentle and generous spirit, as well as a willingness at all times to endanger one's life for the sake of public order or to save a friend, then Wild Bill Hickok has a considerable claim to fame. He was, in his time and in his environment, this country's greatest peace officer. He stood for law and order when there was neither. And as a pistoleer in the presence of bad men running wild, he was the *ne plus ultra perfecto*.[7]

Moviegoers in the 1930s were just as impressed with Cooper, who effortlessly embodied the heroic western lawman that William S. Hart had popularized. In his 1959 autobiography, Cecil B. DeMille reflected:

> I need hardly describe to anyone who ever goes to the movies that combination of assured authority and apparently effortless ease of manner which makes Gary Cooper so distinguished a performer. Gary is an embodiment of the old saying that art consists in concealing its own artfulness. After seeing him on the screen, any young man might say, "Shucks, I could do that." The young man would be wrong. Gary Cooper, off screen as well as on, is an affable, modest American gentleman; but he is also an accomplished artist in his profession.[8]

Jean Arthur, Cooper's co-star in *The Plainsman*, was more succinct. Of working with Cooper, she said simply, "You feel like you're resting on the Rock of Gibraltar."[9]

John Wayne traveled a longer and tougher road to stardom. Raised in Glendale, California, he attended the University of Southern California on a football scholarship, and turned his attention to the film industry after an injury ended his football career. Wayne later told Peter Bogdanovich that he was hired for his first job, in the props department at Fox studios, because he got Tom Mix a box seat for USC football games.[10] Tales of his first encounter with director John Ford, who would become a lifelong mentor, are legendary. Wayne remembered their meeting on the set of *Mother Machree* (1928) as follows:

> [Ford] said, "You're a football player, aren't you?" I said, "Yes," and he said, "Do you think you could block me?" and I said, "Yes." So he said, "Get down on your three-point stance," which is where you have one hand on the ground and the other in front of you. So I got down, and he kicked my hand away, and I went facedown in the dirt. Ford and everyone just laughed, but I was steaming mad. I said, "I'd like to try that again," so I got down, but this time, I didn't wait for him to make a move. I just suddenly drove into him and sent him flying over tables and chairs—and there was a horrified silence from everybody who obviously thought, "That guy won't work here again." But Pappy just laughed and said, "You'll do all right."[11]

Ford and Wayne became close friends, but the actor's first big break came courtesy of Raoul Walsh, who cast him in the lead role in *The Big Trail*.

Unfortunately for Wayne, *The Big Trail* was a commercial failure, and the young actor was consequently relegated to low-budget B westerns and serials for the rest of the decade. Year after year, he struggled to chisel out a unique screen persona, as he explained in later years:

> I made up my mind that I was going to play a real man to the best of my ability. I felt many of the western stars of the twenties and thirties were too goddamn perfect. They never drank nor smoked. They never wanted to go to bed with a beautiful girl. They never had a fight. A heavy might throw a chair at them, and they just looked surprised and didn't fight in this spirit. They were too goddamn sweet and pure to be dirty fighters. Well, I wanted to be a dirty fighter if that was the only way to fight back. If somebody throws a chair at you, hell, you pick up a chair and belt him right back. I was trying to play a man who gets dirty, who sweats sometimes, who enjoys really kissing a gal he likes, who gets angry, who fights clean whenever possible but will fight dirty if he has to. You could say, I made the western hero a roughneck.[12]

Wayne certainly helped to reinvent the western hero for a more sophisticated audience in more uncertain times, but his return to big-budget films was a long time coming. The same was true for the western genre in general.

In 1931, *Cimarron*—a grandiose depiction of the Oklahoma Land Rush of 1889 starring Richard Dix as an adventurous lawyer and newspaperman—took home the Academy Award for Best Picture, but the film's success was haunted gold for the genre. Instead of inspiring more prestige westerns, *Cimarron*'s success spurred the creation of countless low-budget westerns. Throughout the Great Depression, formulaic oaters flooded theaters. Work was steady, if seldom inspired, for recognizable cowboys like Wayne, Hoot Gibson, George O'Brien, Ken Maynard, Buck Jones, Tom Keene, Bob Steele, Tim McCoy, and Johnny Mack Brown. The biggest success story of the decade was Gene Autry, the singing cowboy who rose to fame as the star of *Tumbling Tumbleweeds* (1935) and the sci-fi/western serial *The Phantom Empire* (1935). Autry's flamboyant persona, somewhat reminiscent of Tom Mix, turned the genre toward more lighthearted fantasy. A few years later, Roy Rogers captured a similar tone in his breakout film *Under Western Stars* (1938). For the next two decades, these two singing cowboys remained highly bankable stars.

The Western hero as roughneck: John Wayne with Marguerite Churchill in *The Big Trail* **(1930, Fox).**

Running parallel to their success story was the rise of the roughneck hero and the birth of a more nuanced myth of the American West.

CHAPTER I

Year of the Gun
(1939)

> *Anyone speculating on our great migration westward is struck with the human parallel between the driving force behind that migration and the driving force behind the great social exploration we are carrying on today. [...] Today, under new conditions, a whole nation, the critical thirteen states and all the West and South that has grown out of them, is on a mental migration, dissatisfied with old conditions, seeking like the little band that came to Marietta to create new conditions of security.*
>
> —Franklin D. Roosevelt, dedication of a memorial to the Northwest Territory, July 8, 1938

Nineteen thirty-nine was a renaissance year for Hollywood, marking the release of classics like *Gone with the Wind*, *The Wizard of Oz*, *Mr. Smith Goes to Washington*, *Gunga Din*, and *Ninotchka*. It was also a renaissance year for westerns—a revival or a coming-of-age, depending on whom you ask. A healthy crop of ambitious "outdoor dramas" signaled the rise of the prestigious big-budget western. Chief among these new westerns were Paramount's old-fashioned historical epic *Union Pacific*, Warner Bros.' jaunty spectacle film *Dodge City*, 20th Century–Fox's populist outlaw movie *Jesse James*, John Ford's legend-making *Stagecoach,* and Universal's bawdy comedy *Destry Rides Again*. Each film is vaguely political, examining the values of a nation that was slowly recovering from the woes of the Great Depression and considering its supranational responsibilities on the brink of World War II.

At the outset, the only major Hollywood studio that had much experience with the western genre was Paramount, and their films tended to be very traditional and politically conservative. In addition to producer Harry Sherman's popular *Hopalong Cassidy* film series (1935–1941), the studio released a string of successful Zane Grey adaptations in the 1930s—including ten films with Randolph Scott, a Southern charmer who got his big break as Gary Cooper's dialogue coach on *The Virginian* and went on to become a conservative icon in his own right. In the later half of the decade, the studio boasted Cooper in Cecil B. DeMille's *The Plainsman* (1936) and rising star Joel McCrea in *Wells Fargo* (1937). Both films were commercial successes, prompting the studio to team DeMille and McCrea in their biggest western epic to date.

The origins of *Union Pacific* date back to June 1938, when Paramount acquired the rights to Ernest Haycox's 1936 novel *Trouble Shooter*. Haycox's story revolves around a gunman named Frank Peace, who is hired to maintain order among Irish immigrants laying track for the Union Pacific railroad. Peace is a reckless orphan who yearns for "permanence and something in life that was serene," but who senses that his job will kill him first.[1] He eventually finds himself at the mercy of a shadowy eastern businessman named Campeaux, who wants to halt the railroad so that he can build a rowdy cow-town at the end of the line. In the end, the heroic trouble shooter squares off against Campeaux's hired gun Al Brett, before abandoning his job to settle down with Nan, a pioneer woman who is as tough and free-spirited as he is.

Although it is not an overtly political novel, *Trouble Shooter* reveals the author's conservative politics, as well as the concerns of many Republicans in the 1930s. In the beginning, a minor character in the novel complains that the "country's no damned good now" because the railroad—a symbol of expanding government influence and interference—is ruining the West.[2] Around the time he wrote the novel, Haycox made comparable statements about Democratic President Franklin D. Roosevelt's New Deal programs, which expanded the size and reach of the U.S. government. He suggested that the New Deal was a threat to individual freedoms: "Simply put, it is the old, old question of how far this government or any government shall reach down into the lives of citizens, how far it shall extend its arm through the shop door and the home door, how far it shall command people to obey its decrees, how far it shall depart from our original concept of democracy as expressed in the old town meeting."[3] Years later, the writer clarified his position, suggesting that big business—rather than big government—might be the real problem:

> I suppose I am some sort of Jeffersonian reactionary. I fear and distrust bigness in anything, government not excepted; and I have a great skepticism concerning the infallibility of my masters. Yet—and now we get to the root of the matter—I also know that private enterprise, for all its marvelous efficiencies in the things that flow from profit, has produced great wastage and break-up beyond the area of profit. If there were no national forests there wouldn't be a damned tree left along the crest of the Cascades.[4]

In accordance with his Jeffersonian politics, the villain of the story is a corrupt businessman who exists beyond the reach of the hero, not to mention the regulatory force of the government. In the end, *Trouble Shooter* is about hard-working, virtuous Americans living at the mercy of corrupt, elitist forces beyond their control.

When screenwriter Jack Cunningham adapted Haycox's story to the screen, he changed most of the names and plot details, and simplified the politics. In *Union Pacific*, Joel McCrea stars as trouble shooter Jeff Butler, who is hired to protect the railroad and its workers. Butler quickly finds himself at odds with Dick Allen, a hired gun working for greedy saboteurs. Unlike Frank Peace and Al Brett in the novel, however, Butler and Allen have a mutual respect. Both men eventually recognize that the real enemy is the unethical capitalist who wants to exploit America's greatest resources—including its people—for personal gain.

The real hero of the film is the woman who brings these two hired guns together. Actress Barbara Stanwyck plays the feisty Irish immigrant who is wild at heart but eager for a man who can "tame" her. She realizes right away that Jeff is the man for the job, but she agrees to marry Dick Allen in order to keep the two men from killing each other. Her motto: "Nobody has ever put any sense into a man's brain through a bullet hole in his head." While the would-be hero Jeff Butler avoids making any concrete plans for the future, rationalizing that "in my job, a man can't look very far ahead," Molly takes a very active role in shaping the future, both hers and his. She keeps everyone working together and committed to the completion of the railroad, and the film culminates with a lavish

Trouble shooter Joel McCrea with Barbara Stanwyck in *Union Pacific* (1939, Paramount).

recreation of the Golden Spike Ceremony of 1869. With this final scene, DeMille's film celebrates the building of the railroad as a project to "bind us together, east and west, as one people," and projects a sense of peace and optimism about the end of the New Deal era.

MGM's star-spangled pre–Civil War westerns *Stand Up and Fight* (1939) and *Let Freedom Ring* (1939) were equally committed to reactionary patriotism. *Stand Up and Fight* initially pits Robert Taylor's meek southern aristocrat Blake Cantrell against Wallace Beery's blustery, blue-collar westerner Boss Starkey. When Cantrell embraces the spirit of the west, however, he turns against the upper class and in the process becomes a "real" man. The drama plays out against the backdrop of a race between a family-owned stagecoach company and a giant railroad corporation. The steam train, although bitterly denounced as an "invention of the devil," wins the race against the stagecoach—but only after Cantrell has exposed the railroad barons as corrupt slavers. In *Let Freedom Ring*, Nelson Eddy plays an eastern lawyer-turned-singing cowboy who also finds himself at odds with a greedy railroad baron. He wins the day by delivering a high-handed speech about American spirit to the immigrant railroad workers: "There's no tyrant to give orders in this country. There's no man bigger or stronger than you are if you'll raise your heads.... This is *your* land. Come on and win it again!" In the end, the common man reclaims America from bureaucratic tyrants.

Compared to the westerns from Paramount and MGM, the early Warner Bros. westerns express more liberal politics, echoing especially President Roosevelt's conservationist concerns and law enforcement reforms. The studio's first attempt at a western epic, *Gold Is Where You Find It* (1938), echoes largely Democratic concerns about the unregulated exploitation of America's natural resources. Set in the "mushroom mining town" of Tenspot during the California gold strike of 1877, the film follows a Yankee mining engineer named Jared Whitney (played by George Brent) who finds himself in the middle a war between farmers and miners over the future of the land. Whitney eventually sides with the farmers—owing to the influence of farmer's daughter Olivia de Havilland—and the film concludes with a paean to America's natural bounty. Unfortunately, the conservationist western failed to strike gold at the box office.

Studio executives Jack Warner and Hal B. Wallis quickly decided that they were missing a key ingredient in their western formula: namely, Errol Flynn. The Tasmanian actor, who had risen to fame as the dashing hero of *Captain Blood* (1935), *The Charge of the Light Brigade* (1936) and *The Adventures of Robin Hood* (1938), was promptly cast as cowboy-turned-sheriff Wade Hatton in *Dodge City*. Flynn protested, saying that while he could appreciate the appeal of the western genre—calling it "expressive, simple, native"—he felt ridiculously miscast in the role.[5] *Dodge City* screenwriter Robert Buckner, who had written *Gold Is Where You Find It*, was equally nervous about becoming the studio's go-to western scenarist. In a 1988 interview, he confessed, "I don't know why I got hooked with so many westerns. I didn't grow up around horses. I was just a Virginia boy who had no connection with the West."[6] Flynn's misgivings and Buckner's lack of experience posed no problem for the studio execs, who were reportedly less interested in historical authenticity than in repeating their formula for "spectacle pictures."

Dodge City begins with Hatton reflecting on his glory days as a trail hand. The hero exclaims, "Railroad's finished, and so's our country." As it turns out, this is just the beginning of a new era in America, with a new set of challenges. Hatton finds a place for himself in Dodge, a frontier town "that knew no ethics but cash and killing." The death of an innocent child and the moral judgment of a beautiful woman (Olivia de Havilland) shame Hatton into taking a job as town marshal, and squaring off against an unconscionable villain. By the end of the film, he

Olivia de Havilland with Tasmanian cowboy Errol Flynn in *Dodge City* (1939, Warner Bros.).

has rescued the girl, dispatched the outlaw, and restored law and order—answering a specific need in this new America for tough and trustworthy authority figures. Drawing inspiration from Stuart N. Lake's 1931 popular novel *Wyatt Earp: Frontier Marshal*, Buckner had produced a pivotal law-and-order western.[7]

Buckner continued to push the theme in his script for *The Oklahoma Kid*, a misguided western featuring James Cagney and Humphrey Bogart as outlaw bandits. The writer remembers, "That was very funny, because it was the first time that Cagney had ever sat on a horse in his life. And Bogart didn't like horses. They took it as a great lark, and the picture came off that way."[8] Despite the setting, the film strongly echoes the plots and politics of Warner Bros. gangster movies. When asked if he has any respect for law and order, or any pride in "empire building," Cagney's cowboy quips, "The strong take away from the weak and the smart take it away from the strong. This is the only law that's worth a hoot in this part of the country." In an effort to satisfy Hollywood's moral arbiters, he is eventually converted into a model citizen—albeit rather unconvincingly—by the righteous behavior of his estranged father and brother, and by a cursory marriage to a woman who vows to domesticate him.

The Oklahoma Kid plays out like the brainchild of producer Daryl F. Zanuck, who was head of production at Warner in the early 1930s. Zanuck believed that Depression-era moviegoers would be able to relate to outlaw characters pitted against a corrupt society. With that in mind, he oversaw the making of several popular urban crime dramas at Warner, including *The Doorway to Hell* (1930) and *The Public Enemy* (1931). Both films revolved around Prohibition-era gangsters, and implied that their criminal behavior was a logical response to unrestrained capitalism. Reflecting on *The Public Enemy*, Zanuck explained that the criminals in his films have inherited a dangerous behavioral code: "People are going to say the characters are immoral, but they're not because they don't *have* morals. They steal, they kill, they lie, they hump each other because that's the way they were made, and if you allow a decent human feeling or pang of conscience to come into their makeup, you've lost 'em and changed the kind of movie we're making."[9] To appease the censors, these films routinely contrasted their amoral characters with moral foils. In *The Public Enemy*, for example, James Cagney's gangster has a morally upright brother who tries to save the villain from himself. To be fair, however, Cagney is not completely inhuman. He does have one redeeming quality: he loves his ma.

In 1933, Zanuck left Warner Bros. to start his own production company, 20th Century Pictures, which later merged with Fox pictures to become a major new Hollywood studio—and, like every other studio head in Hollywood, Zanuck seemed driven to resurrect the western. His studio answered *Dodge City* with an official adaptation of Stuart N. Lake's *Wyatt Earp: Frontier Marshal*, helmed by veteran western director Allan Dwan and starring stalwart Randolph Scott in the lead role. (Due to protest from Earp's widow, however, Scott's character wasn't named Wyatt Earp, and the film was known simply as *Frontier Marshal*.) Dwan's old-fashioned B western was eclipsed by the sheer spectacle of *Dodge City*, but Zanuck did manage to reclaim his gangster-movie formula with the western biopic *Jesse James* (1939).

History tells us that the real Frank and Jesse James grew up amidst guerrilla warfare in the war-torn state of Missouri. As teenagers, they sympathized with the Confederacy and were eventually accused of committing atrocities against Union soldiers. After the Civil War, both brothers tried to surrender to Union forces. In the process, Jesse got shot in the chest. Based on these historical facts, it is easy to imagine that the James brothers felt disillusioned about law and order in the Reconstruction Era, and that their disillusionment led them to a life of crime. Zanuck's film, written by Nunnally Johnson and directed by Henry King, dispenses with this backstory in favor of a simpler explanation. The screen story begins with a confrontation between the two brothers, played by Tyrone Power and Henry Fonda, and a gang of greedy railroad agents who burn their childhood home and cripple their mother. As established in *The Public Enemy*, even notorious criminals love their mothers, so the attack immediately transforms Frank and Jesse into outlaws.

From that point forward, the film is a tale of Frank and Jesse's revenge against a corrupt and powerful institution. When the boys rob their first train, Frank gleefully advises the passengers, "Don't forget to sue the railroad for everything you give us, cause it's responsible." Later, the upstanding citizens of a nearby town take the criminals into their homes based on a mutual contempt for the railroad administration. According to historian Ted Yeatman, this depiction of Frank and Jesse as local heroes is not inaccurate. He explains the context in which poor people embraced the two outlaws in the wake of economic crises in the Midwest in 1873:

Nancy Kelly with blood brothers Tyrone Power (top) and Henry Fonda in *Jesse James* (1939, 20th Century–Fox).

A rash of bank closings came in the wake of the failure of the financial house of Jay Cooke and Company in September 1873, due to its inability to sell several million dollars' worth of Northern Pacific Railroad bonds. More than five thousand businesses closed in the first year alone. Compounding the problem in the plains states was a grasshopper plague that summer, destroying crops. Many farmers lost their farms as banks foreclosed on unpaid crop debt. The displaced were often forced to return to the industrial cities farther east, their dreams shattered. Unemployment became rife, and the "hobo" or "tramp" was a common sight as men drifted from place to place looking for work. Those small farmers who held onto their land often joined the Grange movement in an effort to have government regulate volatile railroad freight rates as wholesale prices dipped some 30 percent. Banks and railroads became despised institutions to many.[10]

As a result, Frank and Jesse's assaults on federal banks and big businesses became a symbol of empowerment for the downtrodden. In subsequent years, reactionary journalists like John Newman Edwards were only too happy to celebrate the outlaws as folk heroes—up to a point.

Zanuck embraced—and embellished—the legend of the Jesse James as a modern-day Robin Hood, but Hollywood's self-censorship code could only allow so much sympathy for a criminal. If Jesse was to be any kind of hero, he had to be a *tragic* hero who suffered the consequences of his illegal and immoral actions. As in Zanuck's gangster movies, there is a secondary character who acts as a foil, allowing the story to play out as a cautionary tale. 20th Century–Fox appointed Randolph Scott—Hollywood's most upstanding, righteous screen cowboy—to play Will Wright, a fictional Missouri lawman who sympathizes with Jesse's motives, but can't condone the outlaw's actions. In the latter half of the film Wright takes Jesse's wife and child into protective custody—a turn of events that enrages Jesse and sets him on the path to self-destruction. When Jesse becomes so rash that he alienates his own brother, we know it's only a matter of time before he gets his comeuppance.

The James Gang remained at large until 1876, when they hit a well-protected bank in Northfield, Minnesota. This time the authorities were waiting for them, and managed to kill every member of the gang except for Frank and Jesse. The bloody shootout effectively put an end to the criminal association between the two brothers. Frank "retired" to farm life, and later faced a series of (mostly symbolic) trials for his crimes. Jesse returned to a life of crime, and was subsequently murdered by a member of his new gang. The film concludes on a solemn, but still sympathetic, note. A newspaperman at Jesse's funeral eulogizes: "I don't think even America is ashamed of Jesse James. Maybe it's because we understand that he wasn't altogether to blame for what his times made him."

Jesse James clearly reflected the zeitgeist of 1939, becoming one of the highest grossing films of the year—but not everyone was satisfied with the finished film. Jo Frances James, Jesse's granddaughter and the film's "technical advisor," complained, "I don't know what happened to the history part of it. It seemed to me the story was fiction from beginning to end. About the only connection it had with fact was that there was once a man named James and he did ride a horse."[11] Director Henry King, however, stuck to his guns, saying: "In the film we do not glorify [Jesse James]. Neither do we picture him as all bad. We attempt, instead, to trace the psychological causes that led him into train and bank robbery, and to depict with historical accuracy the most famous of his exploits. We have tried to respect the judgment of historians and at the same time keep in mind what those people who were his sworn friends thought of him."[12] By adding a bit of psychological nuance to the traditional white hat/black hat western formula, the film prompted a rash of badmen biopics—including Universal's *When the Daltons Rode* (1940) and Warner's *Billy the Kid* (1941) and *Bad Men of the Missouri* (1941). As a result, *Jesse James* made straightforwardly didactic westerns seem antiquated.

The only 1939 western to rival *Jesse James* in terms of influence was John Ford's *Stagecoach*. Ford was already something of a Hollywood legend, having directed the silent epic *The Iron Horse* (1924) and won an Oscar for *The Informer* (1935), but he had not made a western since 1926's *Three Bad Men*. In 1937, he was ready to get back on the horse and he had very specific ideas about the film he wanted to make. Convinced that what audiences remember most is not spectacle, but rather the "heart-interest stories of plain people interpreting vital emotions," he hired screenwriter Dudley Nichols to adapt Ernest Haycox's character-driven short story "Stage to Lordsburg."[13]

Haycox's story revolves around nine strangers "with nothing in common except a destination." Among them are an "unobtrusively gallant, unexpectedly gentle" gunslinger named Malpais Bill and a worldly-wise prostitute named Henriette. At the beginning of the trip, both are fatalists, believing that their past actions have determined the narrow course of their lives. At the end of a hard journey, however, they find hope for a new beginning together. It's a simple story with minimal dialogue, but that's precisely what appealed to Ford.

While trying to develop the film, Ford fought hard for his choice of leading man. He wanted a roughneck everyman, rather than a romantic lead—John Wayne, not Gary Cooper. At the time, however, nobody in Hollywood wanted to produce an A-western with B movie star John Wayne. Biographer Dan Ford explains:

> In 1938 Wayne was under contract to Republic Pictures, grinding out a "B" western every eight days. He was well-established in Hollywood, but only in the realm of children's pictures. Every agent and casting director knew who he was, but they all had the same mental notation beside his name: "John Wayne, Ex-jock, western leading man, Mascot, Monogram, Republic, Looks good, moves and rides great, Can't act." Wayne had no money to speak of, no prestige, no importance in the eyes of his peers. He was frustrated at being a second-rate actor and bored by trite, cliché-ridden, shoot-em-ups.[14]

Ford remained resolute, convinced that John Wayne was the man for the job. Eventually, independent producer Walter Wanger agreed to let the director make the film his own way—with Wayne in the lead. The shoot was particularly grueling for the actor, who later told Peter Bogdanovich that Ford forced him to re-think his acting style: "[Ford] taught me that a reaction is the most valuable thing you can have on a picture. Having made so many cheap quickie pictures, I'm in a position to know the difference between the two. The quickie things they imagine that I do, and I have done them certainly, are those kind of pictures in which you tell the audience what you're going to do, then you go do it, and then you tell them what you've done, then you tell them what you're going to do next."[15] Ford's way, the actor explained, was simpler: "When you talk, talk low, talk as little as possible, and say it with sincerity."[16] It was the filmmaker's recipe for an ideal western hero.

The Ringo Kid is a consummate outsider, thoroughly independent, self-made and self-assured. Placed within a microcosm of 1880s America, which is mostly populated by narrow-minded capitalists and moral hypocrites, Ringo is the still point of the turning world. That was Ford's simple ideal, as he described it: "These men are natural. They are themselves. They are rugged individualists. They live an outdoor life, and they don't have to conform. I think one of the great attractions of the western is that people like to identify themselves with these cowboys. We all have an escape complex. We all want to leave the trouble of the civilized world behind us. We envy those who can live the most natural way of life, with nature, bravely and simply."[17]

At the beginning of the film, Ringo is pursuing a vendetta against the man who killed his brother. By the end of the film, the gunslinger and his future bride—another consummate outsider—surrender the past and leave the motley crew of self-righteous travelers to create their own outpost in the wilderness. Unlike *Dodge City*'s Wade Hatton, who becomes a devoted guardian of civilization, and Jesse James, who actively rebels against civilization, Ringo simply withdraws into a libertarian Eden. An envious lawman observes, "Thus they're saved from the 'blessings' of civilization."

Ford's biographer Joseph McBride theorizes that the filmmaker's vision of the West reflects his family background, supposing that first-generation Americans like Ford "saw better than most people that the true democracy they were seeking in America was represented in the idealism of the westward impulse," "a vicarious journey into wide-open spaces where a person's past meant nothing and individual initiative still counted for everything."[18] With this in mind, the biographer reads *Stagecoach* as "a justification of American Manifest Destiny on the eve of World War II, a scathing critique of capitalist corruption and Republican hypocrisy, and a celebration of the egalitarian values of the New Deal."[19] Ford frankly admitted, in 1937, that he was "a definite socialist democrat—*always* left."[20] Screenwriter Dudley Nichols was also a prominent Hollywood leftist at the time, so McBride's assessment of the film's politics seems fair.

What is perhaps more interesting than the director's perspective on partisan politics, however, is his perspective on the war in Europe. In the late 1930s, Ford was an outspoken member of the Hollywood Anti-Nazi League. At the same time, he was acting as a spy for U.S. Naval Intelligence, using his private boat to look for Japanese military activity off the coast of Mexico. Whatever his fears about the future, however, *Stagecoach* is definitely not a call to war. Robert Sherman suggests that audiences flocked to the film in 1939 precisely because it provided an escape from real life horrors: "*Stagecoach* was released at a time when the American people were growing increasingly uneasy about the news emanating from Europe. Hitler had just signed a friendship treaty with an old arch-enemy, Russia. Hitler was reported to be mobilizing troops and tanks along Germany's eastern border. And finally, Hitler was preparing to invade Poland. As rumors intensified, Americans sought escape—and found it in John Ford's brilliant new western."[21] Until the bombing of Pearl Harbor in December 1941, the United States government maintained an isolationist policy toward events in Europe. Like Ringo, America's decision-makers spoke softly and tried to go their own way. *Stagecoach* is a pre-war vision of America, captured two years before Japan awakened the "sleeping giant." At this point the Man of the West may have violence and justice on his mind, but he still has a naïve hope in his heart.

Ford's subsequent film, *Drums Along the Mohawk* (1939), retreated even further into innocence, delving deeper into American history to present a grandiose but simple-minded story about 18th century American pioneers. John Wayne and Claire Trevor—the stars of *Stagecoach*—reteamed in RKO's *Allegheny Uprising* (1939), an even more bland colonial-era western. Republic's *Man of Conquest* (1939) focused on the nation-building history of Sam Houston, but it carefully avoided looming questions about the future of America.

Destry Rides Again tackles the subject more directly and, as a result, is one of the most prescient western films of its day. The project began its life simply enough, as a straightforward remake of a 1932 Tom Mix vehicle, but producer Joe Pasternak concocted a plan to make a new kind of western by reversing the roles of the male and female characters. The girl in the original *Destry Rides Again*, Pasternak remembered, "was a frail, silly child waiting for her man to come home." In the remake, Frenchie would be a tough and unpredictable dance-hall girl, "the equal of Destry in looks, drive, and personality."[22] He borrowed James Stewart from MGM to play Destry, the pacifist sheriff of Bottleneck, and pursued Marlene Dietrich to star opposite him. Having worked with Dietrich years earlier, Pasternak believed she would be a perfect fit for the role.

There was only one problem. Following the commercial failure of three of her recent films, Dietrich was more of a pariah in Hollywood than John Wayne. No one wanted to finance a film with her in the lead role. Further complicating Pasternak's plan, Dietrich herself had no interest in making a western. The producer remembers her reaction: "I

Claire Trevor with laconic outsider John Wayne in *Stagecoach* (1939, United Artists).

was vacationing in Monte Carlo when I put through the call. The line crackled! 'Why do you want me?' asked Dietrich. 'Because of the wonderful work you have done.... I know you'll be great in this picture I have for you.' 'Okay,' said Dietrich. 'What is it?' 'It's a western.' 'Oh, no! You must be crazy!'"[23] Perhaps because Pasternak was willing to gamble on her when no one else would, Dietrich gambled on *Destry Rides Again*. And it *was* a gamble. When filming began, *Destry* didn't even have a completed script.

For much of the film, Stewart's character gets his way with a wink and an aw-shucks grin. Haunted by the murder of his father in Tombstone, he has replaced gun-fighting with napkin ring-carving. "You'd be surprised," he tells an old friend, "the genuine rage you can work off just by carving a little piece of wood." Dietrich's character, of course, mocks him and his "little piece of wood," and sets out to prove that she's the leading authority in town. Stewart maintains that he's a lover, not a fighter—until a local criminal murders one of his oldest friends. At that point, Thomas Jefferson Destry reluctantly straps on a pair of six-shooters for a traditional western movie showdown.

The rest of the film might easily have been a routine shoot-'em-up, but the filmmakers improvised a last-minute twist. While all the men in town rally behind either Destry or his male nemesis, Frenchie rallies all the women in town to prevent the men from killing each other. The women of Bottleneck are clearly *not* pacifists, but they embrace non-lethal violence over lethal violence and, in the end, they are the ones who emerge victorious from this western's climactic showdown. In much the way that Barbara Stanwyck is the real hero of *Union Pacific*, Marlene Dietrich's character is the real hero of

Lover James Stewart with fighter Marlene Dietrich in *Destry Rides Again* (1939, Universal).

Destry Rides Again. Even though the Hollywood production code requires her to suffer a tragic hero's end, she manages to save the town of Bottleneck.

Stewart's biographer Marc Eliot suggests that, behind its playful tone, *Destry Rides Again* reflected the changing "mood of the country," as America reluctantly contemplated intervening in the war in Europe:

> In *Destry* the hero arrives in peace, unarmed, not wanting any trouble and certainly not looking for any. The town of Bottleneck has, like Europe had been by an earlier generation, "cleaned up" by Destry's unseen father, only to have once more fallen to the forces of evil. Dietrich's presence further cements the Germanic link, giving the saloon she works in a decidedly exotic, foreign flavor. America's struggle with isolationism versus entering World War Two on the side of the Allies hovers all over this movie.[24]

According to film critic William K. Everson, this may have been the producer's explicit intention:

> Friends of producer Joe Pasternak, a refugee from Nazi Germany who arrived at Universal in the mid-thirties, insist that he saw *Destry* as a very specific anti–Nazi allegory, and that it could be broken down point by point, character by character (including Brian Donlevy whose little mustache made his Hitler alignment at least plausible) to prove it. On paper, it made for interesting theorizing, but the ineptitude of Stewart's Destry and his reluctance to take *physical a*ction even though he might adopt a moral stance—and the stress placed on comedic and aggressive women—make it a dubious theory to support.[25]

Viewed in light of these speculations, the film seems to suggest that America might be able to avoid the conflict in Europe. Three years later, however, Dietrich would be starring with John Wayne in a much more jingoistic western film, and Stewart would be headed to war with the United States Army.

In the intervening years, Columbia Pictures captured the uncertain spirit of the times in *Arizona* (1940), a tale of empire building deferred. Actress Jean Arthur plays Phoebe Titus, a pioneer woman regarded as a "female army" with "nothing but iron from top knot to gizzard." Despite her stony exterior, Phoebe is quietly making plans for a more domesticated life (she has even picked out her domesticator: a young drifter named Peter Muncie, played by William Holden), but first she has to help tame the wild frontier town of Tucson, Arizona, and make it safe for law-abiding families.

Unfortunately, the Civil War thwarts her plans. First, the U.S. Army abandons the Arizona territory to the Apaches, and Phoebe has to convince her neighbors to defend their homes without the government's help. Later, when the territory aligns with the Confederacy and all the able-bodied men in the territory go to war, she protests the way that a government "can mess up the plans of a people who want to mind their own business." Adding insult to injury, a slimy businessman named Jefferson Carteret soon wrests control of Tucson, begins supplying guns to the Indians, and initiates a period of lawlessness that outlasts the Civil War.

In the end, the future of Tucson—as well as Phoebe's representative American Dream—depends on a violent showdown between Muncie and Carteret. In a bold departure from western movie tradition, the showdown between the two men is not featured onscreen. Phoebe, fearing the worst, can't bring herself to watch it, and so we wait with her for news of the outcome. When Peter Muncie appears victoriously, Phoebe announces that Tucson, and America, have "quite a future" ahead of them. Despite the reassuring denouement, however, it is impossible to forget the moment of seemingly hopeless waiting—the moment before the shooting begins, when the future of the free world was hanging by a very thin thread.

CHAPTER II

Westerners at War
(1940–1946)

The true goal we seek is far above and beyond the ugly field of battle. When we resort to force, as now we must, we are determined that this force shall be directed toward ultimate good as well as against immediate evil. We Americans are not destroyers—we are builders. We are now in the midst of a war, not for conquest, not for vengeance, but for a world in which this nation, and all that this nation represents, will be safe for our children.
—Franklin D. Roosevelt, fireside chat, December 9, 1941

Westerns remained big business for Hollywood in the early years of World War II, while Americans weighed the pros and cons of interceding in Europe. In that politically-charged atmosphere, studios continued to develop their own distinctive formulas, and filmmakers began to express personal beliefs and political views by rethinking the traditional definitions of heroes and villains.

In 1940, even a star like Gary Cooper could fall victim to this new ambiguity. After headlining *Northwest Mounted Police* (1940), a simple-minded epic from Cecil B. DeMille about a Texas Ranger who pursues an outlaw through the wilds of Canada, Cooper was cast in *The Westerner* (1940), a more intimate psychological western about an eccentric hangman. *The Westerner* is ostensibly named for Cooper's character, but the main character is obviously Judge Roy Bean, the legendary Texas hanging judge who sentences him to death. Bean was a real historical figure, whose quirks alone made him famous. Biographer Everett Lloyd tried to sum up his appeal: "Bean was no saint, but let us give the devil his due. He possessed at least one quality or trait in rare abundance—what the French call *savoir-faire*."[1] As played by character actor Walter Brennan, Bean is indeed a lovably unpredictable old coot, and the film hinges on his surprising rapport with Cooper's laconic drifter—a rapport born of the natural respect and fondness between the two actors, as well as screenwriter Niven Busch's unique conception of the West. Busch explains, "I believe that the single-mindedness of lonely people was a basic motivating power among the western frontier cultures."[2] With its emphasis on characterization rather than moralizing, the independently-produced *The Westerner* became an inspiration for more picaresque postwar westerns.

In the meantime, the major Hollywood studios were trying to repeat the successes of the previous year. 20th Century–Fox perpetuated the legend of Jesse James with *The Return of Frank James* (1940) and *Belle Starr* (1941). Director Fritz Lang helmed the former film, a courtroom drama that relied heavily on Henry Fonda's folksy charm and drew its

Walter Brennan (left) as the lovably unpredictable Judge Roy Bean, with Doris Davenport and Gary Cooper in *The Westerner* **(1940, United Artists).**

only real dramatic weight from a fictionalized confrontation between Frank and his brother's assassin. Actress Gene Tierney, Frank's love interest in the film, went on to play "the female Jesse James" in *Belle Starr*, starring opposite Randolph Scott. Scott, meanwhile, made a killing in Warner's *Dodge City* follow-up *Virginia City* (1940), Universal's badmen biopic *When the Daltons Rode* (1940), and 20th Century–Fox's *Western Union* (1941)—a more compelling western from Fritz Lang, about a reformed outlaw who helps build a telegraph line across the Great Plains. Lang, who championed the genre as "a certain religion of the American people," later said that he would have preferred to tell the story of a *real* outlaw like Billy the Kid—not as a "handsome, dashing" figure, but "as he really was."[3] Unfortunately, somebody beat him to the draw.

By 1940, Billy the Kid already had a history in Hollywood. Director King Vidor had celebrated the youthful gunslinger in his 1930 film *Billy the Kid*, adopting the whitewashed perspective of novelist Walter Noble Burns, who had transformed the notorious outlaw into an ideal westerner—bright, sympathetic, courteous, cheerful, generous, humble, honest and loyal—with only occasional hints of a 'sub-zero vacuum' in his soul."[4] When MGM decided to remake the film, with romantic leading man Robert Taylor in the title role, they maintained the whitewash. In the 1941 version, Billy's first victim is a selfish bully who wants to suppress free speech and corrupt the local government to serve his own goals. In short, the film leaves little doubt in the viewer's mind that the murder is justified. According to film critic Peter Stanfield, that makes *Billy the Kid* "the most overt allegory of the international conflicts facing America in the months before its entry into the war."[5] Viewed in that context, the theme is simple: *It's a dirty job, but somebody has to do it.* Of course, because Billy is a private citizen and not a professional soldier, his actions will not go unpunished.

During the same time period, Warner Bros. was producing even more overt allegories. According to Hal B. Wallis, "Because Jack Warner and I were deeply concerned over the crisis in Europe in the late 1930s, we decided to undertake a policy of opposition to Nazism in our pictures, despite the very strong possibility that isolationist sentiments in America would severely criticize us."[6] The studio's post–*Dodge City* westerns aren't as overtly political as *Confessions of a Nazi Spy* (1939) or *Underground* (1941), but their subtexts were often undeniable.

At the end of *Dodge City*, Wade Hatton's wife promises to follow him on his quest to tame yet another frontier town: Virginia City, Nevada. For better or worse, Hatton and his wife never made the onscreen journey to Virginia City, but Errol Flynn made it into a sequel-of-sorts called *Virginia City* (1940). The film begins during the final weeks of the Civil War, with Flynn's escape from a Confederate prison camp run by Randolph Scott. When Flynn and Scott meet up again on the western frontier, Scott has arranged to smuggle a huge shipment of gold back to Confederate headquarters to help sustain the war effort, *Virginia City* poses a question: *How might the outcome of the Civil War have been different if the Confederacy had been able to compete with the financial resources of the Union?* It was a timely question at a time when Germany was gobbling up Europe, building its national resources at an overwhelming rate.

Errol Flynn and Olivia de Havilland reteamed in *Santa Fe Trail* (1940). Taking significant creative license with American history, the film proposes that future Confederate general J.E.B. Stuart (Flynn) and future U.S. Army cavalry leader George Armstrong Custer (played by future U.S. president Ronald Reagan) met while they were cadets at West Point Academy and fought together against abolitionist John Brown in the months leading up to the Civil War. (Never mind that Stuart graduated in 1854, Custer in 1861, and that John Brown was executed in 1859.) The fictionalized history is mostly a setup for heavy-handed premonitions of the Civil War, in which the West Point classmates will be pitted against each other: North vs. South, Custer vs. Stuart. Key dialogue in the film prompts speculation about an alternate version of American history—one in which the country might have been able to avoid the Civil War altogether.

J.E.B. Stuart argues that John Brown's only crime was being a rabble-rouser who threatened the unity of America, and suggests that if Brown had allowed Southerners to resolve the slavery issue on their own terms, they might have been able to do so to everyone's satisfaction. From this perspective, forcing an end to slavery led only to wounded pride and a fractured nation. For moviegoers in 1940, this dubious perspective might have had a contemporary equivalent. *If America left Europe to its own devices, would the warring nations resolve their problems in a way that might be acceptable to the international community?* Certainly, many American isolationists of the period did not view the war in Europe as a big enough threat to the international community to justify risking American lives, so they could have embraced such vague hopes. Today, with hindsight of the Holocaust, the idea seems unthinkable—but, in 1940, things were changing fast.

In 1941, Errol Flynn headlined a fourth epic western from Warner Bros. *They Died with Their Boots On*, released a few short weeks before the bombing of Pearl Harbor, takes place in a much more complicated world than that of *Santa Fe Trail*. In this depiction, Custer (now portrayed by Flynn rather than Reagan) is a foolhardy but principled romantic who negotiates a truce with the Sioux Nation on behalf of the U.S. government, only to be betrayed by his superiors. The message is that a few greedy businessmen, rather than Custer or Sioux chief Crazy Horse, are the warmongers. Rumors of a gold strike in the Black Hills prompt Uncle Sam to knowingly sacrifice Custer's regiment for the sake of money. At the subsequent Battle of Little Big Horn, Custer essentially commits suicide—not for money or even to serve Washington, but to protect innocent pioneers who are caught in the middle. He offers one additional reason: "There's one thing to be said for glory—you can take glory with you when it's your time to go." *They Died with Their Boots On* grants the controversial historical figure his glory, championing an independent-minded soldier above the government he serves. It was a troubling message to deliver to a country on the brink of war.

In early 1942, just weeks after the bombing of Pearl Harbor, Universal Pictures released *The Spoilers* starring Marlene Dietrich and John Wayne. In the film, Dietrich plays a saloon entertainer in turn-of-the-century Alaska, where the discovery of gold creates an atmosphere of lawlessness. The lawbreakers are not gun-slinging cowboys, but upstanding bureaucrats (including a wonderfully sleazy Randolph Scott) and a high-profile judge who has solemnly vowed to keep the peace at the expense of the common man. When these lawmen steal from the local blue-collar miners, including Wayne and his pal Harry Carey, they incite a riot that threatens to destroy the entire settlement. Based on a 1914 novel by Rex Beach, it's an old story with a new relevance.

Wayne's and Carey's characters respond very differently to the chain of events. Wayne, who has a certain weakness for the corrupt judge's pretty niece, wants to believe that the institutions of law and order will prevail, so he convinces Carey and his fellow miners to wait for justice instead of taking the law into their own hands. Over the course of the film, however, it becomes clear that Lady Justice serves only the rich in this town, and the corrupt leaders all but crush the spirit of the settlement. Wayne belatedly leads the revolt, advising the miners, "What we're doing tonight is gonna be a warning to any crooks headed this way." The sleeping giant has been awakened.

Wayne would continue to play the righteous rebel for many years to come, in a slew of propagandist war films—including the 1942 film *Pittsburgh*, which once again teamed him with Marlene Dietrich and Randolph Scott. For the most part, however, the development of the Hollywood western was stymied by current events. The bombing of Pearl

Errol Flynn as a foolhardy but principled George Armstrong Custer in *They Died with Their Boots On* (1941, Warner Bros.).

Harbor instantly changed the tone of American films, and the studios all but abandoned prestige westerns as Hollywood's heroes went to fight the war in Europe and the South Pacific, both onscreen and off. Between June 1942 and September 1945, the United States Office of War Information (OWI) played a significant role within every major Hollywood studio, helping to craft entertainment that would boost national morale. During that time, John Wayne and his fellow westerner Henry Fonda were particularly instrumental in rallying moviegoers to the cause.

Following his breakout role as the noble outlaw Frank James, Fonda had portrayed a colonial American patriot in the frontier epic *Drums Along the Mohawk* (1939), embodied one of the country's most effective wartime presidents in the courtroom drama *Young Mr. Lincoln* (1939), and symbolized the enduring spirit of Depression-era Americans in *The Grapes of Wrath* (1940). With these three films, director John Ford had transformed Fonda into the face of America. That was precisely why director William A. Wellman cast him in *The Ox-Bow Incident* (1943), a wartime western that helped transform the genre.

The Ox-Bow Incident originated as a 1940 novel by Walter Van Tilburg Clark. Clark was not a western enthusiast, but he found a way to use the genre to reflect personal and cultural fears. Years later, he remembered:

> I was disturbed by what had happened in Italy with fascism there, and was growing in Germany with the Nazi horror, and I thought that was the great threat to the modern world, and specifically to American

democracy. I saw the seeds of Nazism in our own country, and maybe especially in the Old West—or if not, then in a simple dramatic incident in the West you could get a sort of test-tube sample, the local version of what had been standard treatment of the Indians and many free-thinking white men all the way from the Pequot War.[7]

The resulting novel—about a man who stands up to a lynch mob—was a literary variation on a decidedly unliterary genre.

Filmmaker William Wellman liked it so much that he bought the film adaptation rights with his own money, then pitched the project to the studios. According to the director, "They all thought I was nuts."[8] The story was simply not what most people expected from a western at the time; it was a small-scale, psychological drama with very little action and even less opportunity for lavish scenery. Like Wellman, producer Darryl F. Zanuck was equally moved by the story, but he remained skeptical of its commercial value. Zanuck reputedly told screenwriter Julian Johnson, "Maybe today's psychology calls for stories so shocking that they compel one to forget the current bad news by blotting it out with something worse.... But I doubt it."[9] In the end, he still greenlighted the project. According to Wellman, Zanuck concluded, "I don't think it'll ever make a dime, but it's something I want my studio to have. I want to have my name on it and I know you want to have your name on it."[10] Wellman agreed to a three-picture deal and *The Ox-Bow Incident* went into production.

"The face of America": Henry Fonda in *The Grapes of Wrath* (1940, 20th Century–Fox).

Fonda was the obvious choice for the lead role of Gil Carter, an everyman who finds himself at odds with friends and neighbors that threaten to hang three murder suspects without a trial. Although he's no crusader, Gil speaks out against the crowd, reminding them of the better angels of human nature. When they make assertions about the need for justice, he counters: "Justice? What do you care about justice? You don't even care whether you've got the right men or not. All you know is you've lost something and somebody's got to be punished."

In his autobiography, Fonda says that he felt those words personally, because they reminded him of an experience from his own life. When he was a boy, his father took him to witness the lynching of a black man. Fonda remembered, "It was the most horrendous sight I'd ever seen.... Aside from the lynching, there was something else. It was my father. He never said a word to me. He didn't preach, he didn't make a point, he just made sure I saw it."[11] Wellman's film does the same thing—it doesn't preach about right and wrong; it simply allows us to see a moral mistake for what it is.

At the end of the film, Fonda's character tries to put his own feelings about mob violence into perspective. It wasn't the first time that the actor had been given such a platform. In *Young Mr. Lincoln*, Fonda's character addresses a hanging mob directly, urging caution and human decency: "[The] trouble is, when men start taking the law into their own hands, they're just as apt in all the confusion and fun to start hanging somebody who's not a murderer as somebody who is. Then the next thing you know, they're hanging each other for fun. Till it gets to a place where a man can't pass a tree or look at a rope without feeling uneasy. We seem to lose our heads in times like this. We do things together that we'd be mighty ashamed to do ourselves."

As Tom Joad in *The Grapes of Wrath*, he explains why we have to be kind to our fellow man. We are all "one big soul," Joad says, "that belongs to everybody." Witnessing the beauty and the horror of life during the Great Depression, he contemplates his place in the world: "Wherever you can look, wherever there's a fight so hungry people can eat, I'll be there. Wherever there's a cop beating up a guy, I'll be there. I'll be in the way guys yell when they're mad. I'll be in the way kids laugh when they're hungry and they know supper's ready. And when the people are eating the stuff they raise, and living in the houses they build—I'll be there, too."

The content of these two speeches reverberates in the final moments of *The Ox-Bow Incident*, as Gil reads aloud a private letter written by one of the three hanged men:

> A man just naturally can't take the law into his own hands and hang people without hurting everybody in the world, 'cause then he's just not breaking one law but all laws. Law is a lot more than words you put in a book, or judges or lawyers or sheriffs you hire to carry it out. It's everything people ever have found out about justice and what's right and wrong. It's the very conscience of humanity. There can't be any such thing as civilization unless people have a conscience, because if people touch God anywhere, where is it except through their conscience? And what is anybody's conscience except a little piece of the conscience of all men that ever lived?

All of these speeches seem to anticipate the now-famous reflections of German theologian Martin Niemöller on the rise to power of the Nazi party: "First they came for the Communists, and I didn't speak up, because I wasn't a Communist. Then they came for the Jews, and I didn't speak up, because I wasn't a Jew. Then they came for the Catholics, and I didn't speak up because I was a Protestant. Then they came for me, and by that time there was no one left to speak up for me." Collectively, the films were powerful reminders to wartime audiences that everyone has a responsibility to be the change we want to see in the world—right now.

Fonda, eager to fight for the rights and freedoms of his fellow man, wanted to be one of the foot soldiers in World War II. In 1942, he enlisted in the U.S. Navy, but Zanuck managed to delay his military service by casting him in a propaganda film called *Immortal Sergeant* (1943). Fonda, who told his wife that he wanted "to be with real sailors not [Hollywood] extras," dismissed the film as "a silly picture," summing up for his biographer: "You want to hear the plot? I won World War II single-handed!"[12] After the film was completed, Fonda joined his fellow filmmakers—Gene Autry, James Stewart, Tyrone Power, Robert Montgomery, William Holden, Ronald Reagan, William Wyler, John Huston, John Ford, and eventually even Darryl Zanuck—overseas.

In Hollywood, meanwhile, John Wayne accepted (some say reluctantly) the mission of winning World War II onscreen. Over the course of the previous decade, Wayne had built a screen persona as the noble cowboy who rode into town and delivered truth, justice and the American way. After Pearl Harbor, he rode into World War II with the same agenda. Between 1942 and 1945, Wayne starred in four combat pictures set in the South Pacific: Republic's *Flying Tigers* (1942) and *The Fighting Seabees* (1943), RKO's *Back*

The face of America at war: John Wayne in *Back to Bataan* (1945, RKO).

to Bataan (1945) and John Ford's *They Were Expendable* (1945). As a result, the roughneck cowboy became the face of America at war.

As Wayne's biographers Randy Roberts and James Olson point out, *Flying Tigers* and *The Fighting Seabees* both bear strong similarities to *Only Angels Have Wings* (1939), a prewar film by director Howard Hawks which drew inspiration from Hawks' experiences as an Air Force pilot in World War I. The central character in *Angels* is Geoff Carter (played by Cary Grant), the thick-skinned leader of a group of daredevil pilots who confront death every time they take to the sky. When one of the pilots gets killed in action, Geoff responds stoically, praising his fallen comrade's sense of duty: "He'd sooner be dead than quit." The sentiment is shared by all of Geoff's pilots, except one.

The arrival of a new pilot named Bat Kilgallen (played by Richard Barthelmess) challenges the group's solidarity. According to rumor, Kilgallen once caused the death of a fellow pilot by bailing out instead of fulfilling his duty. Hawks later claimed that the character was based on a real person he met in Mexico:

> One day Howard Hughes was making a picture. He had an old bomber fixed up and it was supposed to go up and start into a spin, light smoke pots and spin down, and then these two guys were supposed to parachute out. One guy came out in a parachute and the other guy stayed in there, calmly lighting smoke pots until he crashed. I saw the plane start down and got in a car and started over there, and the guy was still in there, deader than a doornail. Then we found the fellow who parachuted out. He wouldn't have gotten out until he saw the other fellow get out, too. Well, he spent the rest of his life trying to prove that he was brave.

He flew at every air circus in some little pusher plane that he'd built until he finally cracked up and killed himself.[13]

In *Only Angels Have Wings*, Hawks gives the guilty pilot a shot at redemption, allowing him to sacrifice himself for his fellow pilots. With this basic plot, the filmmaker created an image of the War Office's ideal American warrior: a dedicated soldier who is prepared to die for the good of his fellow man.

Flying Tigers grants the same shot at redemption to Woody Jason, the "glamour boy" whose selfish antics appear to cause the death of a fellow fighter pilot. Wayne, playing Jason's thick-skinned commander, uses the incident as an object lesson, reminding his pilots that they have to work together. "Don't try to win this war by yourself," he says. "Results here are based on cooperation and understanding." In *The Fighting Seabees*, the roles were reversed. This time, Wayne himself is the outsider—an arrogant lone wolf whose mistakes humble him and slowly transform him into a dedicated company man. By the end of the film, his motto is simple: "That's the Navy way and that's the way you're gonna do it!"

Wayne's biographers observe that these two war movies are "really little different from his westerns; he played only variations on the same hard moral man—ornery and uncompromising, but truthful, loyal, and likable."[14] That certainly sums up his character in *Tall in the Saddle* (1944), the only western that Wayne made during the war, about a drifter who helps a small-time rancher expose the villainy of a murderous land baron. It was a precursor to the types of roles he would play in the future.

After the war, Wayne reunited with his mentor John Ford. *They Were Expendable* relegated him to a supporting role, but one that gave him another opportunity to be a mouthpiece for the U.S. military. This apparently irked Ford, who seems to have harbored a grudge against Wayne for failing to serve active duty in the real war. (Wayne, a father of four, was initially deferred for dependency reasons, and later deferred "in support of national health, safety or interest" due to his iconic status as an onscreen hero.) Ford himself had proudly served at the forefront of action in the South Pacific, not with a gun but with a camera. In 1942, he formed the Field Photographic Branch of the U.S. government's Office of Strategic Services and personally filmed the battle at Midway on June 4th. He later turned his footage into an Oscar-winning documentary short "for the mothers of America."[15]

In subsequent years, Ford produced dozens of documentaries and training films for the public, the soldiers and the military brass. By the time he made *They Were Expendable*, his filmmaking style had changed. Dispensing with the epic scenery of his earlier films, he gave *They Were Expendable* a stark documentary quality. The film was also a departure from the heroic grandstanding of Wayne's earlier war movies, conveying a solemn message about the human cost of war and the bond among those who risked everything.

When Ford returned to the western genre in 1946, he carried that same solemnity with him. *My Darling Clementine* is Ford's re-telling of the legend of Wyatt Earp, the most famous (or infamous, depending on your viewpoint) lawman of the Old West. Earp was a pro–Union, anti-slavery Republican from Abe Lincoln's Illinois, who began exploring the western frontier at a young age. By his mid-twenties, he had earned a reputation in the rough-and-ready cow towns of "Bleeding Kansas" as a tough but fair lawman, quick-witted and even quicker on the draw. The most famous stories about Earp revolve around his years as marshal in the aptly-named town of Tombstone, Arizona, where the lawman's Northern politics fueled a violent clash with a disparate band of rowdies known as The Cowboys, culminating in the legendary gunfight at the O.K. Corral on October 25, 1881.

Hollywood depicted the gunfight in the 1932 film *Law & Order,* followed by two screen adaptations of Stuart N. Lake's novel *Wyatt Earp: Frontier Marshal,* one in 1934 and another in 1939. In the intervening years, Richard Dix tackled the "frontier marshal" role (as a thinly-disguised peace officer named Clay Tallant) in *The Arizonian* (1935). Filmmaker Allan Dwan, who claimed that he had once directed the real Wyatt Earp as an extra, added a love triangle subplot to his version of *Frontier Marshal*. At the beginning of the 1939 film, Wyatt's partner-in-crime Doc Holliday is living in Tombstone with a trouble-making saloon girl named Jerry (modeled on a real-life companion known as "Big-Nosed Kate"). The relationship becomes tense when Doc's ex-girlfriend Sarah arrives in town, so Wyatt does his best to keep Sarah occupied.

The subplot later found its way into *My Darling Clementine*, with Doc's ex-girlfriend (now named Clementine) representing the coming of civilization to the West. In Ford's film, Wyatt is a humble, funny, kind-hearted man, who becomes endearingly nervous in the presence of Clementine. He clearly recognizes his duty to protect people like her from dehumanizing lawlessness, and this is what distinguishes Ford's postwar hero from a pre-war hero like *Stagecoach*'s Ringo Kid: In *My Darling Clementine*, the hero safeguards civilization instead of trying to escape from it.

Henry Fonda as postwar hero Wyatt Earp, with Cathy Downs in *My Darling Clementine* (1946, 20th Century–Fox).

The secondary hero of Ford's tale is Doc Holliday, who becomes more than simply a cold-blood killer with a strong sense of loyalty. As played by Victor Mature, Doc is a tragic figure, like the Shakespearean characters he admires. Once a successful physician back east, he turned to the bottle and the gun after being diagnosed with tuberculosis and became his own worst enemy. When Clementine arrives in Tombstone, ostensibly to save Doc from himself, the outlaw tells her that the man she knew is already dead. He reconsiders this self-indictment only briefly, when confronted with an opportunity to perform a life-saving surgery.

If Henry Fonda's Wyatt Earp is a revision of The Ringo Kid, Doc Holliday is a variation on Doc Boone, the tainted physician in *Stagecoach*. The Boone character mostly served as comic relief, until the plot called for him to sober up and become a doctor again. Doc Boone's story was a tale of redemption: he delivers the baby that symbolizes hope to a group of world-weary travelers. In *My Darling Clementine*, however, Doc's shot at redemption turns out to be a cruel joke. When his patient dies, he has only one other chance to give meaning to his life: by sacrificing himself for a worthy cause. Doc eagerly rides to war with Wyatt because Wyatt stands for something. By association, Doc stands for something too: community.

After the Cowboys have been defeated and order has been restored, Wyatt leaves Tombstone—and Clementine—in a final scene suggesting that the main hero of the film is ultimately a tragic figure too. According to Earp biographer Allen Barra, Ford didn't want to end the picture with Wyatt riding off into the sunset. "I wanted Wyatt to stay there," the filmmaker said, "and become permanent marshal."[16] Such an ending would have offered hope that Clementine could effectively civilize Wyatt, just as he had civilized the town. Resolutely happy endings, however, are a rarity in postwar westerns, and the existing ending has much more ominous implications.

Violence transfigures the scene—for the best, as far as the community is concerned—and ultimately transforms the characters. The real Wyatt Earp moved from Ellsworth to Wichita to Dodge City to Tombstone because, in Lake's words, "the gunman had to go, forced out by the growing sentiment against him."[17] By civilizing the frontier through violence, the marshal creates towns where violent men are no longer necessary or welcome; lawyers and politicians replace the gunman. To the people of Tombstone, and to himself, Wyatt Earp is a killer. That separates him from the law-abiding, God-fearing people of the newly-secured community. It also raises the question of whether soldiers can ever become "good" citizens again after they've been to war. Perhaps this is what producer Darryl F. Zanuck had in mind when he suggested his own alternate ending to *My Darling Clementine*: "Earp instead should say good-bye to Clementine at the edge of town and, before riding away, hint that he may return."[18] The film certainly hints at darker roads ahead for western heroes.

Chapter III

Blood on the Moon
(1947–1949)

> *Many of our people still suffer the indignity of insult, the narrowing fear of intimidation, and, I regret to say, the threat of physical injury and mob violence. Prejudice and intolerance in which these evils are rooted still exist. The conscience of our Nation, and the legal machinery which enforces it, have not yet secured to each citizen full freedom from fear.*
> —Harry S. Truman, address before the NAACP, June 29, 1947

In *Hollywood Goes to War*, authors Clayton R. Koppes and Gregory D. Black conclude that the psychological and sociological effects of World War II "doomed the old Hollywood" and its "symbols of a unified, harmonious society."[1] American cinema in the post-war years took on a more pessimistic tone and a darker hue, which French journalists labeled "film noir." The most obvious examples of film noir are urban crime pictures that wallow in the shadowy underworlds of lascivious and sadistic characters, but the bleak impressionistic style and somber quality of film noir also infected the western genre. Although major studios continued to produce hoary epics like *Buffalo Bill* (1944) and *The Virginian* (1946) with Joel McCrea, *San Antonio* (1945) with Errol Flynn, and *Unconquered* (1947) with Gary Cooper, independent filmmakers crafted darker, edgier visions of the West. Superficial hybrids like *Station West* (1948) and *The Capture* (1950) transplanted the plots and characters of the urban crime picture onto western settings, while more ambitious crossovers re-imagined traditional horse operas as classical tragedies, psychological dramas, and metaphysical thrillers.

One of the key figures in the transition was author and screenwriter Niven Busch. After co-writing *The Westerner*, Busch helped to create two very different psychological westerns. While his original screenplay *Pursued* went into development at Warner Bros., independent producer David O. Selznick adapted Busch's novel *Duel in the Sun* to the screen. The finished films were worlds apart: *Pursued* (1947) is a small, dark, claustrophobic drama; *Duel in the Sun* (1946) became a grand-scale, lavish epic, filmed in full color on a massive budget. Initially, however, both films were conceived as intimate character studies. According to King Vidor, the nominal director of *Duel*, nearly everything about Selznick's film changed during production:

> [Selznick] called me over to tell me about [*Duel in the Sun*]—it was a little book by Niven Busch, a little paperback. It was about the length of *High Noon*, and he said, "I want you to do this as an intimate story of these people, and I will let you alone. I will have nothing to do with it, it's your film." I saw it as a possibility of an intense new angle on a western situation—a small, really small frame. He said no big stuff. But as we

got into it, he wanted me to run *Gone with the Wind* and he wanted to have the biggest ranch and the most cattle and the biggest cast and the script was being rewritten and he suddenly had the idea this should be another *Gone with the Wind* of the West, you know. And it was a question of blow up, blow up, expand, expand, expand. In fact, the beginning, the opening shots, I didn't shoot—you know, big Mexican border dance hall—but he had become the writer then and it just got blown up all out of size and got a long way from [that] intense little study.[2]

Jennifer Jones as ill-fated Pearl Chavez in *Duel in the Sun* (1946, Selznick).

The final film, as Busch observed, is "an extravaganza rather than realistic"—a classical tragedy set in the wild West.[3]

In *Duel*, Jennifer Jones stars as Pearl Chavez, a hot-blooded half-breed who tries hard to be morally upright, but who always falls victim to the carnal "curse" of her Indian blood. The noble Joseph Cotten tries to win her hand through love and respect, but she gravitates instead toward his ne'er-do-well brother—a sniveling Gregory Peck, who "tames" her by force and then discards her. In contrast to Niven Busch's source novel, which ends with the death of the bad brother and the union of Pearl with the good brother, Selznick's film ends with Pearl's death. Peck remembers, "We couldn't stand to be apart, and we couldn't stand to be together, so we ended up killing each other. David was actually out there on the set with a bucket of blood, splashing us."[4] Despite the bright, warm Technicolor hues, *Duel in the Sun* is coldly fatalistic.

Pursued tells a similar story of love and hate, but it offers Freudian psychology as an alternative to fatalism. The film begins with an aftermath, evidence that bad things have happened and cannot be undone. Piece by piece, a man tells his tragic tale as his repressed memories come into focus for the first time. He re-lives his early childhood in shadowy, dream-like fragments. Once the dark spots are removed, the would-be hero promises, we'll see something about him that "explains everything." Unlike *Duel*, which follows its characters toward inescapable finale, *Pursued* tells its story in reverse, searching for the beginning.

Along the way, supporting characters help to unravel the mystery for us. At ten years of age, we learn, Jeb Rand was unknowingly hunted by a stranger from Santa Fe who vowed to kill "every Rand on earth," believing that murderous instincts resided in the family blood. The stranger later explains to Jeb's stepmother that the boy is cursed, both by his blood and by memories of a formative experience that he can't possibly repress forever. All of these forebodings converge around one symbol: a seemingly haunted house where Jeb's parents were murdered in front of him. "What happened to him," the hunter explains, "will make him do things, just like spirits whispering in his ear, saying, 'Kill! Kill!'" Jeb, the stranger insists, is as doomed as Pearl Chavez.

Jeb's stepmother has a different vision of the future. She hopes that her son can escape the past by ignoring it, and advises him, "Don't ask questions of the past. It has no answers for you. Grow up strong in the love that's here for you. As long as you love in return, nothing can happen." Jeb does grow up strong, but love is a continual challenge for him. He enlists to fight in the Spanish American War, and learns that he has a knack for killing. When he returns from war, he accidentally kills his stepbrother—a tragic event that turns his stepsister Thor, the only person whose love can save Jeb from his inner demons, against him.

Jeb and Thor both become consumed by rage, but this is not the end of their story. Eventually they realize that love is "the only hope and the only answer," the only way to escape their horrible past. As Jeb regains full access to his memories and confronts the dark rider who has pursued him throughout his life, he and Thor face the future together. The final act of *Pursued* plays out like an endorsement of Freudian psychoanalysis, although Busch insists his goal was much simpler: "My objective was to make the people real and to give them three dimensions in terms of modern culture. People in westerns weren't often like that. And maybe some of my characters are more modern in psychological terms than people of that period really were. Certainly their actions were self-revealing."[5]

Reportedly, director Raoul Walsh was annoyed by the psychological complexities of Busch's story, and asked the writer "to stay nearby during shooting and be ready to tell him what the hell was going on."[6] Walsh was a traditionalist, and may have thought that *Pursued* was a misguided deviation from the simple, classic western formula. He may also have been baffled by the film's leading man, who projected a very different persona from the likes of Gary Cooper and John Wayne. Whereas Cooper was simple and straightforward, Mitchum was cynical and suspect. Whereas Wayne was outspoken and dogmatic, Mitchum was cool and seemingly indifferent. He was a new type of hero for the postwar era.

Mitchum came of age

Star-crossed lovers Jeb (Robert Mitchum) and Thor (Teresa Wright) in *Pursued* (1947, Warner Bros.).

during the Great Depression. He left home at fourteen and rode the rails across the United States, eventually settling in Los Angeles, where he was employed as a sheet metal worker in an airplane factory on the eve of World War II. In May 1942, he auditioned for Paramount producer Harry "Pop" Sherman, who observed that the young actor looked "kinda mean around the eyes" and cast him as the villain in a series of *Hopalong Cassidy* quickies.[7] Over the following years, Mitchum was mostly relegated to two roles: cowboy or soldier. After playing the hero in a pair of cheap Zane Grey westerns, *Nevada* (1944) and *West of the Pecos* (1945), his portrayal of a gruff World War II veteran in *The Story of G.I. Joe* (1945) made him a star. He brought the same smoldering intensity to the character of Bill Tabeshaw in *Till the End of Time* (1946), a postwar drama that features him as a decorated war hero who can't readjust to civilian life. In war, Tabeshaw explains, "you didn't know where you were going, but everybody else was going to the same place, so what difference did it make? Now we're civilians again. Rugged individuals with no one to tell us what to do or when to do it. We're on our own."

Director Robert Wise helped Mitchum to hone his image as Hollywood's Byronic hero, with the RKO western *Blood on the Moon* (1948). Unlike Raoul Walsh, Wise clearly understood that Mitchum was a different kind of screen icon, and *Blood* was a different kind of western. Unlike most classic westerns, which take place outdoors during the day, this one was shot mostly on lamp-lit interiors at night (hence the title, which seems like a direct response to *Duel in the Sun*). Mother Nature also played a part in determining the aesthetic of the film, as the director explains:

> We were down in Sedona, Arizona, for all those marvelous shots; the weather changes so fast down there. You'd be at one end of the valley to shoot something, and it would be dark and gray and rainy, and you would look at the other end of the valley and it would be sunny. So, you would pack everything up and run to the other end of the valley for another location, and by the time you got there the weather had changed. We were constantly jumping around, grabbing what we could between—and during—these stretches of bad weather.[8]

The result is a film that looks like it was shot on the dark side of the moon, far from the shining lights of Hollywood and high above the sun-bleached, cloudless desert. Style reveals substance: *Blood on the Moon* is an interior narrative, gothic rather than mythic, and its would-be hero is as mysterious as the shadowy landscape.

The screen story, adapted by Luke Short from his novel *Gunman's Chance*, revolves around Jim Garry, a rugged cowboy who finds himself on the wrong side of a feud between cattle ranchers and homesteaders. Garry is tempted to run away from the whole mess, but he's also tempted by the daughter of one of the homesteaders, who talks him into fighting for the other side—not just for her sake, but for his own sake. "You've been in hard luck and you've made mistakes," Amy says, probing his conscience. "You've hated those mistakes, but you've never admitted them except to yourself." Echoing the themes of *Pursued*, she tells Garry that he can't "wipe out the past" by running from it, and urges him to stand up for what he believes in. Once Amy stands up for him, Garry takes charge of his own destiny. In the end, he realizes that a man defines himself with every decision he makes and every action he takes. The past has no power in this version of postwar America.

Mitchum's brand of hero obviously made an impression on Hollywood. Many of the silver screen's most established westerners soon began to darken their images as well. In *Abilene Town* (1946), Randolph Scott played a lawman who derives a bit too much pleasure from doing his job. When a woman accuses him of wanting to see a man dead on

Femme fatale Veronica Lake hides behind "real westerner" Joel McCrea in *Ramrod* (1947, United Artists).

the ground, he says menacingly, "Being afraid [of murder] would take half the fun out of life for me." A few years later, in Columbia's *Coroner Creek* (1948), Scott's gunman would threaten to shoot a man near a stovetop, so he could watch the man's face fall on the burner and begin to cook. Such sadism was common in crime pictures of the day, but it came as more of a shock in westerns—especially westerns starring Randolph Scott.

Actor Joel McCrea was likewise determined to make grittier western films, and he got his chance when he teamed up with director André de Toth. In his 1947 film *Ramrod*, de Toth cast Joel McCrea as Dave Nash, "a real Westerner" who could "fall for temptation and not lose his backbone."[9] Opposite McCrea, the filmmaker cast his wife Veronica Lake as one of the genre's first femme fatales—a character who fit the title of the film better than McCrea. Lake's Connie Dickason is the real ramrod, a modern-day Lady Macbeth who orchestrates all the violence in the picture without ever lifting a finger. Dave Nash is just a pawn who realizes too late that he has been duped by the woman he loves. By then, innocent people all around them are dead; the damage is irreversible and there is nothing left for Nash to do except walk away from the battlefield, leaving his femme fatale alone among the ruins.

McCrea's subsequent western was equally unconventional, but not so bleak. Over the years, *Four Faces West* (1948) has achieved some fame as the only western in which no guns are fired and no punches thrown. It's a story about inner-conflict rather than external conflict—but that doesn't mean there's no action. The story begins when McCrea's character, Ross McEwen, rides into a sleepy southern New Mexico town and (peaceably) robs the local bank right under the nose of famous lawman Pat Garrett. On the way to Gallup by way of El Morro National Monument, he meets a young nurse named Fay Hollister (played by McCrea's real wife, Frances Dee) and falls in love with her. The couple makes plans to start a new life together, but McEwen is hampered by his past. While he takes some comfort in Fay's liberal philosophy—she says, "It isn't what a man does in the past that matters; it's what he does in the present"—he knows that lawmen and bounty hunters of the Old West adhere to a more unforgiving code of justice. When Garrett and his men finally catch up with McEwen, the remorseful bank robber abandons Fay and flees into the Mexico desert, haunted by her last words to him: "You can't run away from yourself. You're not a criminal ... but if you don't stop now, you will be. You'll go on, and now you'll have to steal to live, and then one of these days you'll have to shoot your way out. And then it *will* be too late. You'll be just another outlaw. A killer."

Fay later pleads with Pat Garrett, saying, "This man *wants* to do the right thing." Ultimately, McEwen proves her right when he halts his escape in order to save a family that has been stricken by diphtheria. When the righteous lawman finally catches up to him, Garrett offers McEwen a choice: keep running from the past or accept justice and face the future. McEwen opts for the hard road to moral redemption.

After *Four Faces West*, McCrea went to work for Warner Bros., starring in two recycled narratives: *South of St. Louis* (1949), a slick Civil War western that repurposed the plot of Raoul Walsh's gangster film *The Roaring Twenties* (1939), and *Colorado Territory* (1949), which modeled itself on the same director's *High Sierra* (1941). In the latter film, McCrea stars as Wes McQueen, an escaped convict planning an elaborate heist from a ghost town among the Colorado Mountains. The desolate imagery of the place casts a pall over the film's proceedings, as an old prospector ominously warns that the town is cursed: "The Spaniards moved in first. Indians come along and massacred them. Then the pox came along and took care of the Indians. Nothing left but scorpions and Gila monsters. Then an earthquake came along and took care of *them*. Ain't nobody gone there since ... [except a] rattlesnake maybe that got itself lost." McQueen insists, "I ain't lost." He thinks he knows exactly where he's headed in life. When the heist is over, he plans to settle down with an innocent girl who reminds him of his dead wife. In her, he sees a chance to become a new man and an honest citizen. Unfortunately his partners and his intended have other plans: they want him captured or killed.

McQueen survives only with the help of a Spanish dance-hall girl named Colorado. After the heist, the couple flees to Old Mexico, where they renounce their crimes and give the stolen money to a Spanish mission, purifying themselves in God's eyes. Unfortunately, the lawmen on their trail want *earthly* justice, and Colorado quickly recognizes that they're just "a couple in a dead village, dreaming about something that will probably never happen." The lovers make their last stand in the City of the Moon, a village of stone where a tribe of renegade Indians made their last stand against the U.S. government. A counterpoint to *Four Faces West*, *Colorado Territory* takes place in a world with no place for a reformed killer.

In contrast with the noir westerns of the day, John Ford's *Fort Apache* (1948) hinges less on the moral dilemma of any particular character than on the strength of the bond between *all* the characters. Ford's subsequent films in his celebrated Cavalry Trilogy, *She Wore a Yellow Ribbon* (1949) and *Rio Grande* (1950), are shorter, more restrained pieces, but the same thing can be said of them: they are testaments to the strength of a community. Behind the scenes, Ford built his own personal cavalry troupe, using actors and crew members from his previous films, in order to convey a deeply personal philosophy about America in the postwar years.

In *Fort Apache*, Ford cast Henry Fonda in the role of Lt. Col. Owen Thursday, a warmongering character based on General George Armstrong Custer.[10] The liberal-minded actor's portrayal of Thursday as "an unsmiling, bitter, strict hardass" (to borrow the words of his son Peter Fonda[11]) was a far cry from his portrayal of Wyatt Earp as a soft-spoken moral crusader. Fonda's Earp was the self-appointed guardian of modern America; Lt. Thursday is a self-serving maniac who foolishly sacrifices his entire regiment for personal glory. In contrast, John Wayne's character in the film, Captain Kirby York, is a rational and peaceable leader. In the end, it is clear that the storyteller's sympathies are with Wayne's character—not just because York is a better leader, but because he is a better soldier. At the end of the film, York loyally defends Thursday's actions and secures the dead man's legacy, because John Ford believed that communal bonds were more important than political differences. Only the former would help the nation to survive the type of mistakes and tragedies that occur in *Fort Apache*.

Howard Hawks set out to explore this idea further when he cast Wayne in *Red River* (1948), as a character even viler than Col. Thursday. In fact, Wayne's character in *Red River* was gruffer, more violent and more thoroughly unlikable than any western hero to date. (For that reason, Gary Cooper had turned down the role, believing that he would appear "too mean and unsympathetic for an audience to tolerate."[12]) Hawks, however, believed that the extreme characterization was necessary to tell the type of story he wanted to tell. "The western is the simplest form of drama," he explained, "and they all fall, really, into two kinds. One is the history of the beginning of the West, the story of the pioneers, which was the story of *Red River*. Then there's the phase when law and order comes."[13] Ford had made the definitive law and order western with *My Darling Clementine*, so Hawks set out to make the definitive pioneer western. As Tom Dunson, John Wayne became the embodiment of American progress—good, bad, and ugly. The film asked a simple question about the country's past and future: *Can a community really endure the rugged individualist's concept of "destiny"?*

Red River begins on the Chisholm Trail in 1851, when Dunson leaves a cattle drive to start his own herd. Soon after, his former traveling companions—including the woman he loves—are massacred by Cherokee Indians. This hardens Dunson's already-stubborn heart. He now has only one reason to live: to build his own empire and see it flourish. As he amasses his herd, Dunson becomes a mentor and father-figure to a young man named Matthew Garth (played by Montgomery Clift). After ten years of preparation, they hire a group of cowboys to drive the huge herd north to Missouri.

From the outset, Dunson makes his expectations clear to the others: "Every man who signs on for this drive agrees to finish it. There'll be no quitting along the way—not by me and not by you." Some of the cowboys find out the hard way that Dunson means what he says: the punishment for quitting is death. Matt backs him up initially, but as Dunson's actions become more and more reprehensible, he proves to be more soft-hearted than his surrogate father. Eventually, Matt stands up to Dunson to save a man from unlawful hanging, and Dunson promises to kill him for it. After the betrayal, Dunson becomes ghostlike, haunting Matt for the remainder of the cattle drive—even as the younger cowboy tries to settle down with Tess Millay, a strong-willed pioneer woman he meets on the trail. At this point, Dunson becomes a man without empathy.

The director was acutely aware that he was "walking a tightrope in telling a story like that." The slightest nuances could turn the audience against the main character, and thus against the film itself. On set, Hawks reassured Wayne that "the great thing in your favor is the boy is standing up for you all the time."[14] If the audience cares about Matt Garth, and Matt cares about Tom Dunson, then the audience can't hate Dunson. In the end, however, the only thing that prevents Dunson from killing Matt is an intervention by Tess, who reminds both men that their familial bond is stronger and more important than their egos. The ending deviates from Borden Chase's source story, in which Dunson tries but fails to kill his surrogate son. Chase remembered: "Wayne gets really badly hurt and then finishes the trip on the wagon with the gal. And he's just about dead. Montgomery Clift draws, but he simply can't bring himself to shoot, whereas Wayne tries like hell, is shooting, but he's so far gone he can't hit him. He fires a half dozen shots at him and then falls face down."[15] Reflecting on the revised ending, Hawks said: "I certainly would have hated to kill one of them."[16] The director's ending suggests that Hawks shared Ford's basic vision of America—his belief that we survive the threats of greed and power not by acting as individuals, but by coming together as a community.

While the western traditionalists sounded these rallying cries, other filmmakers expressed less optimism about the spirit of America in the postwar years. In *The Man from Colorado* (1948), also written by *Red River* scribe Borden Chase, ex–Marine Glenn Ford played a Civil War veteran who can't stop killing even though he knows that the war is over. Violence is no longer simply a part of his world; it is a part—and perhaps the larger part—of his own soul. Upon returning home, Ford's Col. Owen Devereaux accepts an appointment as a federal hanging judge and quickly finds himself at odds with some of his own former soldiers, who have returned home to lesser prospects. Most of them are learning that their land has been legally, but unfairly, confiscated while they were away. When the veterans rebel, Devereaux goes "crazy with power." Even an old friend and fellow officer, played by William Holden, can't change the fact that the war has already killed Devereaux. He's hellbound, and determined to take everyone down with him.

Madness is also the central obsession of John Huston's contemporary western, *The Treasure of the Sierra Madre* (1948), an adaptation of B. Travern's novel that also drew on

"Crazy with power": Glenn Ford as hellbound Col. Owen Devereaux in *The Man from Colorado* (1948, Columbia).

the writer/director's experiences as a horseman in the Mexican army. The film features Humphrey Bogart as a down-on-his-luck drifter in 1920s Mexico who teams up with a kindly old prospector who warns him about the dangers of gold fever. "I know what gold does to men's souls," the old-timer says ominously. He doesn't have to explain. Before long, Bogart's wild eyes say it all. After Bogart murders his partner for money, the desert landscape takes on a spectral quality; dancing firelight turns sharp-edged plants and tree branches into vengeful spirits.

Like many popular examples of film noir, *Treasure* paints a pessimistic portrait of human nature—a portrait counterbalanced only by the final scene, with the vague suggestion of a higher moral arbiter at work in the world. In the end, death claims the unrepentant killer and the wind carries away his gold. The moral message seems to be that greed is the root of all evil and murder does not go unpunished. The message was reiterated in a number of imitative westerns, including *Lust for Gold* (1949) with Glenn Ford and Ida Lupino, and *The Walking Hills* (1949), an early John Sturges western starring Randolph Scott and Ella Raines.

Gregory Peck faced a similar moral crisis in director William Wellman's *Yellow Sky* (1948), one of the most overtly religious westerns of its day. In the beginning of the film,

"A Dante-esque jurney": Gregory Peck (front) leads his gang of outlaws through the inferno in *Yellow Sky* (1948, 20th Century–Fox).

Peck is a hardened criminal concerned only about money. Later, after he and his gang of bank robbers get lost in the desert, he begins to re-think his priorities. Much as the midnight landscape in *The Treasure of the Sierra Madre* made Bogart believe in ghosts, so the desert landscape in *Yellow Sky* makes Peck believe in Hell. The filming location in Death Valley perfectly conveys the allegorical quality of W.R. Burnett's source novel about a Dante-esque journey through the Inferno and Purgatory.

When the outlaws reach the town of Yellow Sky and find that it is nothing but a dried-up old ghost town, they abandon all hope. Moments later, a woman shows up and leads them to water. Some of the men are grateful; the rest are oddly determined to drown each other. Lamar Trotti's script continues to develop as a spiritual allegory. After the outlaws have been plucked from the Inferno by grace or providence ("something bigger" than themselves), they learn that the town is literally a gold mine. From that point forward, each man's actions determine his fate. Peck's character reassures his angelic rescuer and her elderly father that he's "from good people"—his mother raised him in the church, he explains—and he promises to deal with them fairly and honestly, even if it turns his companions against him. It does, of course, and the hero has to fight for his own salvation. For the actor, it was an important role. Peck was raised in Catholic and Episcopalian churches, and he later said that Christianity was for him "like an anchor to windward—something that's seen me through troubled times and some personal tragedies."[17]

Films like *The Treasure of the Sierra Madre* and *Yellow Sky* are rare examples of vaguely metaphysical westerns. While most western films of the day dealt with crises of morality and ethics, very few addressed the supernatural. John Ford's remake *3 Godfathers* (1948), in which John Wayne is literally guided through the wilderness by the ghosts of his dead friends, is one notable exception, as are a handful of films that show the influence of RKO producer Val Lewton. Lewton produced one western, *Apache Drums* (1951), and his protégés Jacques Tourneur and Robert Wise each directed two significant examples of western noir.

Biographer Edmund G. Bansak points out that "one continuing thematic thread in the Tourneur films is the presence of an inescapable dark force."[18] In *Canyon Passage* (1946) and *Stars in My Crown* (1950), the force has dual aspects. One threatens the community from the outside and one threatens the community from the inside. In *Canyon Passage*, Indians are the exterior threat, while political corruption and mob violence are the interior threat. In *Stars in My Crown*, the faceless menace of the Ku Klux Klan is the exterior threat and an outbreak of typhoid (or, more to the point, the townfolk's reaction to the outbreak) is the interior threat. In the latter film, small-town preacher Josiah Grey (played by Joel McCrea) finds himself at odds with the local doctor on the issue of how to rid the town of its dark force. The doctor recommends quarantine; the parson suggests faith and prayer. Tourneur's film ultimately sides with Josiah, and the dark force is eradicated by "the will of God."

Robert Wise's first western, *Blood on the Moon*, demonstrated his ability to import the nightmarish existentialism of film noir into the genre. His second western was even darker. Based on a story by Frank Nugent, *Two Flags West* (1950) revolves around a Confederate prisoner of war played by Joseph Cotten. After a presidential pardon, he and his fellow soldiers agree to join the U.S. cavalry to help fight the Indian Wars on the western frontier. Naturally, there is some tension between the Southerners and the Union cavalrymen. It is broken only by the need to unite against a common enemy.

The second half of the film showcases an epic siege on Fort Thorn by an army of Apache warriors, followed by a dread-filled night of waiting for the battle to resume. The film tells us that Apaches won't fight in the dark, so the cavalrymen must wait to die. One character sums up the atmosphere with eerie calmness, saying, "I guess tomor-

Robert Mitchum in "the most Lewtonesque western ever filmed," *Track of the Cat* (1954, Warner Bros.).

row'll be the end of the world." As it turns out, tomorrow *is* the end of the world—but only for one character. Jeff Chandler's disabled Union vet sacrifices himself to save the Southerners he hates. Under the circumstances, his surrender is as devastating as any epic battle scene. Darkness and the ominous sound of native drums transform the soldier's heroism into a moment of sheer horror. After the Indians leave, one of the survivors struggles to summon feelings of hope for the future, but it is clear that she remains traumatized. "Doesn't the end of war have to be a beginning?" she asks, desperate for some reassurance. Her question hangs on the air for a long moment, until she finally answers her own question in the affirmative and a swell of reassuring music brings the film to a close. That initial silence, however, carries far more dramatic weight.

Val Lewton himself produced only one western, for director Hugo Fregonese, and it is strikingly similar to *Two Flags West*. *Apache Drums* (1951) tells the story of a diverse group of white settlers who get trapped inside an old presidio, surrounded by hostile Mescalero Indians. While the settlers await an inevitable siege, the Apaches beat their drums in ceremonial fashion, terrorizing the insiders in much the same way that the voodoo practitioners terrified the heroine of Lewton and Tourneur's horror film *I Walked with a Zombie*. Amid the growing tension, the supposedly civilized characters turn against each other. Some waste time and energy denouncing a half-breed and a killer in their midst, while others counsel tolerance and try to create a united front against the external threat. When the preacher among them denounces the "vile music of the heathens" and refers to the Indians as "evil," the killer expresses contradictory sympathy for the "savages." "The Apaches are dying," he says, reminding the others that the Indian culture has been destroyed by white men, and speculating that they are now on a mass suicide mission, intending to transform themselves into "ghost warriors." The speech suggests that the siege might only be the beginning of a different kind of war, and the rest of the film is pervaded by an overwhelming sense that fear is the real enemy.

Edmund G. Bansak tracked Lewton's spirit to yet another spiritual western made a few years later. *Track of the Cat* (1954), stars Robert Mitchum as a doomed hunter, trapped with his family in a blinding snowstorm that threatens to swallow them all, body and soul. Bansak calls it "the most Lewtonesque western ever filmed," noting that it uses symbolism and suspense techniques from Lewton's horror film *The Leopard Man* (1943) to convey tension between these white characters and the ghostly Native Americans outside their door.[19] Director William Wellman, however, later regretted following the model too closely, as he explained in his autobiography:

> The black panther was the symbol of the picture. It was the black panther that represented all that was bad in Mitchum and that finally kills him. In a fit of sophomoric thinking, I decided that we should never see said panther killing our hero. We should just hear it, and the audience could use their imagination, and the effect would be much more powerful [...] I was wrong. The audiences' imagination failed to imagine, and my arthritis became my black panther and the son of a bitch has been prowling around my system ever since.[20]

Audiences in the late 1940s may have been willing to accept such metaphysical conceits, but the style and techniques of film noir were already becoming passé in the early 1950s. By then, most western films—with rare exceptions like Edgar G. Ulmer's *The Naked Dawn* (1955) and William Witney's *Stranger at My Door* (1956)—were rooted firmly in the human psyche rather than the soul.

CHAPTER IV

High Noon
(1950–1956)

> *The American people have learned a lot from two world wars and from the last seven years of working to keep the peace. They know that as long as communism is loose in the world we must have allies and we must resist aggression. The American people are living in the atomic age, and they know that the ideas of the stone age won't work any more—if they ever did work.*
> —Harry S Truman, Jefferson–Jackson Dinner, March 29, 1952

Renowned French film critic André Bazin, writing about the evolution of the western film in 1955, coined the term "super-western" to define the post-war American western that is "ashamed to be just itself, and looks for some additional interest to justify its existence—an aesthetic, sociological, moral, psychological, political, or erotic interest, in short some quality extrinsic to the genre and which is supposed to enrich it."[1] *The Westerner* (1940), *The Ox-Bow Incident* (1943) and *The Outlaw* (1943) are early examples that fit Bazin's definition, but the influence of these films was minimal during the war. More ambiguous postwar westerns like *I Shot Jesse James* (1949) and *The Gunfighter* (1950) heralded a new age for the genre—an age in which the basic hero myth would embody conflicting ideas about America's new identity as the world's dominant superpower.

In the years leading up to World War II, social liberals and progressives of many stripes—including card-carrying communists—were united against fascism. Filmmaker Edward Dmytryk remembered, "Anyone who was against Fascist Spain or Italy, or Nazi Germany *after* Pearl Harbor was okay—obviously. But anyone who was against the fascists before Pearl Harbor had to have strong leftist leanings because only the Communist countries of the world officially resisted the spread of fascism at that time."[2] When the Soviets signed a non-aggression pact with Germany in 1939, however, many conservative Americans began to voice longstanding suspicions about the Communist Party and communist sympathizers. After the war, the U.S. government reinforced those fears by citing international communism as a threat to western society. In 1947, the FBI began investigating allegations of subversive activity in Hollywood, pitting ultra-conservatives like John Wayne against more liberal-minded peers. Three years later the United States went to war in Korea, launching a four-decades-long Cold War against international communism. At the same time, Hollywood filmmakers mobilized along party lines for an even longer propaganda war between American "liberals" and "conservatives."

Like many of his fellow filmmakers, John Ford underwent a political transformation during the years following World War II. In 1937, two years before he made *Stagecoach*,

Ford had declared himself "a definite socialist democrat—*always* left."³ His experiences during the war apparently changed his political bias, such that ten years later he was declaring himself a conservative Republican and routinely speaking out against communism.⁴ For the time being, however, his films continued to espouse a distinctly anti-war message. Ford followed up *Fort Apache* with two very different cavalry films, *She Wore a Yellow Ribbon* (1949) and *Rio Grande* (1950). The former begins with a pronouncement that Custer is dead, and focuses its story on Custer's successor, Captain Nathan Brittles. As Brittles, John Wayne projects a sturdy sense of duty and loyalty, but also the weariness of an old soldier who has witnessed too much death. When ordered to lead his men into another Little Big Horn–type battle, Brittles refuses, saying, "Old men should

"Old men should stop wars": John Wayne with Shirley Temple in *She Wore a Yellow Ribbon* (1949, RKO).

stop wars!" After doing just that, the character prepares to ride off into the sunset. His poignant farewell ceremony is Ford's tribute to a community of World War II soldiers who gave their lives for the greater good. The filmmaker later called it "the best thing I've ever done."⁵

In the final scene of the film, however, Captain Brittles is summoned back to duty. Ford and Wayne likewise went back to war movies. After *She Wore a Yellow Ribbon*, Wayne returned to the South Pacific to lead a Marine platoon in Allan Dwan's chest-beating World War II drama *Sands of Iwo Jima* (1949). Wayne's character, Sgt. John Striker, became the most indelible example of the actor's onscreen persona: a hard-headed, no-nonsense American cowboy ordering the younger generation to "saddle up!" In contrast, Ford opted for a more restrained exercise with his film *Wagon Master* (1950), an intimate story of two brothers who help a band of Mormon pioneers pursue a pure and simple dream of finding the "promised land" in the American West. Noting that Ford named *Wagon Master* as another personal favorite film, biographer Joseph McBride suggests that it represents the filmmaker's "indirect protest of the darkness, suspicion, and hatred that had enveloped America by the middle of the twentieth century."⁶ Like *She Wore a Yellow Ribbon*, *Wagon Master* is Ford at his most optimistic—arguably, for the last time in his filmmaking career.

When he reteamed with Wayne to make *Rio Grande*, Ford was on a more direct, less optimistic path. *Rio Grande* picks up where *Fort Apache* left off: John Wayne returns to the role of Kirby York, now a colonel who has been hardened by the sacrifices he's made in service of the U.S. Cavalry. The narrative offers him an opportunity to reconcile with his estranged wife and son, but requires him to forsake the military in order to do so: When York's son joins the Army, his wife asks him to discharge their boy from the military. York declines, saying, "If a man's worth anything, even his own destruction must be honored." For him, as for Ford and Wayne, courage and devotion to an honorable cause are more important than life itself. By supporting his son's decision to fight, York feels he has been loyal to both of his families.

Viewed within the context of the times, the plot of *Rio Grande* also has a distinctly political dimension. Wayne, who was positioning himself as *the* symbol of American patriotism at the precise moment when he became Hollywood's most popular star, characterized the film as an allegory for the Korean War, which had broken out ten days into filming. He explained:

> *Rio Grande* was written by James McGuiness as a metaphor for the invasion of South Korea by North Korean Communist forces. In *Rio Grande* it's the Apaches who come across the border to make their attacks, and then go back over the border where the cavalry weren't supposed to go. But Lieutenant Colonel York, the part I played, knew he had to lead his men across the border to save the lives of innocents. In Korea the Communists were making their raids into South Korea and then going back to the North. Well, I felt that our forces should have gone after them, and that's what York did in *Rio Grande*—and it was the right thing to do.[7]

Ford apparently agreed. Biographer Joseph McBride notes that the director strongly supported U.S. Army General Douglas McArthur's desire to pursue the communists into their own territory, rather than President Harry Truman's general policy of containment and "limited war."[8] The director confirmed his loyalties by making *This is Korea!*, a 1951 documentary that celebrated the opening volley of America's protracted war against communism.

By that point, Wayne had obviously undergone his own political awakening. Although Henry Fonda insisted that Wayne "couldn't even spell politics" in 1948, Wayne said that he became suspicious of communist activity in Hollywood as early as 1937.[9] Onscreen he fought alongside Chinese communists in the 1944 film *Back to Bataan* (a film, incidentally, that was directed by self-professed communist Edward Dmytryk), but off-screen he became a strident anti-communist and a committed Republican. By the time he made *Rio Grande*, he clearly associated patriotism with the Cold War policy of defense through aggression. As a result, John Wayne became America's leading symbol of militant liberty.

While Ford and Wayne presented the traditional cowboys-versus-Indians narrative as an allegory for the war on communism, filmmaker Delmar Daves and actor James Stewart (both progressive Republicans) turned a similar narrative into a treatise on racial tolerance and civil rights. *Broken Arrow* was not intended to be an overtly political film; Daves simply wanted to pay homage to his pioneer ancestors, and to share a simple life lesson he had learned from his own father. The filmmaker remembered, "We would be talking about religion and he'd say—before you make any decision: 'Go to every church there is. Go to the Catholic church; go to the Baptist church; go to all the Protestant churches; go to the Episcopalians; go to the Jewish synagogue; add it all up yourself.' Ever since I've had respect for the other man's religion. Don't be too quick to dismiss them." *Broken Arrow* applied the same philosophy of tolerance to Native American culture.[10]

The film revolves around the historical figure Thomas Jonathan Jeffords, a Pony Express mail carrier who rode alone into an Apache camp in the 1860s and negotiated a truce with tribal leader Cochise. According to Elliot Arnold, author of the source novel, Jeffords not only earned Cochise's trust and respect, but also fell in love with a young Apache squaw while he was there. "There is no record of their ever marrying," Arnold writes, but "I have taken a writer's liberty and imagined that such a wedding took place."[11] The union between Jeffords and Sonseeahray symbolizes hope for a future in which the white man and the red man live together in harmony, but that dream is quickly shattered by prejudiced settlers, who attempt to assassinate Cochise and end up killing Sonseeahray instead.

The film reflects several controversial political issues in 1950s America, including debates over racial segregation and so-called miscegenation. From 1863 until 1948, most U.S. states had laws prohibiting the marriage of whites to blacks, Indians or Asians. Many of those laws continued to be enforced until 1967. The U.S. military was segregated until 1948, and public schools until 1954. The racial integration of American society took even longer, culminating with the Civil Rights Act of 1964 and the Fair Housing Act of 1968. *Broken Arrow* anticipated these immanent changes by substituting 1880s Indians for all mid–20th century minority Americans, and African-Americans in particular. As a result, the film resonated strongly with audiences in 1950, and influenced a host of pro–Indian westerns, including *Devil's Doorway* (1950), *Across the Wide Missouri* (1951), *Tomahawk* (1951), *The Battle at Apache Pass* (1952), and *The Savage* (1952).

Some critics, however, interpret *Broken Arrow* in a darker light. Peter Biskind argues that the film expresses a white man's disenchantment with his own culture, rather than voicing a plea for racial equality. Stewart's character, he notes, doesn't simply make peace with the Apaches; he marries into their tribe. "In the context of cold-war politics," Biskind concludes, "if the Apache reds are the Russians reds ... then this film is saying that not only is red better than dead, it's better than white as well."[12] Critics of the day did not accuse *Broken Arrow* of communist propagandizing, but probably only because the name of the screenwriter was not on the finished film. When the film was released in July 1950 Albert Maltz was serving time in prison for refusing to testify before the House Un-American Activities Committee about an alleged communist conspiracy in Hollywood.

By 1951, when the committee launched a second round of hearings, hundreds of film industry employees had been blacklisted due to allegations that they were affiliated with the Communist Party. Director John Huston, whose 1948 film *The Treasure of the Sierra Madre* was suspected of espousing a socialist agenda, remembered, "Suddenly people were made into circus performers. If they didn't jump through hoops, they were disgraced, ruined, and destroyed. I had a great sense of shame at that time."[13] While some filmmakers became "friendly witnesses" for HUAC, others maintained that the investigations were a violation of First and Fifth Amendment rights.

Director Elia Kazan was among those who testified before the House Un-American Activities Committee. He confirmed that he had been a member of the Communist Party in the mid–1930s, explaining, "It seemed to me at that time that the party had at heart the cause of the poor and unemployed people who I saw on the streets about me. I felt that by joining, I was going to help them, I was going to fight Hitler, and, strange as it seems today, I felt that I was acting for the good of the American people."[14] By 1936, however, he had changed his mind and left the party. In 1952, he committed his anti-communist sentiments to the screen in *Viva Zapata!*, a biopic of Mexican revolutionary Emiliano Zapata. Kazan told interviewer Jeff Young about the origins of the film: "[Screenwriter] John [Steinbeck] and I were both ex–Communists, and Zapata's story allowed us to show metaphorically what had happened to the Communists in the Soviet Union—how their leaders became reactionary and repressive rather than forward thinking and progressive."[15]

In the film, one of the first American westerns set during the Mexican Revolution, actor Marlon Brando plays Zapata as a reluctant leader. At first, he is one of many peasant farmers who appear before a totalitarian president to contest land rights. When the president labels him a rabble-rouser and tries to have him killed, however, Zapata rebels with a small but disciplined army. In a crucial moment when he has the opportunity to seize money and power for himself, Zapata remains principled and humble. He tells his followers: "You always look for leaders, strong men without faults. There aren't any. There are only men like yourselves. They change. They desert. They die. There are no leaders but yourselves. A strong people is the only lasting strength." Kazan reflected, "No Communist, no totalitarian, ever refused power. By showing that Zapata did this, we spoiled a poster figure that the Communists have been at some pains to create."[16] Obviously eager to distance himself from the Party, the director named names in his 1952 HUAC testimony—a move that understandably cost him many friends in Hollywood.

At the other end of the political spectrum, screenwriter Carl Foreman refused to testify before HUAC about his alleged affiliation with the Communist Party, and instead channeled his beliefs into the script for his next film. "I used a western background," he explained, "to tell the story of a community corrupted by fear, with the implications I hoped would be obvious to almost everyone who saw the film, at least in America."[17] Foreman's script for *High Noon* (1952) began with an image of a deserted ghost town, which the writer describes "a town that died because it lacked sufficient fiber of its citizenship to stand behind a man on moral grounds."[18] The completed film focuses instead on the town's demise, and on the hero who stood alone.

Gary Cooper plays Will Kane, a noble lawman who has served and protected the people of Hadleyville for years. When a

Communist or anti-communist? Marlon Brando with Jean Peters in *Viva Zapata!* (1952, 20th Century–Fox).

group of vengeful criminals come to kill him, however, he suddenly finds himself without any friends or deputies. Everyone around him cowers in fear, leaving Kane to defend himself against seemingly insurmountable odds. At the end of the film the sheriff survives thanks to the intervention of his pacifist wife, then he decides to leave the town and abandon his duties as a lawman. Foreman's message was glaringly obvious, and as a result the project drew protests from some quarters. John Wayne avoided criticizing star Gary Cooper, a fellow right-winger who told HUAC a few years earlier that he had "turned down quite a few scripts because I thought they were tinged with communistic ideas," but Wayne called *High Noon* "the most un–American thing I've ever seen in my whole life."[19] Howard Hawks was more diplomatic, but opined that Kane was definitely not his idea of a "good western sheriff," suggesting that a *real* western hero would never have asked for help in the first place.[20] Hawks and Wayne alike claimed that the cowardly townfolk in *High Noon* were not representative of the America they knew.

Heroic or un–American? Gary Cooper with Grace Kelly in *High Noon* **(1952, United Artists).**

Regardless of its political subtext, *High Noon* became one of the most commercially successful westerns of its day, inspiring a rash of imitations, including *Riding Shotgun* (1954), *Silver Lode* (1954), *At Gunpoint* (1955), and *The Proud Ones* (1956). In the years since its release, the film has become a modern classic that many viewers regard as a timeless myth rather than a timely allegory. Film historian Michael F. Blake argues that *High Noon* illustrates an ideal cowboy "code of honor," which he sums up as follows: "Keep your word, don't let anyone bully you, never let a friend down, stand up for what's right and for the weak, treat a woman decently and be true to yourself."[21] Blake observes that Will Kane is a thoroughly *human* embodiment of these values; he experiences and expresses fear and anger, but he still manages to rise above those feelings and do the right thing. In the critic's estimation, this inner conflict makes the hero more complex and even more admirable than earlier screen western heroes who never exhibited such vulnerability.

Shane (1953)—perhaps the only western film of the 1950s to cast a longer shadow than *High Noon*—is on the surface a much simpler myth, viewing its hero through the

A symbol of nuclear deterrence? Alan Ladd as *Shane* (1953, Paramount).

eyes of a child. For author Jack Schaefer, who wrote source novel during the final months of World War II, that was a very conscious decision. He later explained: "*Shane* began as a study of the basic legend of the West, the man with a gun using it to right wrongs, in a sense the American version of a knight on horseback. I deliberately presented the story through the eyes of a boy so that the man himself, seen thus, could be thrown up larger than life, more heroic, without the tale degenerating into outright overblown melodrama."[22]

In the novel that boy is named Bob, and the author articulates Bob's first impression of Shane as follows: "He rode easily, relaxed in the saddle, leaning his weight lazily into the stirrups. Yet even in his easiness was a suggestion of tension. It was the easiness of a coiled spring, of a trap set."[23] Bob senses danger in Shane, but also cause for hope. When a greedy cattle rancher tries to bully Bob's family off of their land, Shane comes to their rescue. Up to a point he remains passive, but his eventual actions prove lethally effective. One could argue that Shane is the ideal American hero as defined by Theodore Roosevelt at the turn of the 20th century: He speaks softly and carries a big stick. In the wake of World War II, that same symbol correlates with the political idea of nuclear deterrence. Shane is merely a threat, until he explodes. After that, there is no more argument.

For filmmaker George Stevens, who made *Shane* as the second film in his so-called "American Trilogy" (which also includes 1951's *A Place in the Sun* and 1956's *Giant*), the story was a more poignant wartime metaphor:

> In some sense Shane is a boy called to go into the Marine Corps because he's the strongest and best qualified to carry out his country's point of view. When you ask a man to fight and take a life, you not only ask him to risk his own life but you ask him to make a great sacrifice of his moral ideals. All our sons, like Shane, are gunfighters, but no mother is breeding her son to be a gunfighter. Shane, the gunman, points up to the sacrifices we call on our boys to make. He's a different man at the end of the picture, and we show this change in him through the character development of the boy Joey. [...] When the film ends and Shane rides away saying, "There's no living with a killing, Joey," we believe that audiences will feel that the boy has learned an important lesson about life.[24]

That lesson, according to the director, is twofold. On one hand, Shane reinforces the themes of the classic western that "the good man always comes out on top" and that "right can have violence on its side." On the other hand, it acknowledges a hard truth about the savior at the center of this violent myth: "Heroes can't have the comforts of ordinary men."[25]

Shane, played by soft-spoken Alan Ladd, teaches Joey about the heavy *responsibility* that comes with violence, and Stevens aimed to do the same thing for moviegoers. The director explained:

> In most westerns, everybody shoots and nobody gets hurt. One thing we tried to do in *Shane* was reorient the audience to the horror of a pistol. We used gunplay only as a last resort of extreme violence. There's no shooting in *Shane* except to define a gun shot, which for our purposes is a holocaust. It's not a gesture of bravado, it's death. When guns are used, they're deadly. Our characters have an abhorrence of violence and a knowledge of the responsibility of taking a life that doesn't exist in most westerns.[26]

Once the deed is done, there's no turning back for the man who pulled the trigger. At the end of the tale, Shane rides away because this particular corner of civilization has no further need for a soldier. Like Wyatt Earp in *My Darling Clementine*, Shane understands that the town—if it is to remain a *civilized* town—has no place for him. Even though he has taken sides with sodbusters who want to "grow families" instead of with ranchers who want to "grow beef," he does not belong to their community. He is a perpetual outsider, a permanent soldier, and he knows it. "A man has to be what he is," Shane tells Joey, and disappears into the dark, gritty landscape.

Obviously, Shane's reasons for leaving are very different from those of Will Kane. Shane accepts his responsibility as a soldier without asking for help or support. He becomes a hero to the community, but (unlike Kane) he does not expect to be treated as a member of the community. When John Wayne made *Hondo* (1953), his own personal variation on *Shane*, he sought a middle ground between the two perspectives. In *Hondo*, Wayne plays a notorious gunman living in Apache territory after the collapse of a long-standing peace agreement between Apaches and the U.S. government. Wayne's character once lived among the Apaches and regarded them as family, but now he has taken on the role of husband and father to a white widow and her young son. When the cavalry comes to "rescue" his new family from the savages, Hondo fights alongside the white soldiers without hesitation. After the battle, a fellow soldier predicts that the natives will soon be completely overrun. Hondo briefly laments "the end of a way of life," but his loyalty lies with the future of America. As a result, Wayne's *Shane* is about a primitively violent hero who exists *within* civilization and protects it from other primitively violent men like himself. In one sense, he is his own enemy—but that leads him only to vague feelings of melancholy, rather than to physical or emotional isolation. Such a narrative might have been particularly meaningful to "friendly" ex–Communists like Elia Kazan and Edward Dmytryk.

Director Nicholas Ray's *Johnny Guitar* (1954) took a more rebellious political stance. Although the film is named for actor Sterling Hayden's laconic drifter, the action revolves around a saloon owner named Vienna, played by the film's real star, Joan Crawford. Vienna's nemesis is a fiery young woman named Emma Small, who falsely accuses Vienna of murder, and then—with the help of a bigoted community leader played by Ward Bond—leads an angry lynch mob to hang her. According to film historian Andrew Sarris, screenwriter Philip Yordan intended the story as a veiled criticism of the communist witch-hunt of Senator Joseph McCarthy.[27] According to Yordan himself, however, it was Joan Crawford who was mainly responsible for the story that ended up onscreen: "She says, 'There's Sterling Hayden in the picture and he's not much and some other actor and he's not much and Ward Bond, one of the actors who John Ford is always using in those pictures with [John] Wayne, and he's not much. So I want to play the man. I want to shoot it out in the end with Mercedes McCambridge, and instead of me playing with myself in a corner, let Sterling play with himself in the corner and I'll do the shoot-out.'"[28]

For some viewers, the result is a western film that is feminist as well as anti–McCarthy. Film critic Jennifer Peterson disagrees, concluding that "the anti–McCarthy allegory betrays itself by merely scapegoating another marginalized figure: Emma."[29] Suggestions are made throughout the film that Emma Small is a homosexual, and the implied sexual politics overwhelm any hint of subtle messages about communism and the threat of mob rule. That said, it is still interesting to note the marginalization of Sterling Hayden—who had appeared as a friendly witness before HUAC in 1947—and the vilification of John Wayne's cavalry buddy Ward Bond, a notorious right-wing reactionary and former president of the Motion Picture Alliance for the Preservation of American Ideals. Hollywood insiders of the day could not have missed the implications.

The 1954 thriller *Bad Day at Black Rock*, a western set in post–World War II California, was equally pointed. The film begins when a one-armed stranger arrives in the type of ghost town that Carl Foreman envisioned for the opening of *High Noon*. *Bad Day* screenwriter Millard Kaufman—who, like Philip Yordan, served as a front for at least one blacklisted writer—describes the town of Black Rock as "a wasteland of the American Southwest," a "poisoned" well.[30] The stranger, played by Spencer Tracy, gradually comes to realize that the town and all the people living in it are harboring a dark secret. Tracy's character, John J. Macreedy, fights back the same way Shane fought back—by waiting.

"He's not much": Joan Crawford with Sterling Hayden in *Johnny Guitar* (1954, Republic).

Ostracized like Will Kane, he takes the abuse that is heaped on him by Ernest Borgnine's surly welcoming committee until he simply can't take anymore. Director John Sturges says this was how he achieved the dramatic effect he wanted: "You can have guys forty stories up, fighting on a six-inch ledge, and if you don't care who wins or loses, it's not much of a fight. The thing that makes that a great fight is the five minutes of needling that Tracy endures before he hits Borgnine. We went right up to the point where the audience, in disgust, is about to say, 'Oh, for Christ's sake!'"[31] When the fight is over, we learn what Macreedy was fighting for. He came to Black Rock to investigate the death of a Japanese-American farmer—a man who fought alongside Macreedy in the South Pacific, only to be murdered by prejudiced Americans upon his return home. Once the secret is out, the town suffers in shame.

From the beginning, some film critics suggested that *Bad Day at Black Rock* was an allegory for the communist witch-hunt, but another real-life injustice is even more analogous. On February 19, 1942, President Franklin Roosevelt had issued Executive Order 9066, authorizing the Secretary of War to deport Japanese Americans to internment camps, to prevent spying and sabotage during the war. One such camp, called Manzanar, stood ten miles north of the town of Lone Pine, California, where *Bad Day at Black Rock* was filmed. Unlike the people of Black Rock, however, the people of Lone Pine acknowledged the injustice. The director remembered, "Most people by [1954] sort of recognized the snap judgment of interning the Japanese Americans was wrong and done without justification. There were no known examples of spying or sabotage."[32] The U.S. government was slower to apologize. Executive Order 9066 was rescinded in 1976, but reparations were not made to the victims until 1990, in the aftermath of the Cold War. By then, many of the victims were dead.

As the Cold War continued to heat up, filmmakers Delmar Daves and John Ford continued to explore the theme of racial tolerance, but their films grew increasingly ambiguous. Whereas *Broken Arrow* emphasized an Indian point of view on American history, Daves' *Drum Beat* (1954) focused on the perspective of white settlers in the midst of the Indian Wars. Alan Ladd stars as Johnny McKay, an Indian fighter sent to Oregon by President Ulysses Grant to negotiate peace, only to discover that Modoc chief Captain Jack (played by a steely-eyed young Charles Bronson) doesn't want peace. "President sick of war," Captain Jack barks, but "I not sick of war." McKay tries to convince him that "in war, only one side wins; in peace, both sides win," but Captain Jack's experience with U.S. treaties has taught him otherwise. Even when McKay demonstrates tremendous faith in his reputedly "faithless enemies," the Modoc chief refuses to yield. War seems inevitable.

Following the revolutionary message of *Broken Arrow*, *Drum Beat* may have seemed like a betrayal to some viewers. Historians claim that the real Captain Jack wanted to avoid going to war, but was eventually goaded into conflict by his own followers.[33] The film, on the other hand, decisively depicts him as a warmonger. Film critic Michael Walker suggests that the change in tone, from *Broken Arrow* to *Drum Beat*, reflects changes in the country during the four years between the making of the two films: "In 1950, the political climate was more amenable to a liberal film like *Broken Arrow*. By 1954, after four years of Joseph McCarthy's attacks on the Left, even liberalism could seem politically suspect. *Drum Beat*, with its depiction of the failure of liberalism (the peace council) and the necessity for direct military action against the Indian (read communist) enemy, registers the shift to the right only too clearly."[34] Although the narrative presumes that a violent confrontation between the cavalry and the Modocs is inevitable, at least *Drum Beat* repeats the core message of *Broken Arrow*: Only a human being, not a skin color, can be trustworthy or untrustworthy. The film concludes on a vaguely hopeful note, making the assertion that "among the Indians as among our people, the good in heart outnumber the bad."

White Feather (1955), a subsequent film co-written by Daves, seeks a middle ground between the radical liberalism of *Broken Arrow* and the hopeful resignation of *Drum Beat*—building its narrative around the subject of racial integration, just one year after the desegregation of public schools in the American South. Reversing the narrative of *Broken Arrow*, *White Feather* follows a Cheyenne woman named Appearing Day who abandons her tribe to marry a U.S. Army soldier. When Appearing Day's brother wages war against white settlers, she tries to bring the two cultures together. "Maybe if we could live in the white man's world," she pleads, "there would be no more talk of dying." For the Cheyenne people, facing exile and extinction, the film presents racial integration as the only real hope for the future. The following year, Daves' *The Last Wagon* and the Audie Murphy vehicle *Walk the Proud Land* reiterated the message.

Of course, not everyone in 1950s America supported such a future. Accordingly, some westerns continued to depict the country in terms of "us" and "them." No film did so more powerfully than John Ford's *The Searchers* (1956), starring John Wayne as a morally reprehensible Indian fighter named Ethan Edwards. Something of an antithesis to Wayne's open-hearted character in *Hondo* (1953), Edwards is a bitter ex–Confederate soldier who becomes downright misanthropic after Comanche Indians slaughter his brother's wife and abduct his niece Debbie. He spends the next several years searching for the marauders, with the firm intention of avenging his brother's wife and putting Debbie out of her misery. Edwards is disgusted by the idea of racial integration, and seems prepared to kill every Indian he meets in order to prevent a future in which white men and red men live in harmony.

Years after the film was released, an interviewer boldly suggested to Wayne that Ethan Edwards was an outright villain. The actor vigorously defended his character, saying, "He was no villain. He was a man living in his times. The Indians fucked his wife. What would you have done?"[35] Wayne apparently misremembered the details of the story, but obviously not the raw emotions that he brought to the character. He later claimed to have built his performance on a crucial background detail from Alan LeMay's source novel (itself based on the true story of frontiersman James Parker)—specifically, the revelation that Ethan was in love with his brother's murdered wife. In a more didactic mode, however, he suggested that his motivation was more political: "I just thought of the Apaches not as Indians but as the Communists who'd been trying to kill me. I thought, What if the Commies were the ones who had done this? What if they had managed to burn down my home and kill my family? You see, I can be a method actor too."[36]

To director John Ford, *The Searchers* was simply the "tragedy of a loner.... He was just a plain loner—could never really be part of the family."[37] One character in the film both pities and praises Ethan, saying, "[He's] nothing but a human man way out on a limb—this year and next [and] maybe for a hundred more." The same character adds, hopefully, "But I don't think it'll be forever. Some day this country's gonna be a fine good place to be." The description says as much about Ford's view of America in 1956 as it does about the character. Film historian James Hoberman sums up *The Searchers* as "a movie about pathology—not just Ford's but America's." He views the film within the context of Hollywood's biggest blockbusters of the 1950s, including *The Wild One* (1953) and *Invasion of the Body Snatchers* (1956): "Ethan takes America's sins—racism, cruelty, violence, intolerance—onto himself. He is not just the Necessary Evil, frontier precursor to the Patriot Roughneck, but an utterly unapologetic, self-reliant, pod fighting force of nature—the rootless Wild One given a cause, perhaps even made a saint in his essentially selfless quest to liberate an innocent child from the Redskin Menace."[38]

Hoberman concludes with a nod to the larger-than-life actor at the center of the film: "Only the Cowboy Warrior would have had the swaggering confidence to play an obsessed white supremacist as a true American."[39] And, of course, only the 1950s—a decade during which the U.S. government contemplated an aggressive "rollback" policy against communist countries half a world away, while continuing to deny basic civil rights to its own citizens—could have produced an unapologetic hero as self-righteous as Ethan Edwards. He may not have been an ideal hero, but he was *our* hero.

CHAPTER V

The Masculine Mystique
(1950–1959)

At such a time in history, we who are free must proclaim anew our faith. This faith is the abiding creed of our fathers. It is our faith in the deathless dignity of man, governed by eternal moral and natural laws. This faith defines our full view of life. It establishes, beyond debate, those gifts of the Creator that are man's inalienable rights, and that make all men equal in His sight. In the light of this equality, we know that the virtues most cherished by free people— love of truth, pride of work, devotion to country—all are treasures equally precious in the lives of the most humble and of the most exalted. The men who mine coal and fire furnaces, and balance ledgers, and turn lathes, and pick cotton, and heal the sick and plant corn—all serve as proudly and as profitably for America as the statesmen who draft treaties and the legislators who enact laws.
—Dwight D. Eisenhower, inaugural address, January 20, 1953

The new breed of super-westerns was so commercially successful in the early 1950s that most of the male stars in Hollywood were eventually given a pair of cowboy boots and pressed into the roundup. A few of those stars became iconic westerners, contributing to a new kind of masculine mystique in America. In the wake of World War II, the United States had reached the apex of its military might, wealth and political influence, so it was only natural that Hollywood would project a larger-than-life image of America's mythic hero. Postwar western heroes, however, were strikingly different from pre-war western heroes. Before World War II, most western heroes were humble and altruistic, resorting to violence only when it became absolutely necessary to protect the greater good. After World War II, some western heroes generally became self-righteous, self-absorbed, impulsive and obsessive—or even downright neurotic. In the 1950s heyday of the western genre, larger-than-life actors like John Wayne, James Stewart, Joel McCrea and Randolph Scott, as well as newcomers like Kirk Douglas, Burt Lancaster and Charlton Heston, embodied the continually evolving myth of the ideal American male.

Henry King's film *The Gunfighter* (1950) effectively established the moral ambiguity of the new western hero. The film tells the story of Jimmy Ringo, a historical figure who spent years building a reputation as a gunslinger, and reputedly sacrificed everything else along the way. When Ringo decides to settle down with his estranged wife and son, who are living in secrecy in the sleepy southwestern town of Cayenne, he discovers that he can't trade in his notorious reputation for a civilized life. Everywhere he goes, he's a celebrity—hunted by friends and family of people he's killed (or allegedly killed), or by young glory-seekers who want to kill him.

Gregory Peck as legendary gunslinger Jimmy Ringo, with Helen Westcott in *The Gunfighter* **(1950, 20th Century–Fox).**

Earlier westerns presented the western hero as an outsider, at odds with civilized society because of his tendency to solve problems with violence, but *The Gunfighter* generated unprecedented sympathy for a weary but unrepentant killer. From the moment Ringo arrives in Cayenne, he is a victim (albeit a victim of his own choices and actions). Two men try to kill him, and a group of high-minded society ladies try to run him out of town, claiming that his presence is "demoralizing" for the townsfolk. A sympathetic sheriff observes that the opposite is true: "The trouble so far ain't been him demoralizing the town. It's the town demoralizing him." Ringo complains, "It's a fine life, ain't it? Just trying to stay alive? Not really living … not enjoying anything, not getting anywhere. Just trying to keep from getting killed." He doesn't seem to appreciate the fact that he has sown the seeds of his own destruction. For that reason, it is inevitable that Ringo will die in the end, but his story is tragic because he dies on the verge of a new beginning. In the final analysis, this gunfighter is neither hero nor villain. He is his own enemy.

Director Anthony Mann brought the same moral ambiguity to the westerns he made in the 1950s. Mann was no stranger to classical tragedy, having built his reputation on thrillers like *Strangers in the Night* (1944) and *Raw Deal* (1948), in which "hero and villain are at the mercy of passions molded by events of the inescapable past."[1] He imported the fatalistic philosophy of film noir into his first two westerns, *Devil's Doorway* (1950) and *The Furies* (1950). In the former, Robert Taylor plays a Shoshone Indian who is effectively cursed by the color of his skin. In the latter, Barbara Stanwyck's Oedipal relationship with her father causes the death of everyone and everything she loves. The same fatalistic philosophy informs Mann's subsequent westerns, but the later films are neither classical tragedies (in which the fate of the hero is often predetermined) nor classical westerns (in which the morality of the hero is beyond reproach). Mann helped to redefine the western hero by redefining the persona of one of Hollywood's biggest stars.

At the center of every Mann western is a lone individual struggling against challenges of man and nature with overwhelming determination. From 1950 until 1955, that individual was James Stewart. At the start of the decade, Stewart was a well-known actor and a decorated war hero, but he was beginning to see the limitations of his public persona. The actor later explained to Peter Bogdanovich:

> I realized after the war that I wasn't going across anymore, after a couple of pictures. I remember on *Magic Town*, one critic wrote, "If we have to sit through another picture while that beanpole stumbles around, taking forever to get things out..." The *New York Times* sent a guy out here to do an article on me, and he said, "Now, I'll tell ya right off, the title of this thing is gonna be, 'The Rise and Fall of Jimmy Stewart!'" I realized I'd better do *something*—I couldn't just go on hemming and hawing—which I sometimes overdid too.... I look at an old picture a mine—*Born to Dance*—I wanted to *vawmit*! I had t' ... toughen it up...[2]

Stewart allied himself with producer Aaron Rosenberg to make a western—but not the kind of western for which he was known. The actor remembered receiving hate mail after *Destry Rides Again*, from "people who objected to the idea of a cowboy, especially a sheriff, who refused to use a gun," and "claimed I was distorting the whole tradition of the cowboy in the Old West."[3] In *Winchester '73* (1950), a film named for a gun, Stewart would play a man *defined* by his ability to use a gun.

Screenwriter Borden Chase created the character of Lin McAdam by drawing on the actor's past. Remembering that Stewart was in the Air Force and that he "knew how to kill," Chase wrote to the actor's "ability with a gun, his tenacity, his straightforwardness."[4] Next, Anthony Mann conspired to make Stewart even tougher by challenging the actor's mental and physical strength. According to film critic John Kitses, "Mann was to speak admiringly of Stewart's readiness to do virtually anything from staging a fight under horses' hooves to allowing himself to be dragged through a fire."[5] The director spoke just as enthusiastically about their first collaboration: "As for *Winchester '73*, that was one of my biggest successes, and it's always my favorite western: the gun which passed from hand to hand allowed me to embrace a whole epoch, a whole atmosphere. I really believe that it contains all the ingredients of the western, and that it summarizes them."[6] Indeed, the narrative was so rich that the filmmaker and star continued to mine it for several years, producing a multi-film odyssey for Stewart's "revenge hero."

At the beginning of *Winchester '73*, Stewart is already a different kind of western hero. The opening sequence contrasts him with Wyatt Earp, the classical hero of *My Darling Clementine*. When the two men meet the film's main villain Dutch Henry Brown, Wyatt Earp remains calm, cool and collected. McAdam, on the other hand, is seething and impulsive. While Earp is focused on maintaining law and order, McAdam seeks Old Testament justice. As the story unfolds, we learn that Dutch Henry Brown is actually Matthew McAdam, Lin's patricidal brother—and the two men have much more in common than Lin and Wyatt Earp. When one character in the film observes, "Dutch Henry is a murderer," another responds, "So is Lin." For his part, Lin McAdam claims that he doesn't like killing—but he justifies his actions by saying "there's some things a man has to do, so he does it."

In pursuit of revenge, McAdam has to leave civilization (the town presided over by

Wyatt Earp) and follow his brother into the wilderness—an ominous landscape haunted by persistent rumors of the battle of Little Big Horn. As the environment becomes increasingly hostile, the avenger's resolve hardens. By the time the two men come face to face, Lin is not only trying to kill his brother; he's also trying to kill the darkest part of himself. It is unclear, however, whether revenge will make him a hero or a villain. One character wonders aloud what Lin McAdam will be like if he gets his revenge. Lin admits that he hasn't given it much thought, and Mann's film doesn't give it much thought either. In the final scene, McAdam returns to civilization, to a woman who represents the possibility of a new beginning.

In a sense, Mann, Chase and Stewart picked up where they left off in *Bend of the River* (1952), a film that muses on the hero's "new beginning" and his relationship with society. At the start of the film, Stewart's character Glyn McLintock is trying to escape his violent past by heading north to become a peaceful rancher. Along the way, he crosses paths with Emerson Cole, a man with an equally dark past. When Cole asks his new friend what he's running from, McLintock answers pointedly, "A man by the name of Glyn McLintock." Cole promises, "He'll catch up with you one of these days." As film critic Jeanine Basinger points out, he already has—in the form of Emerson Cole.[7]

Over the course of the film, both men learn that they cannot permanently escape violence. In Mann's West, violence is as inevitable as sunshine in the desert and as necessary as rain. Before long, the reformed hero is once again seeking revenge—hunting down his alter ego like Lin McAdam in *Winchester '73*, or John Wayne in *Red River*. Unlike Cole, however, Glyn is ultimately able to shake off his primitive impulses and join a peace-loving community. "Men can change," he says hopefully. "Some men." The hero kills Cole not for revenge, but in order to protect the community that has given him a second chance.

The Naked Spur (1953) charts a similar moral recovery, but from a much more vulnerable place. This time Stewart's character, Howard Kemp, is coping with the betrayal of a woman he loved—an emotional trauma that makes him even more volatile and unsympathetic than Lin McAdam in *Winchester '73*. Kemp directs his rage toward an outlaw named Ben Vandergroat, but Vandergroat—a more rational, if not more principled, man—quickly recognizes the hero's fragility and tries to psychologically dismantle him. The outlaw enlists the help of an innocent young woman named Lina, who must ultimately decide whether or not to help push Kemp over the edge. In the end, her decency neutralizes the other woman's betrayal, allowing Kemp to overcome his dark half once and for all.

Mann and Stewart worked together on two more films, both of which emphasized the would-be hero's need for love and community on the path to redemption. In *The Far Country* (1954), Stewart plays Jeff Webster, a drifter with very little faith in civilization. When he finds himself in the middle of a gold rush in the Yukon, he does his best to avoid getting involved in a violent struggle between working-class miners and corrupt businessmen, insisting, "I don't need other people. I don't need help. I can take care of *me*." After claim-jumpers attack him and leave him for dead, however, Jeff rethinks his philosophy of life. A young woman nurses him back to health, explaining, "You've got to help people when they need help." She follows up, "What kind of a world would it be if everybody was...?" Jeff knowingly finishes her sentence, "Like me?" Following his recovery, he dedicates himself—and his gun—to the community.

In *The Man from Laramie* (1955), Stewart's character Will Lockhart emerges as the

Emerson Cole (Arthur Kennedy, on horseback) stares down his alter ego Glyn McLintock (James Stewart) in *Bend of the River* (1951, Universal).

sum of the actor's roles in Mann's cinematic West. The director remembers, "I wanted to recapitulate, somehow, my five years of collaboration with Jimmy Stewart: that work distilled our relationship. I reprised themes and situations by pushing them to their paroxysm."[8] Like Lin McAdam in *Winchester '73*, Lockhart arrives in town at the beginning of *The Man from Laramie* with revenge on his mind. He is searching for a man who sold repeating rifles to a band of Apaches, holding that man indirectly responsible for the murder of his brother. Almost immediately, however, he finds himself in the middle of a local range war, and at the mercy of a hot-headed young gun named Dave Waggoman. At first it appears as if Waggoman is the man Lockhart is looking for, but the real villain turns out to be a more sympathetic character.

Played by Arthur Kennedy (who starred as Emerson Cole in *Bend of the River*) Vic Hansbro is a hard-working, level-headed cowboy who becomes almost like a brother to Lockhart. When Lockhart learns that Hansbro sold the rifles, he is reluctant to exact revenge. In the end, thankfully, he doesn't have to. Hansbro's reprehensible actions lead to his murder by Apaches, as circumstances beyond human control divide Mann's world into men who can tame their impulses and men who can't. The latter are consumed by life. The former emerge as true western heroes. With *The Man from Laramie*, Stewart's revenge hero finally manages to escape the cycle of violence and become a more traditional western hero.

Unfortunately, Anthony Mann and James Stewart never made another western together after *The Man from Laramie*. Stewart turned down the lead role in Mann's *The Last Frontier* (1956), and Mann abandoned the Stewart vehicle *Night Passage* (1957).[9] Nevertheless, the themes of their five collaborations continued to resonate in their later works and in the work of other western filmmakers.

During the same period that Mann and Stewart forged their alliance, independent producer Hal B. Wallis was busily grooming three new stars to become iconic western heroes. "At the time," Wallis remembered, "there was a shortage of rugged leading men. I went east in 1945 determined to find actors of this type."[10] His first discovery was "a lithe, barrel-chested, six-footer with a mop of wavy blond hair" and "a jauntiness, a self-confident grace that commanded attention."[11] The actor's name was Kirk Douglas.

Wallis promptly cast Douglas in a string of film noir thrillers, which led to a breakout role in the boxing drama *Champion* (1949). The performance earned Douglas an Oscar nomination and a non-exclusive contract at Warner Bros., where he was tested as a leading man in the western genre—much to the actor's chagrin. In *Along the Great Divide* (1951), Douglas played a U.S. marshal named Merrick who has to lead a suspected murderer across Death Valley and through the Alabama Hills, to stand trial. Along the way, he is hunted by an angry lynch mob and haunted by memories of his own dark past. By the end of the film, Merrick is practically walking dead, but more determined than ever to deliver the old man to a fair trial. That undying determination was, for the actor, the core of the film, as he explained in early script notes to Warner Bros.: "To dramatize Merrick's inner conflict, to achieve the point of this story, Merrick *must* go to the other extreme before he is straightened out. His determination to deliver his prisoner must be *more* than that of a good law officer. It must be an *obsession*—an obsession with the law, manifested by absolute *refusal* on his part to concern himself in any way prior to the start of his transformation, with guilt *or* innocence, in other words, *justice*."[12] Over the following years, Douglas's screen persona was defined by obsession.

In *Man Without a Star* (1955), a film written by the equally hardboiled Borden Chase (who remembered Douglas as "a forceful actor, a forceful man,"[13]), the actor played Dempsey Rae, a drifter obsessed with personal freedom. He migrates to the open range of Wyoming for one simple reason: "I just don't like barbed wire." Rae has the physical scars to explain his distaste for being "fenced in," but they are nothing compared to his emotional attachment to open land and living in peace. For a time, he contemplates putting down roots on a Wyoming ranch. He seduces the female ranch owner (or is it the other way around?) and cultivates a paternal relationship with a younger cowhand, teaching him how to shoot a gun and how to be a man. Conveniently, he offers the same advice on both topics: "Get it out fast, then put it away slow." When fences and range war threaten his new home, however, he prepares to head north into the wilds of Canada—until a woman appeals to his sense of responsibility. "No matter where you go," she tells him, "you're going to run into that same fence. And it always has wire on it. You know those killings is going to go on and on. Till the wires come here to stay. You know it better than anybody in the world." In the end, Rae stays to help to erect the fences, acknowledging the inevitability of "progress," and making the ranch safe for his would-be son. Once this is done, he heads north alone—unable to surrender his obsession.

In André De Toth's *The Indian Fighter* (1955), the actor plays an equally strong-willed explorer who negotiates peace with the natives through the sexual conquest of a "wild" Indian squaw, daughter of a tribal chief. In his characteristically bold manner,

V. The Masculine Mystique

"A forceful actor, a forceful man": Kirk Douglas in *The Indian Fighter* (1955, United Artists).

Douglas stakes his claim on the girl and the land: "To me, the West is like a beautiful woman. *My* woman! I don't want to see her changed [or] civilized." The film's sexism is as bold as its racism, but both reflect the times in which the film was made—a time when men asserted themselves unreservedly, when such hyper-masculinity was celebrated. By mid-decade, Douglas's virile screen persona was so resonant that Hal Wallis decided to cast him in the iconic role of wily gunslinger Doc Holliday, opposite an equally hyper-masculine Wyatt Earp, played by Burt Lancaster.

When Wallis first met actor Burt Lancaster in the mid-1940s, he saw a ladies' man. The producer remembered, "Looking at Burt's huge shoulders and big, capable hands, I knew women would be delighted with him."[14] In contrast to Douglas's fiery obsession, Lancaster exhibits smoldering intensity—the kind of cool confidence that defined Robert Mitchum, but backed by an even more formidable physical presence. The actor made his western film debut in MGM's *Vengeance Valley* (1951), a period melodrama about stepbrothers set at odds by the arrival of one brother's illegitimate child. Lancaster acquitted himself admirably in the film, but he had much more remarkable westerns ahead of him.

In Robert Aldrich's *Apache* (1954), he stars as Massai, the legendary last Apache warrior. Massai fled from captivity after the surrender of Geronimo in 1886, only to return to his homeland and conduct a series of border raids between 1887 and 1890. In the film, Massai returns home to lead an insurrection, but a young Apache woman prompts him to re-think his priorities. "Many men have wronged you," she argues, "but now you make yourself worse than they are. Now there is nothing in you but hate." According to Lancaster's biographer Gary Fishgall, the original script called for Massai to be killed by federal troops, but the studio ordered a revised ending in which the warrior's outlook changes when he hears the first cries of his newborn son.[15] In that moment, Massai decides that he has a greater responsibility to his family than to his own ideals. It was a tacit acknowledgment of the traditional (family) values of the era—one that the filmmaker came to regret. Aldrich said later, "It made a joke out of the whole film."[16] Although the revised ending blunted the hard edge of Lancaster's performance, the film was a commercial success, significantly raising the actor's profile.

Next, Lancaster appeared opposite one of the silver screen's biggest stars and most iconic westerners—a sure sign that he had become an icon in his own right. *Vera Cruz* (1954), co-written by Borden Chase and directed by Robert Aldrich, paired Lancaster and Gary Cooper as professional gunfighters looking for work in the midst of the Mexican Revolution. The two men strike up a friendship (Lancaster tells Cooper "you're the first friend I ever had"), while acknowledging that any friendship between mercenaries is tenuous at best. It is inevitable that the two men will face off against each other eventually, and Lancaster's personal code seems to give him an edge over his older, softer-hearted friend. He advises Cooper, "Don't take any chance you don't have to, don't trust anybody you don't have to trust, and don't do no favors you don't have to do." In effect, the younger man was articulating a new cowboy code for a forthcoming generation of "professional" westerners in films like *The Magnificent Seven* (1960), *The Professionals* (1966), and *The Wild Bunch* (1969). The film represented a passing of the torch.

Ironically, the following year Lancaster used his clout to direct an old-fashioned pioneer western. *The Kentuckian* (1955) charts the westward migration of a father and son from Kentucky to Texas, where they plan to live the life of "natural men." Lancaster's character, Big Eli Wakefield, sums up their idealistic ambitions: "It's a big place for the likes of us. No people there much. No neighbors to crowd you. Only wild game to see and to shoot at. And when you take a breath, it's got a clean taste to it. Like nobody ain't never used it before.… That's the way Texas is and that's the way for us. It ain't we don't like people. We like room more. Room to stretch in. Room to see and hunt. And where you set your foot, no foot's been set before." Big Eli's dream is slowly squashed by a spiteful lawman and by Eli's "civilized" brother, who resolves to "work the buckskin out of him" and turn Eli into a businessman instead of a dreamer.

Little Eli faces the same trial. A schoolteacher tells him, "You'll never get anywhere looking out the window." Eventually the boy learns to focus on what's in front of him, and the story develops into a conflict between Big Eli and Little Eli, over the central debate about how a modern man should live his life. Should he be a sensible and constructive member of society, or should he remain independent, however impractical? Lancaster's answer is unsurprising, but his idealistic message may have been a bit untimely in mid-1950s America. *The Kentuckian* was a commercial failure, and it was nearly twenty years before the actor directed another film.

No doubt disappointed by the film's failure, Lancaster was initially reluctant to take the lead role in Hal Wallis's next western, *Gunfight at the O.K. Corral* (1956), envisioned by the producer as a revisionist narrative. Wallis wrote: "At Warners, I made three popular westerns, *Dodge City* and *Virginia City*, starring Errol Flynn; and *Oklahoma Kid*, with Cagney and Bogart. But these pictures were based on fiction, not fact. At Paramount I decided to make hard-hitting western films debunking the myths audiences believed to

Smoldering intensity: Burt Lancaster as the legendary warrior Massai in *Apache* (1954, United Artists).

be true."[17] Dismissing John Ford's *My Darling Clementine* as "romantic fiction, fantasy," the producer regarded Earp as a two-faced businessman who both protected and exploited the people of Tombstone, and his pal Doc Holliday as charming bigot.[18] Director John Sturges apparently agreed with his perspective on history, saying, "I thought Jack Ford was a hell of a director and *Clementine* an interesting movie. But it's ridiculous to say it had anything to do with Earp and Holliday."[19]

Gunfight at the O.K. Corral stripped away all potential subplots and supporting characters in order to focus entirely on the "real" identities of two men. Once Lancaster finally signed on to play Earp, he shaped the character as a cold, calculating figure that inspires respect but rarely admiration. The most revealing moment for the character comes when he tries to convince Billy Clanton (played by a young Dennis Hopper) not to become a gunfighter. "All gunfighters are lonely," Earp says, "They live in fear and die without a dime, a woman or a friend." There is no Clementine at the center of this story to help the lawman tame his violent instincts. Wyatt's brothers pester him about settling down and getting married, but he ignores them just as surely as he ignores his fiancée's pleas for him to him to stop fighting. For all the effect she has on him, she might as well be in a different movie. Wyatt is a greedy opportunist and a cold-blooded killer, plain and simple.

The only character who can understand him is Doc Holliday. Just as Wyatt's relationship with his wife is ultimately meaningless, Doc's relationship with his prostitute girlfriend is blatantly sadomasochistic. The core of the film, as in the narratives of Borden Chase, is the bond that forms between the two men. Lancaster sarcastically explained the dynamic to his co-star in the bluntest terms: "You know, we're playing two pre-Freudian fags. We're in love with each other and we don't know how to express ourselves that way—so we just kind of look at each other and grunt and don't say very much, but you know we love each other."[20] Douglas's take was not quite as bold; years later he defensively described *Gunfight* as a film about a platonic "love between the two men, which has been the most important theme in many movies—starring Spencer Tracy and Clark Gable, Dean Martin and Jerry Lewis, Robert Redford and Paul Newman."[21] No doubt he had heard something similar from his *Man Without a Star* collaborator Borden Chase, who maintained that "a man can actually love and respect another man more so than he can a woman."[22] Sturges, who had also learned a thing or two from Borden Chase—the two worked together on *Backlash* (1956)—charted the middle ground between Lancaster and Douglas: "They shared a common sense of values, a common sense of integrity. Earp was a very straight-on guy. He discovered to his amazement that so was Holliday. Doc didn't lie. He didn't kill without cause. He never pretended to be anything he wasn't. Wyatt liked him for that reason. Each was kind of amazed by the uprightness of the other."[23]

At the end of the day, however, Sturges' focus was on action, not psychological drama. The legendary gunfight at the O.K. Corral, shot on the dusty streets of Old Tucson, is a captivating ballet of violence, and it is what truly distinguished *Gunfight at the O.K. Corral* from its competition, making the film one of the most commercially successful westerns of the decade, and elevating Sturges into the pantheon of great western filmmakers.

Soon after he had made stars of Douglas and Lancaster, producer Hal Wallis struck gold a third time when he hired "a pleasant, giving human being" named Charlton Heston. "Like Kirk and Burt," he reflected years later, "Chuck was exactly the type of he-man I was looking for."[24] Like Douglas and Lancaster, Heston quickly became a regular in westerns. In a trio of Paramount westerns—*The Savage* (1952), *Pony Express* (1953), and *Arrowhead* (1953)—he played larger-than-life characters with very different loyalties: an Indian, an Indian scout, and an Indian hater. The young actor casually avoided the political implications of these early films, telling gossip columnist Hedda Hopper in 1953 that he thought "actors, on any subject other than their work, should keep quiet."[25] For the time being, this man of the west was all sound and fury, signifying nothing.

Within a few years, however, Heston began expounding personal political views. During the making of *The Ten Commandments* (1956), the larger-than-life actor gave a public speech decrying the "dread disease" of bigotry.[26] A few years later he became active in America's Civil Rights movement, and his involvement culminated with a prominent appearance alongside Martin Luther King, Jr., at the March on Washington in 1963. Clearly, Heston no longer believed that a hero should—or could—exist within a vacuum. A man must stand for something. Like Kirk Douglas and Burt Lancaster, Charlton Heston was a member of the vanguard of young Hollywood Democrats who saw a new era on the horizon.

For the time being, the Hollywood West was in a transitional phase and some westerners preferred to celebrate traditional values rather than looking to the future. For much of the decade, actor Joel McCrea projected an image of the heroic cowboy as a God-fearing, community-serving family man in minor westerns like *Saddle Tramp* (1950),

Cattle Drive (1951), *The Lone Hand* (1953) and *Border River* (1954). Even when he played a death-dealing gunslinger in Jacques Tourneur's films *Stranger on Horseback* (1955) and *Wichita* (1955), McCrea was straightforward and altruistic. In *Stranger*, he plays a circuit judge who rides into town with a law book and a gun, as intent on delivering a murderer to justice as a circuit-riding preacher would deliver a sermon. The film makes righteous justice seem like an irrepressible force of nature. In *Wichita*, the actor played Wyatt Earp as a man in service of a greater power than himself. A local newspaper man observes: "There's a lot more to him than just his ability to handle a gun. Personally, I think he's a lawman with ancient desire just fighting against him [...] I know a blacksmith back in Boston acted the same way, only it was about religion. Natural born preacher. It was fighting against him. One day, the regular preacher got sick of us. Blacksmith substituted for him. Spent the rest of his life serving God." When the town mayor opines, "Serving God and serving the law are two different things," the reporter responds: "I disagree. To do either one takes a dedicated man."

McCrea embraced his roles as a mythic western hero in decidedly simplistic terms: "Whether the story was based on fact or fiction was hardly important. What was important was the struggle between virtue and evil. I am proud to have been a western actor, would be proud to act again in any good western, as long as it represents what the westerns of old represented: Americana."[27] For McCrea, "Americana" was synonymous with conservative Christian values. "I don't care what your religion is," he told interviewer Patrick McGilligan, "you must believe that there's a force for good, and you must believe that if you do right, it's gonna win out in the end."[28] As western films became increasingly dark and pessimistic in the latter part of the 1950s, the actor found himself at odds with his material. After portraying a pair of thoroughly grim characters in *Trooper Hook* (1957) and *Fort Massacre* (1958), he decided to hang up his spurs. He explained, "I had kind of established an image, such as it was. I saw no reason to become an anti-hero."[29]

McCrea's fellow trail-rider Randolph Scott faced a similar choice. By the early 1950s, Scott had cultivated an indelible screen persona: polite, humble, reserved, humorless. Director Roy Huggins, who worked with the actor on *Hangman's Knot* (1953), reflected, "He created the 'Randolph Scott' character and played it to perfection. I'm not sure that that's 'acting.' It may even be something superior to acting."[30] André De Toth, who directed Scott in a series of smaller westerns for Warner Bros. in the early 1950s, was less gracious: "Good actor, he wasn't. He was Randy Scott. Which had advantages, but no surprises."[31] Apparently DeToth, who always had a penchant for thematically dark material, became increasingly frustrated by the actor's boy scout persona. After *The Bounty Hunter* (1954), their sixth film together, the director coldly concluded, "I couldn't get blood out of an abacus anymore."[32] He went on to make his best western, *Day of the Outlaw* (1959), with Robert Ryan. Director Budd Boetticher, meanwhile, orchestrated the apotheosis of Randolph Scott's B movie cowboy.

Boetticher was an ex-bullfighter who made his directorial debut in 1951 with *The Bullfighter and the Lady*. During filming, the director reputedly locked horns with producer John Wayne. Years later, he remembered: "Duke was Duke, and he was wrong about a lot of things, I thought, and I was the only one around who ever told him so. He was a tough, wonderful son-of-a-bitch, but he was wrong about a lot of things. We didn't agree on anything, politically or otherwise. Politically myself, I'm right down the middle."[33] Neither could have been too offended, because a few years later Wayne hired Boetticher to helm *Seven Men from Now* (1956) starring Randolph Scott. Boetticher had already made several respectable westerns—including *Horizons West* (1952) with Robert Ryan and Rock Hudson and *The Man from the Alamo* (1954) with Glenn Ford—but his partnership with Scott allowed both men to realize their full potential. Together, they made seven westerns between 1956 and 1960, comprising a multi-film odyssey comparable to the Anthony Mann/James Stewart collaboration.

The big difference between *Seven Men from Now* and the early Mann/Stewart films was the nature of the hero. Scott's Ben Stride is motivated by revenge, but he never appears as volatile as Stewart's characters in *Winchester '73* and *The Naked Spur*. According to Boetticher, that was the strength of the film—a "straight-line hero" who "didn't have a psychological problem, like today's directors think western heroes should have. His wife was killed; he's going out to get the guys who did it. Period."[34] The narrative reveals Stride's moral strength through a series of trials and temptations—particularly the romantic temptations of a pioneer woman named Annie Greer, and the violent provocations of an outlaw named Bill Masters (played by Lee Marvin).

According to Boetticher, the character of Mrs. Greer existed only in relation to the hero. "What counts is what the heroine provokes, or rather what she represents," he said, "In herself, the woman has not the slightest importance."[35] Although Bill Masters serves a similar function in the narrative, the filmmaker felt more strongly about the nominal villain of the piece. In his autobiography, Boetticher wrote that he and screenwriter Burt Kennedy realized that Masters had to be more than a stereotype: "Burt and I agreed that western 'heavies' over the years had been portrayed as much *too* heavy. They rode black horses and wore black hats. You never saw anything *good* about any of them. And they always died at the end of the show. Well, we set out to make our villains extremely attractive. Sure, they were going to get killed—eventually—by our hero, but we wanted our audience to really love 'em while they were still kickin'."[36] The director went on to argue that the villains in his westerns, because they admitted their desires, were "more human" than the (emotionally repressed) heroes, and therefore more sympathetic to viewers.[37] In *Seven Men from Now*, Lee Marvin's character is primarily motivated by greed and lust. Throughout the film, he operates as the Id to Scott's Ego, whispering in his ear like a devil on the shoulder.

Boetticher's films gave the audience two characters to root for, but in the end only one could survive. In *Seven Men from Now*, the

"Something superior to acting"? Randolph Scott in a studio publicity still.

hero wins the day—but he does so by making an emotional sacrifice, unlike Stewart's revenge hero who gave in to an emotional impulse. The director explains: "Before, in westerns, the hero always shot the villain and gloated. In *Seven Men from Now*, after Scott is forced to shoot Lee Marvin, he sits down on a rock and mentally vomits. Scott didn't want to shoot him. He liked Marvin. But he had to."[38] Stride cannot allow Masters' greed to trump the law. In the end, his actions confirm him as a *civilized* hero—a man who, like the heroes of the later Mann/Stewart films, puts moral responsibility ahead of personal feelings.

Pat Brennan, Scott's character in *The Tall T* (1957), is more of a loner—an ex-ramrod who only wants "something of my own." He has his own ranch and, despite a friend's assertion that "it ain't natural" for a man to live alone, a solitary life is enough for Brennan. His perspective begins to change when a trio of stagecoach robbers murders two of his friends and an innocent boy. After the murderers take Brennan hostage, the hero admits to the lead bandit, Frank Usher, that he's afraid of dying. His honesty creates an instant rapport with the villain, who shares Brennan's dream of "having something of my own." Despite similarities between them, however, the two men remain at odds because Brennan adheres to a moral code. Usher, on the other hand, is willing to break the law to get what he wants.

In the end, Brennan turns the tables on his captors, killing the two hardened criminals and offering the vaguely repentant Usher a chance to walk away. Like Lee Masters in *Seven Men from Now*, Usher can't embrace the opportunity for a new beginning. Boetticher explains: "All of my villains have definite ideas about what they want to do. They may realize halfway through their association with Scott that they're wrong, but by then they're too far committed. They're past the point of no return. That's why, morally, [actor Richard] Boone had to come back, maybe knowing that he was going to die. He was a kamikaze pilot; he saw a battleship, and he had to take a chance."[39] For both hero and villain, there are some things a man can't ride around.

Decision at Sundown (1957) and *Buchanan Rides Alone* (1958), both written by Charles Lang, deviated from the established formula. The former replaces the stoic Boetticher/Scott hero with a volatile and vulnerable avenger, comparable to Howard Kemp in *The Naked Spur*. *Decision at Sundown*, however, leads to a very different conclusion. After Scott's gunslinger gets his revenge, he proceeds to drown his anger and sorrow in whiskey, while the townsfolk look on in pity. His actions have served and protected those around him, but his heroism is tainted by the impurity of his motive. His anger destroys everything, including himself. *Buchanan Rides Alone* adopts a more comic tone, as Scott's hero moves beyond stoicism and tragedy to an almost Eastern light-heartedness. When he manages to get himself jailed and nearly executed for casually—and inexplicably— aligning himself with a killer, Scott's character coolly observes: "Man's gotta be loyal to something." The way he says it suggests that maybe it doesn't matter much *what* that something is.

With *Ride Lonesome* (1959), the Boetticher/Scott series returns to familiar territory. The film features Scott as a bounty hunter named Ben Brigade, who is tracking a wanted murderer through Indian country. Brigade gets his man, but then comes under attack by Indians. Reluctantly he enlists two outlaws to help him deliver the murderer to justice. Along the way, one of those outlaws (played by James Coburn) contemplates giving up a life of crime to pursue "something of his own," echoing the hero/villain dynamic of *The Tall T*. In this case, however, the nominal villain appears genuinely willing to change, and the hero begins to look increasingly villainous.

Brigade identifies himself as "the kind who would kill a man for money," and he seems perfectly willing to murder the outlaws in order to keep them from sharing the bounty. Anticipating a conflict, Coburn's outlaw echoes Boetticher's mantra: "There's some things a man can't ride around." As it turns out, he's wrong. In the end, Brigade doesn't care about money; he simply wants his wife's murderers brought to justice. Once the two outlaws help him get that, he allows them to claim the bounty for themselves. This ending effectively reverses the final notes of *The Tall T* and *Decision at Sundown*, leaving the would-be villains laughing good-naturedly and allowing the avenger to avoid a violent tragedy.

The final scene is one of the most powerful in Boetticher's canon. Scott's hero watches the smoke rise from a burning hang-tree that symbolizes his thirst for revenge. For Boetticher, this image says it all: "Here is this whole man's life. That tree represents everything bad in his life. And he personally is burning it, having accomplished what he needed to do in order to have the right to light that match. [...] I said it very simply, and that's why I make my pictures."[40]

Like *The Man from Laramie*, *Ride Lonesome* brings the revenge hero's odyssey to a natural conclusion. "Before," Boetticher explains, "we always let Randy 'ride off into the sunset.' We always gave you the feeling that there was a tomorrow. I never knew what the tomorrow was in *Ride Lonesome*. I could write fourteen original scripts starting with the burning of that cross."[41] As it turned out, Boetticher made only one more film with Randolph Scott. In *Comanche Station* (1960), the hero concludes: "A man does one thing in his life, one thing he can look back on, [he can] go proud. That's enough."

CHAPTER VI

The Lost Cowboys
(1955–1959)

> *Crises there will continue to be. In meeting them, whether foreign or domestic, great or small, there is a recurring temptation to feel that some spectacular and costly action could become the miraculous solution to all current difficulties. A huge increase in newer elements of our defense; development of unrealistic programs to cure every ill in agriculture; a dramatic expansion in basic and applied research—these and many other possibilities, each possibly promising in itself, may be suggested as the only way to the road we wish to travel. But each proposal must be weighed in the light of a broader consideration: the need to maintain balance in and among national programs, balance between the private and the public economy, balance between cost and hoped for advantage, balance between the clearly necessary and the comfortably desirable, balance between our essential requirements as a nation and the duties imposed by the nation upon the individual, balance between actions of the moment and the national welfare of the future. Good judgment seeks balance and progress; lack of it eventually finds imbalance and frustration.*
> —Dwight D. Eisenhower, farewell address, January 17, 1961

In the mid-1950s, Hollywood turned its focus toward a new audience: baby boomers. Children of the generation that fought and won World War II came of age at a time when the filmmaking industry was preoccupied with atomic-age anxieties and juvenile delinquency. (In the minds of some cultural critics, the two are inextricably related.) Charismatic young actors like Marlon Brando and James Dean became cultural icons overnight, with Brando kicking off a generational rebellion in *The Wild One* (1953). Although generally recognized as the first of many counterculture biker movies, Peter Bogdanovich has suggested that *The Wild One* was also "the start of the modern western."[1] Brando's motorcycle cowboy Johnny Strabler was an extension of the actor's character in *Viva Zapata!*: a consummate rebel. Unlike Zapata, however, Strabler was a rebel without a revolution—or, to borrow the phrase that came to epitomize James Dean—a rebel without a cause.

Around the same time, the traditional western film, and the masculine mystique of the "G.I. Generation," entered a transitional phase. On television, the conservative western myth continued to thrive, as film critic Richard Schickel explains: "*Gunsmoke, Wagon Train, Bonanza, The Virginian* and *The High Chaparral* featured all-wise elders rallying a real or surrogate family against the anarchic threat posed by the outsider, the other. It says something about the popular culture's raging need for a particular kind of order that this pattern was imposed on the television western, thereby creating a spurious historical example to reassure the suburban middle-class family that it had made the right choice, should be wary of intruders, adventurings, passionate emotions."[2] On the big screen, the narrative was more ambiguous. Many popular western films of the mid to late 1950s depict the sunset of an era.

Raoul Walsh's *The Tall Men* (1955), for example, plays like an elegy for the old-fashioned American cowboy. Leading man Clark Gable isn't just "what every boy thinks he's gonna be when he grows up," but also what he "wishes he had been when he's an old man." This Man of the West is as wild and majestic as the Montana landscape, but the landscape is changing fast. In the later part of the decade, as Russia pulled ahead of the U.S. in the space race and the Cold War heated up, the entire country seemed to be yearning for a new sense of security and direction. Years later, President Dwight Eisenhower reflected: "That was a period of anxiety. Sputnik had revealed the psychological vulnerability of our people. The Communists were steadily fomenting trouble and rattling sabers; our economy was sputtering somewhat, and the ceaseless and usually healthy self-criticism in which we of the United States indulge had brought a measure of genuine self-doubt."[3] Onscreen, young rebels voiced their anger and frustration, while some traditional westerners seemed to be lost and wandering.

One of the most emblematic Hollywood stars of this transitional era was war hero-turned-actor Audie Murphy. After serving his country in North Africa, France and Italy, Murphy emerged from World War II as America's most decorated soldier, and his innocent and youthful good looks became the face of the popular war. During subsequent years, however, he struggled to find a new purpose in life. "At home," he remembered, "some wanted to hire me because I was a famous killer, others wouldn't for the same reason. I couldn't get a job that left me any self-respect."[4] On the advice of James Cagney, the increasingly disillusioned war hero came to Hollywood and made his acting debut in 1947, appearing as a traumatized soldier in the Alan Ladd vehicle *Beyond Glory*. Two years later he landed his first starring role, as a modern-day Billy the Kid in *Bad Boy* (1949). Murphy thought the part suited him well. "When I was younger," he said, "I might have become another Billy the Kid if I hadn't had wonderful neighbors who pitched in and gave me jobs in numerous ways."[5] Universal executives instantly recognized the commercial appeal of Murphy's "killer kid" persona, and signed him to a seven-year contract. Soon after, he was cast as the real Billy the Kid in *The Kid from Texas* (1950), and then as a young Jesse James in *Kansas Raiders* (1950). Within a few years, he had gone from being a real-life hero of the G.I. generation to being a movie cowboy for baby boomers.

After a celebrated performance in John Huston's war movie *The Red Badge of Courage* (1951), he continued to play baby-faced killers in respectable westerns by Budd Boetticher (*The Cimarron Kid*, 1952), Don Siegel (*The Duel at Silver Creek*, 1953), Nathan Juran (*Gunsmoke*, 1953; *Tumbleweed*, 1953; *Drums Across the River*, 1954), Jesse Hibbs (*Ride Clear of Diablo*, 1954), and George Marshall (*Destry*, 1954). With each film Murphy's persona matured, his characters becoming less and less rebellious. His popularity reached its peak in 1955, when Murphy played himself in the hugely successful biopic *To Hell and Back*. The actor referred to the film as a "western in uniform."[6] It was, however, a traditional western rather than a modern western. Although the actor still had some of his best work ahead of him (most notably, in the 1959 film *No Name on the Bullet*), Murphy was already being replaced by younger, more impetuous gunslingers.

Director Nicholas Ray's *Run for Cover* (1955) cast John Derek in the role of a disaffected youngster named Davey Bishop. After being crippled by a bullet, Davey becomes

VI. The Lost Cowboys

Bill Mauldin nervously watches war-hero Audie Murphy in *The Red Badge of Courage* (1951, MGM).

bitter and violent—a transformation that his father-figure Matt Dow (aptly played by Audie Murphy's Hollywood benefactor James Cagney) understands only too well. The wise elder tries to steer the boy away from the path of rebellious violence, but Davey throws in with a gang of bank robbers, prompting this stern rebuke from his mentor: "There's a lot of people in this world who've had a tougher time than either you or me. It comes with the ticket. Nobody guarantees you a free ride. The only difference is most people don't run for cover. They keep right on going, the best way they can. But you never hear about them.... [It's] the ones who can't take it, like you, the ones who want a free ride, who cause all the trouble everywhere." *Run for Cover* serves as a prelude to Ray's most famous film, *Rebel Without a Cause* (1955), which empathizes with the rebellious teenagers rather than with the older generation.

Later, the director tackled another J.D. western, demonstrating an equally strong loyalty to its troubled young characters. In contrast to the 1939 film *Jesse James*, *The True Story of Jesse James* (1957) focuses on the outlaw's formative experiences during the Civil War, when he was tortured by Union soldiers and shot while trying to surrender. The film's narrative, fragmented by frequent flashbacks to these events, illustrates the concept of arrested development. The traumas of the Civil War continually haunt Jesse as World War II—and the omnipresent specter of eventual nuclear annihilation—haunted the baby boomer generation in the 1950s. When Jesse's wife accuses him of "thinking like a child,"

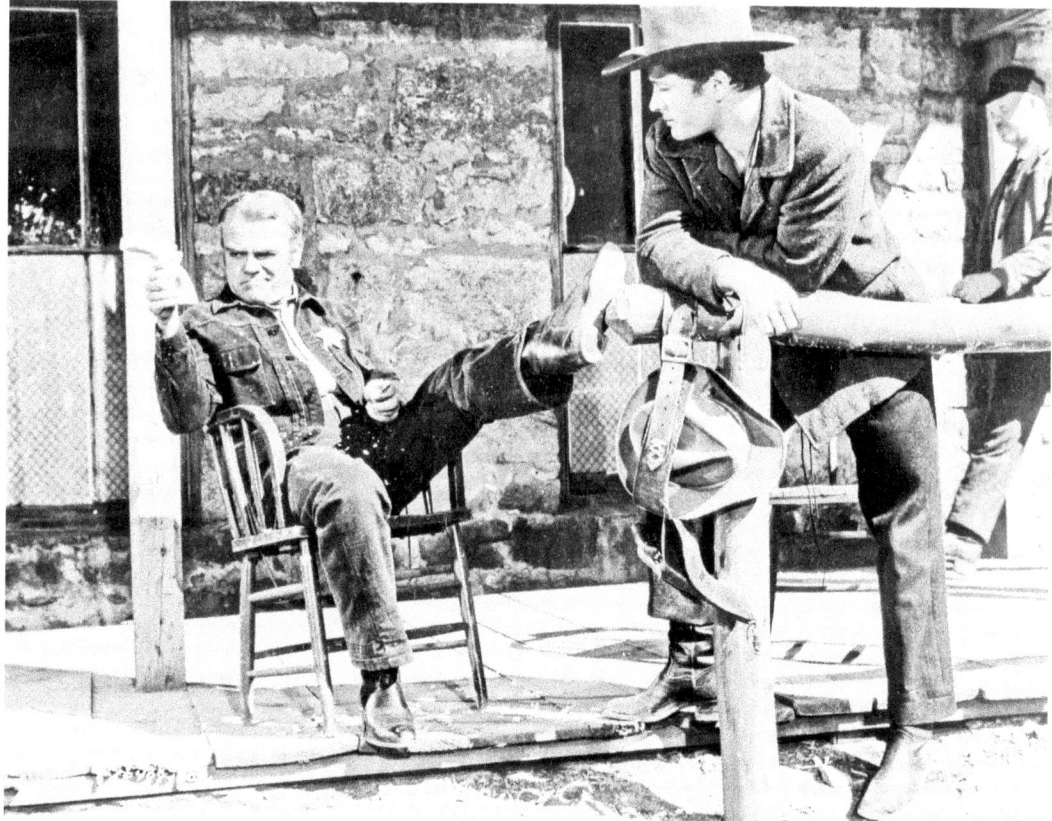

"Nobody guarantees you a free ride": Matt Dow (James Cagney) and his surrogate son (John Derek) in *Run for Cover* (1955, Paramount).

he admits that he is concerned "mostly about the past" and complains that he doesn't "like the way grownups think." Through violent rebellion, he aims to get even with the adult world that wronged him and transformed him from a "gentle boy" into an anxious killer. As in *Run for Cover*, however, the only way he can grow up and move forward is by letting go of the past and taking responsibility for his own future. In the end, his brother Frank helps him to see that his crimes are nothing more than expressions of infantile neuroses. The rebel needs a cause.

Arthur Penn's *The Left-Handed Gun* (1958) explores the same idea by rewriting the legend of Billy the Kid. Billy, played by a young Paul Newman, turns violent after his only role model is murdered, and for the duration of the film he acts out like a spoiled child, thoughtlessly responding to violence with violence. The character is occasionally sympathetic, but resolutely un-heroic—even to himself. There is an element of sadness in his voice when he tries to explain his personal code: "I don't run. I don't hide. I go where I want. I do what I want." He looks stunned when he literally blasts another man out of his boots, as if aware that he wields more much power than he can possibly hope to understand or control.

Elaborating on the perspective of screenwriter Gore Vidal, Penn suggests that Billy the Kid's problems were psycho-sexual: "He had an infantile sense of justice, a kind of pre–Oedipal sense of justice: an inability to reconcile that someone had *really* slept with his mother, so that these men were constantly transgressors. They were constantly failing his system of justice, his unbearable system of justice."[7] The director explains in consistently Freudian terms: Billy *penetrates* by using a gun, because real sex requires intimacy and Billy doesn't trust intimacy.[8] Because he is so disillusioned about the world around him, the outlaw remains a perpetual outsider, unable to make any meaningful, lasting connections in life—and it is that tragic quality that appeals to the filmmaker. Penn reflects:

> I would say that the only people who really interest me are the outcasts from society. The people who are *not* outcasts—either psychologically, emotionally, or physically—seem to me good material for selling breakfast food, but they're not material for films. What I'm really trying to say through the figure of the outcast is that a society has its mirror in its outcasts. A society would be wise to pay attention to the people who do not belong in it if it wants to find out what its configuration is and where it's failing.[9]

Penn's version of Billy the Kid is a spokesman for the younger generation in 1950s America—a generation in rebellion against traditional postulations of truth, justice and the American way.

Predictably, many traditionalists took issue with this (mis)appropriation of the western genre. Veteran director Howard Hawks bluntly dismissed Penn's film, saying, "Some people have tried silly things, like a picture called *The Left-Handed Gun*, which compared a western gunman with a modern-day hophead or something. It's no good [because] it doesn't live up to what people want."[10] Hawks argued that contemporary problems

Paul Newman (far left) as an infantile Billy the Kid in *The Left-Handed Gun* (1958, Warner Bros.).

shouldn't be examined within the western's historical milieu. Apparently he failed to realize that his generation had done the same thing, presenting conflicts of the Old West in terms of post–World War II anxieties. Regardless, there was no bucking the trend. Penn and other young filmmakers continued to modernize the western by adapting it to changing times and changing political perspectives in America.

Writer/director Richard Brooks offered a pointed criticism of the defining American philosophy of Manifest Destiny in *The Last Hunt* (1956). The film tells the story of two friends: Sandy McKenzie, a sympathetic frontiersman, and Charlie Gibson, a gun-crazy hunter who believes that "the more you kill, the more of a man" you are. Gibson represents the wave of opportunistic and sometimes psychopathic men who swarmed across the Great Plains in the late 19th century, killing everything in their path and decimating the population of American bison—a careless act that had grave repercussions for Native Americans. Brooks succeeded in turning the western genre on its head, but the harrowing nature of the film was too much for contemporary audiences—especially the scenes depicting the slaughter of the buffalo, which were filmed during an annual thinning of the herd in South Dakota's Custer State Park. The director blamed himself for the film's commercial failure, concluding, "When you deal with a subject in films that is traditional, don't deny it to the public, because the western and its gunplay is like a musical—it's a fantasy and it should be kept as such."[11]

Despite the resistance, some filmmakers continued to produce anti-myths. Samuel Fuller's *Run of the Arrow* (1957) echoed the contemporary Civil Rights debate by railing against the treatment of Indians in the Old West and in traditional Hollywood westerns. Ideally, Fuller insisted, "Indians would be depicted as a community of people with their own rules and rituals, not—as in most studio movies—like a pack of marauding killers."[12] The only marauding killer in Fuller's western is a white soldier, played by Rod Steiger, and the filmmaker definitively characterizes him as a "sore loser, not a gallant hero."[13] The psychotic ex–Confederate swears allegiance to the Oglalla Sioux so that he can continue murdering Yankees, while pretending that he is still a soldier at war rather than simply a murderer. Over the course of the film, the Sioux help him to overcome his hatred and re-join his own nation. *Run of the Arrow* ends on an uncertain note, with a bloody battle between the U.S. Cavalry and the Sioux. Steiger's character has found peace, but a title card insists that "the end of this story can only be written by you"—a reminder to audiences that many Americans were still struggling for their civil rights.

Fuller's subsequent film was even more liberal-minded. *Forty Guns* (1957) stars Barbara Stanwyck as a powerful woman named Jessica Drummond, backed by forty armed men and determined to protect her hotheaded brother from an equally hotheaded stranger. When she and the stranger become trapped together during a tornado(!), she falls in love and convinces him that real strength requires roots. She offers him a personal and professional partnership, saying, "I need a strong man to carry out my orders." Unfortunately, the men in the film think only with their guns. The stranger not only rejects Jessica's offer and kills her brother, he also shoots Jessica and leaves her for dead. Fuller explains: "*Forty Guns* is not only about strength. It's about modesty, too. Jessica rides in on a horse followed by forty men, but, at the end, she's on foot, running after the guy she loves. Her power is just as great, but it's been altered by love, forgiveness, and humility."[14]

In the filmmaker's original concept, Jessica died from the bullet wound and the stranger was forever hardened by his actions. The studio, however, demanded a more upbeat ending. In the final film, Jessica survives the gunshot wound and reconciles with

VI. The Lost Cowboys 77

Charlton Heston as he-man Steve Leach in *The Big Country* (1958, United Artists).

the stranger—and eradicates his violent impulses through love, forgiveness and humility. Fuller lamented the change, believing that it softened the film's message too much. In essence, the filmmaker says, he designed this western to bluntly protest the traditional western movie philosophy of righteous violence:

> Guns in movies are fantasy objects. In real life, there are just too many guns and too many violent people who have access to them. The argument that our Constitution gives everyone the right to carry guns is stupid. It was written in 1789, when we were afraid that the British might return and we'd have to fight again for our independence. The situation is crazy today, and something clear-cut must be done to keep the tools of violence away from destructive people, especially youngsters. We must teach our children tolerance and forgiveness, not how to resort to guns.[15]

Filmmaker William Wyler echoed the same message in *The Big Country* (1958). The film stars Gregory Peck as James McKay, a privileged New Englander who travels to Texas to win the hand of a cattle rancher's daughter. Upon arrival he meets Steve Leech, a hyper-masculine man's man (played by Charlton Heston) who is eager to fight him for the lady's hand. When Peck refuses to fight, his intended becomes embarrassed. "Don't you care what people *think*?" she begs. "I'm not responsible for what people think," he answers, adding, "There are some things that a man has to prove to himself alone, not to anyone else." In fact, McKay *is* willing to fight—but not to serve some kind of masculine code. In the most telling scene in the film, he dukes it out privately with Heston's ramrod. After both men have been bloodied and beaten to a standstill, Peck says, "Now tell me, Leach, what did we prove?" Director William Wyler shared the character's ideas about the futility of violence, saying, "I have never seen any great virtue in the American tradition of punching a guy in the nose if he said something you didn't like. It only proves who can punch the quickest or the hardest—nothing else. The problem that intrigues me is whether people can have faith in a man that doesn't punch."[16] Peck ultimately tries to prove his manhood by preventing violence rather than perpetuating it. He uses his money and influence to bring an end to a protracted Hatfield-vs.-McCoy type range war that has tormented his fiancée's family for years. The outcome, as Peck himself once said, illustrates the theme of "an anti-macho western."[17]

Another Gregory Peck western released the same year conveyed a related message, albeit via a more conventional narrative. In Henry King's *The Bravados* (1958), Peck plays a vengeful gunslinger named Jim Douglas who is on the hunt for four convicted killers. The hero executes the killers one by one, only to realize later that he has executed four innocent men who were framed for murder. After realizing his mistake, Douglas falls on his knees and repents. For the actor and the director (who was, perhaps knowingly, making his final film), the ending justified the picture. Peck explained:

> *The Bravados* was interesting because of Henry's change of the original script, which was a pretty straight story of a man who finds his wife raped and murdered. In this outpost his tiny daughter is left psychologically damaged. He goes after the murderers and he kills them one by one. Henry's sense of morality, his Christian belief, is that revenge is wrong, that it is immoral for a man to set himself up as the judge, jury and executioner. He would not swallow that story of pursuit and revenge.[18]

Instead, *The Bravados* was a critical reaction to a near-decade of revenge westerns.

Even Anthony Mann, the filmmaker who turned James Stewart into a vengeful tough guy, sensed that the future belonged to a different kind of hero. Mann's *The Tin Star* (1957) tells the story of Morg Hickman, a cynical former lawman who threw away his badge when he learned that ordinary people are often unwilling to fight for their own rights, and his successor Ben Owens, a young greenhorn who seems ill-prepared for the cutthroat realities of being a sheriff in the Wild West. Despite his cynicism, Morg—played by elder statesman Henry Fonda—remains kind-hearted enough to support Owens when he finds himself outnumbered, outgunned and abandoned by his friends and colleagues. The younger man, played by rising actor Anthony Perkins, holds his own with conviction if not the kind of authority that a western hero generally embodies. "Man can't run away from his job," Owens says, perhaps hoping that this mantra will help him internalize his mentor's fearless resolve. Inspired by the younger man's sincere dedication, the weary old western hero manages to muster some hope for an uncertain future.

Film historian Stephen McVeigh suggests that *The Tin Star* conveys a vision of late 1950s American politics. Specifically, he views the relationship between Morg Hickman and Ben Owen as a parallel to the relationship between then-president Dwight Eisenhower, who earned his authority as a five-star general in World War II, and Vice President Richard Nixon, a youthful lawyer and career politician.[19] During the course of his presidency, Eisenhower suffered several brief but serious illnesses, which prompted the public to question his comparatively inexperienced successor's readiness to lead the country. Viewed in this light, Mann's film anticipates the nervous end of a decade in which conservatives dominated American politics.

In some respects, Edward Dmytryk's *Warlock* (1959) seems to extend the narrative. The film begins with a group of rowdy cowboys running off the ineffectual sheriff of the titular town. In the wake of this embarrassing incident, Warlock's "citizen's committee" hires a more authoritative gunslinger—Henry Fonda again—to clean things up. Fonda's Clay Blaisdell takes the job, but with stated reservations:

VI. The Lost Cowboys

Protégé Anthony Perkins (left) and mentor Henry Fonda in *The Tin Star* (1959, Paramount).

People generally begin to resent me. It will happen. I come here as your salvation, at a very high wage, and establish order. Ride roughshod over offenders. At first you're pleased because there's a good deal less trouble. Then a very strange thing happens. You begin to feel that I'm too powerful. You begin to fear me. Not me, but what I am. When that happens, we shall have had full satisfaction from one another. It'll be time for me to leave.

The story unfolds exactly the way Blaisdell predicts it will, up to a point. The new marshal restores order, falls out of favor with the citizen's committee, and is subsequently replaced by a younger, "more civilized" lawman. His successor, played by Richard Widmark, promises to uphold the letter of the law rather than abiding by a personal moral code. In the end, that's not enough to maintain the peace. When outlaws threaten to kill the new sheriff, Blaisdell—feeling vindicated and purposeful again—offers to back him up. At this point, however, the story diverges sharply from the Eisenhower/Nixon narrative of *The Tin Star*. The young sheriff denies Blaisdell's help, and ultimately doesn't need it. Once the gunslinger realizes that he is no longer needed, he suffers an identity crisis. The final battle is essentially a battle between Blaisdell and himself, as the old-fashioned hero confronts the reality that the "times are changing" and there is no place for him in the new West.

For many viewers, the classic western finally reached the end of its trail with the passing of Gary Cooper in 1961. The actor's last three films in the genre *Man of the West* (1958), *The Hanging Tree* (1959) and *They Came to Cordura* (1959)—all convey a sense of loss, while trying to project some hope for the future. *Man of the West* and *The

Hanging Tree also represented final statements from two of the genre's most influential filmmakers: Anthony Mann and Delmar Daves.

In Anthony Mann's *Man of the West*, Cooper plays Link Jones, a rogue outlaw-turned-community leader who travels to Fort Worth to hire a schoolteacher on behalf his one-horse Texas town. When bandits rob his train, Link is drawn back into his old life. Blamed for the crime, he reluctantly returns home to the family that raised him—a pack of ruthless criminals who have kidnapped his would-be schoolteacher. Torn between primal instincts and civilized ideals, Link realizes that "there's a point where you either grow up and become a human being or you rot like that bunch." He decides to fight for a better way of life and effectively kills his past by killing everyone associated with it.

Although the hero resorts to violence in stereotypical western movie fashion, the violence in *Man of the West* is ugly rather than exhilarating, and Cooper looks consistently weary and remorseful behind the gun. Despite all of his demoralizing experiences, however, the film offers hope that Link can still start over. He falls in love with the schoolteacher and, in the final moments of the film, tells her, "I've never *loved* anyone or anything before. I always wondered what it would feel like…. I wouldn't change this feeling, not for anything." Significantly, it is this *feeling* that Mann chooses to end on, rather than any speculations about the future. In this moment, *Man of the West* expresses the filmmaker's ultimate statement on the themes he had spent a decade exploring: A man is defined not by his past, but by the choices he makes and the action he takes *in each new moment*. Equally important is Mann's belief that anger and violence can never harden a man's soul so thoroughly that love cannot penetrate it.

In Delmar Daves' *The Hanging Tree*, Cooper tries to resist such a transformation. At the beginning of the film his character, Dr. Joseph Frail, seems to be a lost cause—he introduces himself in a new mining town as a man with "frail hope." The gun-toting physician proves to be a useful member of the community, but his neighbors remain suspicious of him. When he takes in an equally frail woman who has been burned and blinded, Doc becomes even more secretive, and his neighbors turn against him.

Cooper projects the pain of a man who neither expects, wants, nor hopes to be loved. When he diagnoses his horribly disfigured patient with the chilling words "inside: that's where the damage is done," we know he's talking about himself. Doc Frail is a dead man walking, a ghost who is unable to forgive himself for a lifetime of secret sins. His inability to heal himself, however, doesn't prevent him from being saved. Just as Mann's final western reassures us that the hero can still love, Daves' final western insists that he still *deserves* to be loved. Western fans wouldn't have had it any other way. For the generations of Americans who drew inspiration from films like *The Virginian*, *The Plainsman*, *Sergeant York* and *High Noon*, Cooper *was* a healer.

When he made his final western, Cooper himself was dying inside. Under the circumstances, *They Came to Cordura* seems especially harsh—up to a point. The film cast Cooper in the role of aged cavalryman Thomas Thorn, a man tormented by the memory of a crucial moment when he succumbed to fear and cowardice. For years Thorn has suffered from guilt and shame, which have gradually worn him down. Now he invites suffering because he feels that he deserves it. A scene in which the repentant soldier allows himself to be dragged behind a train car is particularly hard to watch. For some viewers, such a moment represented the defilement of an American hero. For others, the scene (and the film) carried a different message.

According to one supporting character, the hero willingly endures constant punishment in an effort to prove that "something else lives in men"—something more than the treachery, viciousness, dishonesty, fear and cowardice that define so many other characters in the film. *Cordura* reiterates the message of *The Hanging Tree*, that no man is defined by a single action or decision: "One act of cowardice doesn't make a man a coward forever. Just as one act of bravery doesn't make a man a hero forever." That was the overriding message of all three of Gary Cooper's final films, suggesting a new, more nuanced western myth: Heroes sometimes make mistakes, but they never stop trying to make a better world.

There was, of course, one other screen western hero who was still waving the flag more fervently than ever. In 1959, John Wayne and director Howard Hawks delivered their own end-of-decade mission statement in *Rio Bravo*. Hawks claimed that he conceived the film as a counterpoint to liberal-minded westerns, including *High Noon* and *3:10 to Yuma* (1957). In the former, he noted, Gary Cooper's hero asks for help to fight off a group of assassins. "That isn't my idea of a good western sheriff," Hawks reflected, explaining, "A good sheriff would turn around and say, 'How good are you? Are you good enough to take the best man they've got?' The fellow would probably say no, and he'd say, 'Well, then I'd just have to take care of you.'" In *3:10 to Yuma*, the director continued, "the sheriff caught a prisoner, and the prisoner taunted him and made him perspire and worry and everything by saying, 'Wait till my friends catch up with you.' And I said, That's a lot of nonsense, the sheriff would say 'You better hope your friends don't catch up with you, 'cause you'll be the first man to die.'"[20]

Hawks had no trouble convincing his leading man. By 1959, Wayne was arguably the country's most potent symbol of conservative values. As Gary Willis writes in his book *John Wayne's America*, "He stood for an America [that] people felt was disappearing or had disappeared, for a time 'when men were men.'"[21] With that in mind, Hawks made a film that was more about character and integrity than plot and action. What matters most are the decisions that Wayne and his motley crew of lawmen make about if, when and how to fight—because, as Hawks implies, the battle between good and evil isn't fought with guns; it's fought with hope and fear.

Regardless of political agendas, that was the prevailing theme of 1950s westerns. Whether a film was macho or anti-macho, its heroes were defined by their willingness to fight—and, if necessary, die—for what they believed in. Such heroes could not be stopped by bribery or intimidation. Often, they could not even be stopped by bullets. In the end, the he-men of the 1950s westerns could only be stopped by time.

Chapter VII

The New Frontier
(1960–1965)

> *I stand tonight facing west on what was once the last frontier. From the lands that stretch three thousand miles behind me, the pioneers of old gave up their safety, their comfort and sometimes their own lives to build a new world here in the West. They were not the captives of their own doubts, the prisoners of their own price tags. Their motto was not "every man for himself" but "all for the common cause." They were determined to make that new world strong and free, to overcome its hazards and its hardships, to conquer the enemies that threatened from without and within. Today some would say that those struggles are all over—that all the horizons have been explored—that all the battles have been won—that there is no longer an American frontier. But I trust that no one in this vast assemblage will agree with those sentiments. For the problems are not all solved and the battles are not all won—and we stand today on the edge of a New Frontier—the frontier of the 1960's—a frontier of unknown opportunities and perils, a frontier of unfulfilled hopes and threats.*
> —John F. Kennedy, acceptance of the Democratic Party nomination, July 15, 1960

In the early 1960s, a youthful president and his successor presented a vision of America's future that emboldened the rising generation. John F. Kennedy's "New Frontier" and Lyndon Johnson's "Great Society" symbolized a national mission to eradicate oppression and poverty at home and abroad. These policies energized the Civil Rights debate in the American South and the ongoing war against communism in the Far East and Cuba. As the new liberalism reshaped American politics, Hollywood westerns fell into two warring categories. Conservative westerns looked back on the historical winning of the West—the old frontier—with nostalgia, while more liberal-minded westerns reflected the trials and tragedies of present-day struggles toward a new ideological frontier.

A few weeks before the 1960 presidential election, two Hollywood westerns offered very different visions of America. Since the mid-1950s, John Wayne had been planning *The Alamo* (1960), his celebration of the Texans who fought and died for their freedom in the famous siege of 1836. The story had already been filmed many times, and had also served as the climax of Disney's popular TV series *Davy Crockett* (1954–1955), but the actor was determined to make the legend his own. He explained:

> I have always been inspired by the story because I don't know of any other moment in American history which portrays the courage of men any better. It's the courage of those men that has always moved me. Since then men—and women—have shown many great acts of courage in the face of adversity. But what for me was the defining moment when men put their lives before all else, was when [Col. William Barret] Travis tells all the volunteers who are on their horses and ready to withdraw from a battle they know they can't win, that they can leave the Alamo without fear of criticism or shame. And every one of those

VII. The New Frontier 83

"A special story for the patriots of America": John Wayne (left), Richard Widmark, Laurence Harvey and the cast of *The Alamo* (1960, United Artists).

volunteers got off their horses and stood behind Travis. It's a story for all the world, but it is a special story for the patriots of America.[1]

Wayne later added that his goal was to remind modern Americans of the nation's founding principles: "We want to recreate a moment in history which will show to this living generation of Americans what their country really stands for, and to put in front of their eyes the bloody truth of what some of their forebears went through to win what they had to have or die—liberty and freedom."[2]

Wayne had his own particular ideas about liberty and freedom in 1960 America. When asked if *The Alamo* was "inspired by the Communists," he responded, "Well, there's always a little truth in everything you hear."[3] He later told Hollywood gossip columnist Louella Parsons that the film was outright propaganda, meant to "sell America to countries threatened with Communist domination."[4] Like Kennedy, he hoped to win the hearts and minds of oppressed people everywhere with his straightforward depiction of fearless heroism. Of course, Wayne wasn't promoting Kennedy. He was promoting his own conservative agenda.

As legendary frontiersman Davy Crockett, Wayne is alternately crude and poetic, humble yet statesman-like. He is a man of the people, a magnet for women, a lover of children, and he can hold his liquor better than anyone else in the saloon. He is, in short, larger than life—not a historical character but a folk hero. Film historian Gary Willis surmises, "Crockett is Wayne philosophizing about his own Wayneness."[5] In one particular scene, the actor delivers a lengthy monologue that fuses his personal history with his public image:

> When I came down here to Texas, I was lookin' for something. I didn't know what. Seems like, if you added up my life, I spent it all either stompin' other men or in some cases getting stomped. Had me some money and had me some medals, but none of it seemed worth a lifetime of pain of the mother that bore me. It was like I was empty. Well, I'm not empty anymore. That's what's important. I feel useful in this old world—to hit a lick against what's wrong, or to say a word for what's right, even though you get walloped for sayin' that word. Now I may sound like a Bible-beater yelling up a revival at a river-crossing camp meeting, but that don't change the truth none. There's right and there's wrong. You gotta do one or the other. You do the one and you're living. You do the other and you may be walking around but you're dead as a beaver hat.

For Wayne, of course, "doing right" was a distinctly right-wing agenda. In 1960, he became a member of the John Birch Society—a radical right-wing group that promoted anti-communism and limited government—and aggressively stumped for Nixon, convinced that the Republican would take a hard line against communism. Putting politics ahead of entertainment, he arranged for *The Alamo* to premiere during the election season, and used press releases for the film to express his disgust with the "lace-curtain arrogance and unctuous liberalism" of the Kennedys.[6] His three-page, star-spangled spread in *Life* magazine hailed Nixon as a man of principle: "In a moment when eternity could be closer than ever before there is a statesman who for the sake of a vote is not all things to all men; a man who will put America back on the high road to security and accomplishment; without fear or favor or compromise; a man who wants to do the job that must be done and to hell with friend or foe who would have it otherwise."[7] Just as Wayne felt that America's future hinged on the election, so he staked his own career on *The Alamo*. He told one reporter, "I've gambled everything I own on this picture—all my money ... and my soul."[8] Unfortunately, *The Alamo* was not the blockbuster he had hoped for, and the film seemed desperately old-fashioned next to John Sturges' *The Magnificent Seven* (1960), which was released the same week.

Foreshadowing the specialization of the American military under President Kennedy, as well as the future of the western genre, *The Magnificent Seven* revolves around a crack team of "professional" gunslingers, the Special Forces of the Old West. At the beginning of the film, the gunslingers—led by Yul Brynner and Steve McQueen—are merely mercenaries for hire, the western film version of wandering *ronin* in Akira Kurosawa's *Seven Samurai* (*Shichinin no samurai*, 1954). In both films, the warriors claim to kill for money, rather than for old-fashioned ideals like honor and justice. When a tormented peasant says that a gunman's help would be a blessing, Brynner responds coldly, "I'm not in the blessing business." Regardless of his claim, the gunslingers do eventually take sides in the Mexican Revolution and liberate an entire town of working-class farmers from a tyrannical president.

In hindsight, the narrative has obvious parallels to contemporary events. In March 1960, President Eisenhower had authorized the CIA to train a brigade of paramilitary soldiers in Mexico. Their mission: to invade Cuba and overthrow the communist leader Fidel Castro. A few months after the release of *The Magnificent Seven*, President Kennedy inherited the mission, which ended disastrously in April 1961, with most of the U.S. soldiers imprisoned in Cuba. In the wake of this foreign policy disaster, the Kennedy administration began developing a more sophisticated plan for combating communism. They could have taken some cues from *The Magnificent Seven*, in which Charles Bronson's

Yul Brynner (bottom) and Steve McQueen (next) lead *The Magnificent Seven* **(1960, United Artists).**

character O'Reilly suggests that the real heroes of the struggle are not the guns-for-hire but the oppressed people who resist and endure, continuing to live their everyday lives in spite of ideological wars. In a pivotal scene, O'Reilly tells a pair of children how to recognize real heroes: "You think I'm brave because I carry a gun? Well, your fathers are much braver because they carry responsibilities.... I have never had this kind of courage.

Running a farm, working like a mule everyday with no guarantee what will ever come of it. *This* is bravery. That's why I never even started anything like that. That's why I never will." In the narrative constructed by self-professed communist Walter Bernstein, only the community—not the selfish individual—can survive this war.

Initially, *The Magnificent Seven* appeared to be as much of a failure as the Bay of Pigs invasion. Box office receipts in the United States were unimpressive, but the film found a more receptive audience in Europe the following year. In hindsight, it is easy to view *The Magnificent Seven* as the link between politically-charged, south-of-the-border westerns like *Viva Zapata!* and *Vera Cruz* and the anarchic, hyper-violent European westerns of the later 1960s. When the film premiered on U.S. television in the fall of 1963, American audiences began to embrace the anti-heroic bent of Sturges' characters. *The Magnificent Seven* was, without question, a harbinger of things to come.

The star of *Viva Zapata!* also helped to pioneer the anti-heroic western. When he set out to make *One-Eyed Jacks* (1961), Marlon Brando explained:

> I have the obligation and the opportunity, in a recently discovered impulse, to try to communicate the things I think are important ... to make a frontal attack on the temple of clichés. Our early day heroes were not brave one hundred percent of the time. My role is that of a man who is intuitive and suspicious, proud and searching. He has a touch of the vain and a childish and disproportionate sense of virtue and manly ethics. He is lonely and generally distrustful of human contacts.[9]

Brando's film certainly wasn't an ordinary western. Loosely based on Charles Neider's novel *The Authentic Death of Hendry Jones*, a fictionalized biography of Billy the Kid, the story passed through the hands of several auteurs (including Rod Serling, Sam Peckinpah and Stanley Kubrick) before Brando took charge. After the star became the director, Neider claims, the film became an expensive improvisation experiment. The author remembers the production atmosphere: "It was as if the place were being run by a Renaissance princeling.... A lot of the shooting was off the cuff (an expensive procedure). At times Brando encouraged actors to forget their lines and make up dialogue as they went along, as if this might produce more authentic stuff. Usually it brought forth silence, or embarrassing lines. It was as if he regarded scripts (and writers) as dispensable."[10]

Such unconventional storytelling methods would be embraced by Hollywood in subsequent years, but at the time nobody knew quite what to make of Brando's self-indulgent tale of a nomadic bank robber named Rio, who hates himself so much that he invites pain. Acknowledging that the film was, if nothing else, unique, Neider summed up: "It has a romantic, perhaps adolescent, bitter-sweetness that distinguishes it from other westerns. And it has the sea, and the beaches, and Brando's genius."[11] Genius or no, the film was a commercial failure that diminished the star's status for the remainder of the decade. Peter Bogdanovich later wrote that *One-Eyed Jacks* also broke the actor's spirit, and viewers can see hints of that truth in *The Appaloosa* (1966), in which Brando plays a luckless hero, ill-fated, none too smart, and too stubborn for his own good. The actor was an ideal anti-hero, but the time was not quite ripe for anti-heroes.

Hollywood was still saying goodbye to its old guard. In 1962, writer/director Sam Peckinpah oversaw the farewell performances of Joel McCrea and Randolph Scott. *Ride the High Country* (1962) presented the two screen icons as a pair of "old timers" at odds with—and almost outmatched by—an increasingly harsh and cynical America. The filmmaker reflected, "What I think my characters have is individuality—which I think is obsolete in today's world. They weren't obsolete then, there was still room to move, now there's no room to move."[12] McCrea's Steve Judd is the true hero of the film, an ex-lawman who may not be as fast or as accurate as he used to be, but whose moral aim remains true. Scott's Gil Westrum is a more jaded, slightly corrupted cowboy who claims to believe only in money. When the two men team up to transport a shipment of gold, Westrum taunts his partner: "You know what's on the back of a poor man when he dies? The clothes of pride. And they're not a bit warmer to him dead than they were when he was alive. Is that all you want, Steve?" Judd responds, "All I want is to enter my house justified." In the end, the self-proclaimed cynic can't argue with that.

Peckinpah later said that McCrea's defining line of dialogue was a paraphrase of a Bible verse he learned from his own father.[13] Like the director, McCrea's character faces the difficult task of applying this simple maxim to a complicated world. After a series of events testifying to the ugliness of human nature, another character questions Judd's principles, saying: "My father says there's only right and wrong, good and evil, and nothing in between. It isn't that simple, is it?" Judd responds, "No, it isn't. It should be, but it isn't." In *Ride the High Country*, the West has moved on. Righteousness doesn't always win the day, but that doesn't stop the true heroes from fighting for what's right. When they die, they won't die for nothing.

"Old timers" Randolph Scott (top) and Joel McCrea face the end of the line in *Ride the High Country* (1962, MGM).

Like Scott and McCrea, iconic director John Ford was also delivering his cinematic last rites on the cusp of a new frontier. Slowly returning to the liberal ideals of his youth— by 1966 Ford was once again referring to himself as "a liberal Democrat"—the filmmaker embraced the socially progressive politics of the day with *Sergeant Rutledge* (1960), a courtroom drama about a buffalo soldier standing trial for murder.[14] It was the first major western to cast a black man in a lead role, and actor Woody Strode recognized the significance, saying, "You never seen a Negro come off a mountain like John Wayne before. I had the greatest Glory Hallelujah ride across the Pecos River that any black man ever had on the screen. [...] I carried the whole black race across that river."[15]

Ford's subsequent film, *Two Rode Together* (1961), was a more ambiguous and meandering narrative about racial prejudice—an effort the filmmaker eventually dismissed as "the worst piece of crap I've done in twenty years."[16] At the time, Ford was struggling earnestly to understand how America was changing. His grandson and biographer Dan Ford remembers:

There was a new, more liberal, more permissive spirit in the air. Minority groups were clamoring for their piece of the American Dream, and there was a new generation of political leaders who seemed willing to give it to them. John was confused and ambivalent. He liked the new liberalism—particularly the struggle for black civil rights, which in his mind was not unlike the struggle for Irish freedom. But he also knew that he was an old warhorse with set ideas, and that his ability to respond to change was limited.[17]

The director's subsequent film, *The Man Who Shot Liberty Valance* (1962), directly addressed his anxiety about being an old warhorse on a new frontier, and offered a kind of eulogy for his old ideals. Onscreen, the eulogy is delivered by James Stewart's elderly senator Ransom Stoddard, as he recalls his rise to prominence on the back of an unsung hero. Decades earlier, Stoddard explains, he was a tenderfoot lawyer who went to Arizona with a head full of high-minded ideas about civilized law and order. Soon after his arrival, he found himself at odds with Liberty Valance, the second toughest gunman in the territory. Unable to defend himself, Stoddard sought help from the toughest gunman in the territory, a man named Tom Doniphon (John Wayne). Unfortunately, the high-minded easterner quickly learned that Doniphon didn't care much for high-minded ideas. The gunman agreed to help Stoddard only because his girlfriend asked him to. As a result, Wayne's character inadvertently lionized the eastern reformer, lost his girl, rendered himself and his way of life obsolete, and ushered in a new era of "civilized" law and order in Arizona.

At the end of the film, the elderly Stoddard finishes telling his story to a group of modern-day newspapermen, and they decide to let the unsung hero's story remain buried. "This is the West, sir," they explain, and "when the legend becomes fact, [we] print the legend." That's exactly what John Ford, and most of his filmmaking peers, had always done in classic Hollywood westerns. In *The Man Who Shot Liberty Valance*, however, Ford does the opposite. He shows us an ugly truth: the death of the western ideal. Coming from the filmmaker most closely associated with the traditional Hollywood western, this untraditional ending seems especially pointed. When the citizens of Arizona celebrate Ransom Stoddard rather than Tom Doniphan, Ford's narrative suggests that modern America has chosen a well-meaning straw man over a true western hero. Film historian Peter Biskind offers a more specific context:

> Conservatives did not, after all, inherit the America of the fifties, the way Ford suggests they would in *Clementine* and *Fort Apache*; on the contrary, the corporate liberals did.... Conservatives who had high hopes for Eisenhower, the first Republican president in two decades, saw him become captive of the corporate-liberal establishment, and they didn't like it. There is real anger in *Liberty Valance*, a sense of betrayal that looks forward to the conservative revival of the late seventies.[18]

For the time being, America belonged to Ransom Stoddard ... or worse.

Three untraditional western films with contemporary settings—*The Misfits* (1961), *Lonely Are the Brave* (1962) and *Hud* (1963)—were even more dispiriting. In *The Misfits*, Clark Gable's cowboy still makes a living by rounding up wild mustangs, but there's no longer any nobility in his work because the mustangs are simply being ground up for dog food. "It's like ropin' a dream now," he laments. In *Lonely Are the Brave*, Kirk Douglas's range-rover is a perennial outsider, a 19th century man at hopeless odds with life in 20th century America, a man persecuted by friends and authorities alike for his inability to conform to modern society's rules. In *Hud*, Paul Newman's title character is a rancher who has lost his connection to the land, to other people, and to any sense of moral obligation. Ruthlessly determined to maintain his hyper-masculine outlook by any means necessary, he becomes a "man with a barbed wire soul."

"Print the legend": James Stewart (left) and John Wayne in *The Man Who Shot Liberty Valance* (1962, Paramount).

The Misfits began as a simple story by Arthur Miller, based on personal experiences. The playwright went to Reno, Nevada, to live for six months so that he could claim residency to get a divorce. While he was waiting, he crossed paths with some real-life modern cowboys. Miller remembers:

> We came upon a little shack, hardly bigger than this room, that cowboys used to rest. Absolutely nothing within fifty miles, just that one little building, and on the floor there were girlie magazines and some about guitar-playing cowboys too. I discovered that they believed those cowboys were the real ones, and not them. They were not something called "cowboys," they were just working men. Reality was in the movies. It was terrible. I remember feeling it was the end of human consciousness that they would devalue themselves and value this nonsense. Because the world didn't respect them, the realities, but respected the facsimiles, they were nothing.[19]

The experience prompted him to write a story about one such cowboy, Guy Langland, who struggles against his sense of loss by trying to make a genuine connection with Roslyn Taber, a sensitive divorcee, and Perce Howland, a shell-shocked rodeo rider. Langland's brief relationship with these fellow misfits only compounds his sense of alienation. Miller explains, "It was a story about the indifference I had been feeling not only in Nevada, but in the world now. We were being stunned at our own powerlessness to control our lives, and Nevada was simply the perfection of our common loss."[20] As it turned out, the casting of the film amplified the sense of loss. Within a year, all three stars of the film—59-year-old Gable, 36-year-old Marilyn Monroe and 45-year-old Montgomery Clift—were dead, enhancing the film's aura of tragic melancholy.

Lonely Are the Brave originated with a 1956 novel by Edward Abbey, called *The Lonely Cowboy*. Producer Edward Lewis and actor Kirk Douglas optioned the novel and hired blacklisted screenwriter Dalton Trumbo to adapt it, convinced that "his relationship to the material," his understanding of the main character's feelings of alienation, "made him right for the project."[21] In the film, Douglas plays a Korean War veteran named Jack Burns who cannot accept an ordinary, stationary life in the new American West. Like Dempsey Rae, Douglas's character in *Man Without a Star*, Burns doesn't want to be fenced in. In *Lonely Are the Brave*, however, the other characters are much more critical of the main character's wanderlust, equating his restlessness with self-delusion and irresponsibility. A friend's wife advises, "The world you […] live in doesn't exist. Maybe it never did." Turning solemn observation into a personal attack, she adds, "You men just act like children, all of you."

To Burns, however, men haven't changed; America has. Today, he reflects, a real man is a "born cripple," because "the only person he can live with is himself." This message resonated strongly with the actor, who casually confessed, "I love the theme that if you try to be an individual, society will crush you."[22] Trumbo, who obviously knew a thing or two about the dangers of nonconformity, recognized Douglas as a genuine "lonely cowboy." In a private letter to the actor, written after seeing the film for the first time, he wrote: "Once in a while when God smiles and the table is tilted just slightly in our favor, something happens. It comes from inside and reveals what we really are. I think it happened to you in [*Lonely Are the Brave*]. I think you are going to leave the theatre saying, 'That is what I really am. Or at least it is what I want to be in my finest hour.' You did it. You showed the heart of a man."[23]

If Douglas's performance in *Lonely Are the Brave* revealed how a man could rise above the pressures of modern America, Paul Newman's performance in *Hud* showed how easily he could be corrupted. Based on a novel by Larry McMurtry, *Hud* tells the story of three Texas cowboys, each representing a different generation of the same ranching family. When one of the cattle in the family herd is diagnosed with foot and mouth disease, each cowboy responds in a different way. The oldest member of the family, representing the G.I. Generation, wants to dispose of every animal he owns to prevent the spread of disease, even though it will mean the negation of his entire life's work. His son,

VII. The New Frontier 91

Kirk Douglas won't be "fenced in" in *Lonely Are the Brave* (1962, Universal).

Hud, would rather sell their livestock immediately, and risk a nationwide epidemic in order to cash in. "This whole country's run on epidemics," the unprincipled capitalist insists, adding, "[If] you don't look out for yourself, the only helping hand you'll get is when they lower the box." The youngest member of the family, Lonnie, is torn between these two perspectives.

Lonnie is played by Brandon De Wilde, an actor best known for his role as Joey Starrett, the wide-eyed kid in *Shane*. As in that earlier film, De Wilde represents the perspective of innocence—a still-undefined generation. The film's vision of America, and its future, hinges on his decision. "Little by little," the grandfather advises Lonnie, "the country changes because of the men we admire." The message is clear: America's heroes are changing, and so are we. Ultimately, Lonnie decides not to follow anyone. He opts to go his own way, turning the cattle loose in an emphatic rejection of both his grandfather's moral responsibility and his uncle's greed. At the end of the film, Lonnie is as much a drifter as Jack Burns and Guy Langland, set loose in search of a better place to call home.

Significantly, the film ends not with Lonnie's departure but with an image of Hud left alone on the ranch. Somehow, director Martin Ritt realized that the title character was the one that audiences would care about the most, although the filmmaker later said he was surprised that younger viewers responded to Hud so warmly. "They ended up supporting him," Ritt observed. "They saw something in him they identified with.... If I had really properly understood that, perhaps I would have known that Haight-Ashbury was coming, and the terrible sixties were going to erupt."[24] Author Larry McMurtry was apparently more percipient. He described Hud as "a twentieth-century westerner, a gunfighter who lacks both guns and opponents," and opined that "the social context has changed so radically that Hud's impulse to violence has to turn inward on himself and his family."[25] Of course, McMurtry neglects to mention the fact that Hud's behavior would have victimized a much larger group of people than himself and his family. This gunfighter doesn't need guns to spread death—and as far as he's concerned, *everyone* is his opponent. Even so, Hud was the anti-hero whose time had come.

The year 1963 was a turning point in American culture, due in large part to the assassination of President Kennedy on November 22. The Italian western *The Price of Power* (*Il prezzo del potere*, 1969) conflated the murder of the president in Dallas with the assassination of President James Garfield in 1881, but Kennedy's death had a more demoralizing and destabilizing effect than Garfield's, precipitating a kind of schism in American culture that led to the Vietnam War being fought at home as well as abroad. No single event can be held responsible for the changes in the culture, or for the gradual demise of the traditional western film, but the effects are clear. Before 1963, it was still possible for Hollywood filmmakers to produce a film like *How the West Was Won* (1962), an epic and hopelessly naïve celebration of Manifest Destiny. After 1963, even traditionalists like John Ford and Raoul Walsh couldn't deny the new perspective. Walsh's final film, *A Distant Trumpet* (1964), protested the U.S. government's historic failure to abide by its own peace treaties. Ford's swan song *Cheyenne Autumn* (1964) offered an apology of sorts to those who suffered most from the imperialist philosophy of Manifest Destiny. In a contemporary interview with Peter Bogdanovich, Ford confessed: "I've killed more Indians than Custer, [Frederick H.] Beecher, and [John] Chivington put together ... [but] I like Indians very much. They're ... they're a very moral people. They have a literature. Not written. But spoken. They're very kindhearted. They love their children and their animals. And I wanted to show their point of view for a change."[26]

Cheyenne Autumn begins in the autumn of 1878, when the Cheyenne people attempt a mass migration from a government reservation in Oklahoma to their native soil in Montana. Along the way they suffer starvation and attack, until a U.S. Cavalry leader reluctantly puts them in a temporary internment camp at Fort Robinson, Nebraska. Most of the Indians choose to die there rather than turn back. Only a few survive.

From the beginning, the filmmaker and his son conceived *Cheyenne Autumn* as social commentary. Pat Ford remembered the initial plan:

> The Cheyennes are not to be heavies, nor are they to be ignorant, misguided savages without plan or purpose to their war-making. Their motives must be clearly expressed in the beginning of the picture. If there is to be a heavy, it must be the distant United States government, a government blind to the plight of the Indians. The Army is to be portrayed as an underpaid, undermanned force, all but forgotten on a distant frontier, a group of dedicated men trying to maintain a virtually impossible peace despite Washington's mismanagement.[27]

The narrative clearly reflected the zeitgeist of 1960s America, equating the Cheyenne with civil rights protesters of every background and color. Unfortunately the didactic western did not appeal to western fans, who no doubt wanted a moral hero to root for. Although the film features James Stewart as Wyatt Earp, the famous lawman seems utterly indifferent to the tragedy at hand. The film's nominal hero, a cavalry officer played by Richard Widmark, seems merely overwhelmed. If John Ford couldn't produce a hero for the times, who could?

Although humbled by the failure of *The Alamo*, John Wayne remained Hollywood's conquering hero. Taking some cues from the character he played in *Rio Bravo*, the actor spent much of the decade building a new screen image as an aging but dignified leading man, humanized by his sense of humor. A more genial John Wayne appeared in *North to Alaska* (1960) and the lighthearted western *The Comancheros* (1961), and really came into his own with the romantic comedy *McLintock!* (1963). After a valiant bout with lung cancer, he returned to the screen in *The Sons of Katie Elder* (1965) with more fighting spirit than ever.

In the film, Wayne played a gunfighter who returns home for his mother's funeral. His presence stirs up trouble with a rival family that's itching for a fight. Initially his four brothers resist the temptation to violence, because they know their mother wouldn't have approved, but the pacifist sentiment doesn't last. As the film transforms into a revenge story, Wayne leads the charge. In one scene, he tortures the sniveling son of his father's murderer (played by rising actor Dennis Hopper), prompting the young man's own father to shoot him just to stop the sniveling. Such a celebration of wanton violence was light years away from Wayne's first postwar western, *Angel and the Badman* (1947), in which a Quaker woman manages to convince the hero that violence only perpetuates violence. In subsequent years, the determinedly-violent gunslinger continued to fight the good fight in a string of blustery westerns directed by fellow conservatives Howard Hawks, Henry Hathaway, Burt Kennedy and Andrew V. McLaglen.

In these final days of the traditional western, McLaglen's name became almost synonymous with winsomely nostalgic vehicles for aging screen heroes like John Wayne and James Stewart. One of his most challenging films of the period was *Shenandoah* (1965), a Civil War western that featured Stewart as a pacifist farmer named Charlie Anderson. At the film's outset, Anderson has managed to keep his six sons at home throughout the war, but the battle literally arrives in his front yard. When Yankee soldiers kidnap and kill his youngest boy, the whole family goes to war. In the end, Charlie stops just short of avenging his son's death. Standing over his wife's grave, he explains that he held back because he suddenly remembered the futility of fighting: "It's like all wars, I suppose. The undertakers are winning it. Or the politicians who talk a lot about the glory of it, and the old men who talk about the need of it. The soldiers, they just want to go home." In a few years, the character could easily have been talking about the war in Vietnam, although the filmmaker insisted that he didn't set out to make an anti-war polemic. "I'm the farthest thing from a pacifist," McLaglen told interviewer Courtney Joyner, "but I think that [those feelings] worked their way out, and for good reason."[28] *Shenandoah* was a product of its time.

Filmmaker Sam Peckinpah was more violently dedicated to anti-war sentiments. Peckinpah made two films in 1965, *The Glory Guys* and *Major Dundee*, both of which undermine the traditional Hollywood western's perspective on war. *The Glory Guys* spends most of its running time humanizing a band of brothers, in order to set up the depressing revelation that they have been deemed expendable, casually discounted by martial strategists. In the end, a Custer-like general leads the inexperienced platoon to their deaths to satisfy his own ego, and the surviving captain waxes poetic on the loss: "I wonder how many of them weren't afraid to take a hold of what they could while they could still see the sun."

In *Major Dundee*, the focus falls squarely on the leader of such a platoon, who displays the kind of mania that Henry Fonda embodied in *Fort Apache*. Major Dundee's rules are as simple and uncompromising as those of Lt. Col. Owen Thursday: "If I signal you to come, you come. If I signal you to charge, you charge. And if I signal you to run, you follow me and run like hell." For Dundee, life is one long endless battle. When an old rival tells him he's fighting a private war, he responds, "The war won't last forever." She knows better. "It will for you, major."

Charlton Heston, who played the surly Major Dundee, later reflected that Peckinpah's film was not as powerful as it could have been, because the director's vision was diluted:

> *Major Dundee* had a lot of problems. One of the most crucial, though none of us realized it at the time, was that Columbia, Sam, and I all really had different pictures in mind. Columbia, reasonably enough, wanted a cavalry/Indians film as much like Jack Ford's best as possible. I wanted to be the first to make a film that really explored the Civil War. Sam, though he never said anything like this, really wanted to make *The Wild Bunch*. That's the movie that was steaming in his psyche.[29]

What a difference a few years would make. By 1969, the United States would be hopelessly mired in a losing war in Vietnam, with public sentiment rising strongly against it. Films like Peckinpah's *The Wild Bunch* would capture the public outrage, but the war in Vietnam would not be the only factor in New Hollywood's red, black-and-blue makeover of the western genre. Within a few short years, an influx of hyper-violent westerns from Europe revitalized and reinvented the genre, and lionized an actor who would supplant John Wayne as the king of the cowboys.

CHAPTER VIII

Blood Money
(1964–1968)

> *History has elected to probe the depth of our commitment to freedom. How strongly are we really devoted to resist the tide of aggression? How ready are we to make good on our solemn pledges to other nations? [...] We demonstrated with a tireless quest for rules to keep the nuclear beast in his cage and with foreign aid programs to help life in the less developed countries—containing two of every three citizens of the free world—to help them to true independence. Now, these are the basic themes of what American foreign policy is all about. They have been essentially the same for more than 20 years now, under all administrations, Republican and Democratic. They are the same themes that are being challenged at this moment and defended by our men in Vietnam. There in South Vietnam, aggression fights not only on the battlefield of village and hill and jungle and city. The enemy has reached out to fight in the hearts and minds of the American people.*
> —Lyndon B. Johnson, remarks at the Conference on Foreign Policy for Leaders of National Nongovernmental Organizations, March 19, 1968

In his 1960 book *Theory of Film*, Siegfried Kracauer proposes that all tragic art is based on a fixed worldview: "The tragic conflict materializes only in a closed universe governed by mythical beliefs, moral principles, a political doctrine, or the like.... Tragedy presupposes a finite, ordered cosmos."[1] In the early 1960s, the American western film was in its tragic phase—the last cowboys bearing witness to the slow death of America's old frontier myth. By mid-decade, John F. Kennedy's myth of a "new frontier" was also dying a slow death, as the country became divided over foreign and domestic policies. Hollywood westerns hovered on the brink of chaos, courting tragedy but not quite anarchy. In contrast, European filmmakers pressed forward, plunging their characters into chaos.

The American West, as imagined by Italian filmmakers from roughly 1964 to 1975, is a land governed by random violence—a land in which the traditional hero cannot reasonably expect to restore order. The lone gunslinger is no longer capable of balancing the scales of justice, and so he generally surrenders to cynicism, becoming a committed anti-hero. Many Italian westerns suggest that the only hope for the future of civilized society lies in grand-scale revolution—a collective movement to establish a new social order. As a result, most of the films focus not on the pioneer stories or law-and-order narratives of traditional Hollywood westerns, but rather on tales of class conflict and the ravages of war. With the Almeria region of southern Spain standing in for the American West, the War Between the States and the Mexican Revolution became popular historical backdrops for the so-called spaghetti western.

Sergio Leone's *A Fistful of Dollars* (*Per un pugno di dollari*, 1964) was not the first spaghetti western, but it was the most influential, prompting the Italian film industry to head west. Ironically, Leone drew his initial inspiration not from American westerns but from Akira Kurosawa's samurai epic *Yojimbo* (1961). Kurosawa himself claimed that his film was influenced by the work of John Ford, but *Yojimbo* was less a film about personal moral codes than about intractable politics. The director explained: "The idea is about rivalry on both sides, and both sides are equally bad. We all know what this is like. Here we are, weakly caught in the middle, and it is impossible to choose between the evils.... And that is why the hero of this film is different from us. He is capable of standing squarely in the middle and stopping the fight."[2]

Leone likewise departed from Hollywood tradition. To him, John Ford's vision of America was naïve, as he explained: "Ford, because of his European origins—as a good Irishman—has always seen the problem from a Christian point of view ... his characters and protagonists always look forward to a rosy, fruitful future. Whereas I see the history of the West as really the reign of violence by violence."[3] Instead of following the established tradition, Leone brought a distinctly modern Italian sentiment—anti-fascist and anti-imperialist—to the western genre. He wasn't interested in creating the kind of "cruel, puritan fairy-story" he had watched as a child; he wanted to show Americanos as he had seen them in real life: World War II "liberators" who turned out to be "materialist, possessive, keen on pleasures and earthly goods."[4] With *A Fistful of Dollars*, he popularized a new breed of western hero: greedy, self-serving, faithless.

Leone originally wanted to cast Henry Fonda, Lee Marvin, James Coburn or Charles Bronson in the role of his irreverent anti-hero, but all of those actors turned down the role.[5] Leone turned instead to a young actor named Clint Eastwood, who was eager to escape his sidekick role on the long-running TV series *Rawhide* ... even if it meant shooting a cheapjack western in southern Spain. Over the years, the director and his star have quibbled over who was ultimately responsible for the mystique of the Man with No Name. Leone says that he and screenwriter Duccio Tessari developed the character after seeing Eastwood in an episode of *Rawhide*. What impressed Leone was Eastwood's "laziness," his economy of speech and movement.[6] Eastwood, however, claims that in the original shooting script his character (then called Joe) had huge chunks of dialogue, which the actor himself whittled down against the director's wishes. The actor remembered: "I felt the less he said the stronger he became and the more he grew in the imagination of the audience. You never knew who he was, where he came from and what he was going to do next."[7] Eastwood also claims that he fought for the removal of a prologue in which Joe saw his mother killed in front of him.[8] The final cut is more cryptic. After Eastwood's one-man army saves a mother and her family, he explains, "I knew somebody like you once, and there was no one there to help."

Regardless of who un-named the Man with No Name, *A Fistful of Dollars* made both Leone and Eastwood famous, and reenergized the Italian film industry by inspiring a glut of imitations. Taking cues from Leone, writer/director Sergio Corbucci made *Minnesota Clay* (1964), about a weary gunfighter who has recently escaped from a Confederate prison camp. For the title character, the war is over. When asked which side he's on, he says, "I'm on my own." His only goal in life is to reunite with his estranged daughter. Like Eastwood's Man with No Name, however, the gunfighter inadvertently finds himself in the middle of a private war.

While *Minnesota Clay* repeated the angry cynicism of *A Fistful of Dollars*, Duccio

VIII. Blood Money

"The less he said the stronger he became": Clint Eastwood as Monco in *For a Few Dollars More* (1965, United Artists).

Tessari's *A Pistol for Ringo* (*Una pistola per Ringo*, 1965) captured the more lighthearted, playful quality of Leone's film. Giuliano Gemma stars as Angel Face, a mischievous and often childish gunman who manipulates both sides of the law, constantly changing sides to his own advantage. Although he is beaten bloody by a group of bandits who recognize his con, Angel Face never loses his air of bemused confidence. In the end, the hero rides off into the sunset with a sack full of money—his reward for not taking *anything* too seriously. The financial success of these two films guaranteed that "Ringo" would ride again in a variety of pseudo-sequels, including Tessari's superior *The Return of Ringo* (*Il Ritorno di Ringo*, 1965), Corbucci's *Ringo and His Golden Pistol* (a.k.a. *Johnny Oro*, 1966) and Mario Bava's *Ringo of Nebraska* (*Ringo del Nebraska*, 1966). These films also established the two-tone nature—alternately dour and comic, pensive and playful—of spaghetti westerns to come.

Having initiated a wildly successful genre of films, Leone set out to top himself. *For a Few Dollars More* (*Per qualche dollaro in più*, 1965) reunited the director with Clint Eastwood for a more epic, almost operatic, story. The film also added a new face to the spaghetti western pantheon. Lee Van Cleef was a veteran character actor who made his screen debut in *High Noon* (1952) and appeared in dozens of minor film and television roles over the course of the subsequent decade. Despite having roles in memorable westerns like Anthony Mann's *The Tin Star* (1957), Budd Boetticher's *Ride Lonesome* (1959) and John Ford's *The Man Who Shot Liberty Valance* (1962), his career was floundering when Leone came calling. The actor remembers: "I was broke! I couldn't pay my phone bill, and it wasn't all that big. They offered me more money than I ever made on any picture, and that's what started it."[9]

In *For a Few Dollars More*, Van Cleef plays a kind of father-figure to Eastwood's laconic Man with No Name. Eastwood refers to him as "old man." Van Cleef responds by calling him "boy." The rapport between the two bounty hunters defines the movie. Van Cleef later said that he strove to convey vulnerability in his role as a "heavy," believing that viewers require "some place to have a bit of sympathy—*not* pity—but *sympathy*; so that the audience feels they're almost—*almost*, I say—as much on your side as they are on the leading man's."[10] The actor also adopted Eastwood's habit of trimming down his character's dialogue, which further emphasizes the kinship between the two men. It was "with *For a Few Dollars More*," Leone acknowledges, "that I directly grappled with my [main] theme for the first time: the friendship that can spring up between two men."[11] Like the films of Anthony Mann and Budd Boetticher, *For a Few Dollars More* shows us that there is oftentimes a marginal difference between heroes and villains. Like the films of Howard Hawks and screenwriter Borden Chase, it shows us that there can be great admiration and respect between them.

By 1967, Italian westerns were certainly making an impression on American filmmakers and audiences. John Ford was bluntly dismissive, while Anthony Mann and Budd Boetticher declared Leone's work cynical and ugly.[12] Moviegoers were generally more enthusiastic, which may have been a result of fortuitous timing. When *A Fistful of Dollars* was released in the United States in January 1967, the nation was reeling from President Johnson's escalation of the war in Vietnam, and the counterculture movement was building rapidly, decrying the government's policy in southeast Asia as aggressive imperialism. Baby boomers were primed for aggressively irreverent westerns that would tell the truth about the American character, and soon Clint Eastwood and Lee Van Cleef weren't the only Hollywood stars roaming the Italian West, skewering Uncle Sam's most popular myths.

"Some place to have a bit of sympathy": Lee Van Cleef as Angel Eyes in *The Good, the Bad and the Ugly* (1966, United Artists).

Joseph Cotten and James Mitchum (son of Robert Mitchum) led the charge in producer/director Albert Band's *The Tramplers* (*Gli uomini dal passo pesante*, 1965), a brutal variation on Joseph H. Lewis's *The Halliday Brand* (1957) that reflected on the Reconstruction era in the United States more bitterly than any Hollywood film had so far. Cotten plays Temple Cordeen, the willful patriarch of a Southern family who refuses to surrender his sword in the aftermath of the American Civil War. At his worst, Cordeen is as bigoted and violent as the most contemptible western villains, but Cotten's portrayal also makes the character sympathetic. His son Hoby, played by Mitchum, is just as proud and just as bitter, but determined to control his hatred instead of letting hatred control him. A confrontation between father and son is inevitable. In the end, however, it won't matter who wins, because the family will be destroyed by their civil war. When the dust settles, a minor character offers a eulogy that reminds viewers of why the United States government turned its attention to the western frontier in the first place: "It'll be a long time before any of us forgets what happened here, but we're gonna have to try." For American audiences, it might have been a warning about the perils of the Vietnam War. Band repeated his war-weary message in his script for Sergio Corbucci's equally savage *The Hellbenders* (*I crudeli*, 1967), which once again cast Joseph Cotten as a hateful, warmongering rebel.

These weren't the only Italian westerns to shatter the decorum of Hollywood's whitewashed version of American history. Director Carlo Lizzani's *The Hills Run Red* (*Un fiume di dollari*, 1966) revolves around a pair of Rebel bandits on the run from Yankee soldiers. Before they can escape to Mexico, one gets captured and imprisoned for five long years. The other takes over his friend's life: bedding his wife and raising his son. The subsequent revenge tale is a hodgepodge of plot twists from popular American westerns (most notably, *Shane* and the Mann/Stewart series), but the film has its own intensity. Sergio Corbucci's *Navajo Joe* (1966)—featuring Burt Reynolds as a renegade Native American warrior—likewise recycles plot points from older Hollywood westerns about the "Indian problem" (*Devil's Doorway*, *Apache*, *The Last Frontier*, etc.), but infuses them with a virulent anger that reflected the political turmoil of the mid–1960s.

At this point, Italian filmmakers were making even the most traditional type of westerns better than American filmmakers. One noteworthy exception was Richard Brooks' *The Professionals* (1966), a cadre western in the mold of *The Magnificent Seven*, about four American mercenaries who become embroiled in the Mexican Revolution. Hired by a wealthy gringo to track down an underground militant named Raza (a stand-in for Mexican revolutionary Emiliano Zapata), the specialists are partly driven by disillusionment about the very idea of revolution. When they finally come face to face with Raza, however, they are forced to reexamine their own values. Raza advises: "La Revolución is like a great love affair. In the beginning she is a goddess—a holy cause ... [but] la revolucción is not a goddess but a whore. Lust but no love. Passion but no compassion. Without love, without a cause, we are nothing. We stay because we believe. We leave because we are disillusioned. We come back because we are lost. We die because we are committed." Burt Lancaster, playing the leader of the professionals, takes these words to heart and reflects: "Maybe there's only one revolution, since the beginning: the good guys against the bad guys. Question is: Who are the good guys?" This moral quandary would hang over the spaghetti western for years to come.

Sergio Leone's most iconic film, *The Good, the Bad and the Ugly* (*Il buono, Il brutto, Il cattivo*, 1966) makes the question even more difficult to answer. The director claimed he wanted to reveal the absurdity of moral distinctions, and he chose to do so by demythologizing America's Civil War. His film revolves around three men, all devoted to a single cause: money. Clint Eastwood plays a cool, self-serving bounty hunter known as Blondie; Lee Van Cleef plays an honest killer called Angel Eyes; and Eli Wallach is a crude, hot-headed criminal named Tuco. Each man pretends political loyalty to the North or the South when it serves him, but all clearly recognize the futility of war. There are no real heroes and no real villains in this story, only differing circumstances and perspectives used to justify violence.

Wallach's character Tuco seems to understand Leone's moral relativity better than anyone; in a scene where he is reunited with his estranged brother, Tuco remembers that he became a bandit simply because he was strong enough to fight. In contrast, his brother became a priest because he was afraid to fight. Tuco observes that if indeed there are only two kinds of people in the world, they are not the Good and the Bad, but the Weak and the Powerful. "An assassin," Leone concurs, "can display a sublime altruism while a good man can kill with total indifference. A person who appears to be ugly may, when we get to know him better, be more worthy than he seems—and capable of tenderness."[13] The small-scale war between the three men in this film is a simple story of survival of the fittest. The ending, according to Leone, represents "the true history of the United States."[14]

Subsequent Italian westerns set during the Mexican Revolution offered even more pointed protests of imperialist and capitalist agendas in the midst of the Vietnam War. The first of these films—dubbed "Zapata westerns"—was Damiano Damiani's *A Bullet for the General* (*Quien sabe?*, 1966). It begins with a fortuitous meeting between an American businessman nicknamed El Niño and a Mexican bandit nicknamed El Chuncho. The two men share revolutionary sentiments, but neither one is overtly political. The American capitalist regards the Mexican Revolution as an opportunity to make money, while the Mexican bandit supports the egalitarian ideals of the revolution more than any actual political movement. The two men part ways, however, when asked to defend a town full of peasants. El Niño suggests that the peasants aren't worth the trouble, to which El Chuncho responds: "Aren't they humans, same as us?" Confronted with this rhetoric, El Niño cynically responds—echoing the worldview of earlier spaghetti western "heroes"—that "you have to look out for yourself." In the end, the reluctant revolutionary shoots the jaded capitalist and gives his money to a peasant, along with the following advice: "Don't buy bread with that money. Buy dynamite!"

Writer/director Sergio Sollima strikes a similar note in *The Big Gundown* (*La resa dei conti*, 1966), staring Lee Van Cleef and Tomás Milián. Milián had made his western debut a year earlier in *The Bounty Killer* (*El precio de un hombre*, 1965), playing an escaped convict whose friends and family mistake him for a "protector of decent folk." The actor remembered: "The character I was supposed to portray was just a bad Mexican guy. He was just plain bad for the American to shoot. I called the producer and the director and I told them I wanted to work on the part with them and give a reason why this Mexican was so bad, right? Then I put kind of a social motive behind this bad attitude towards life, and that's how I did it."[15] This embellishment established the actor's screen persona; for the next decade he continued to play characters with a wavering devotion to revolutionary ideals. "During the hippie revolution," the actor claimed, "I did my revolution in the movies."[16]

In *The Big Gundown*, Milián starred as Cuchillo, a common thief—or, rather, a common peasant and an exceptional thief—on the run during the Mexican Revolution. Sergio Sollima, who based Cuchillo on Toshiro Mifune's character in Akira Kurosawa's *Seven Samurai* (*Shichinin no samurai*, 1954), claimed that Cuchillo represented "the first time in western history [that] the protagonist was depicted as a dreamer, a boy [instead of a man.]"[17] He added, "Young people could see him as one of them, not a cold superhero like Clint Eastwood, but someone really human, who stole when he had to, who lied continually, who had all the human failings of a social class of which the western rarely spoke."[18]

Van Cleef's character, "Colorado" Corbett, hunts the dreamer on behalf of the upper class, initially believing a corrupt politician's assertion that Cuchillo is a rapist and murderer. As he pursues his quarry, however, Corbett realizes that Cuchillo is more merry mischief-maker than black-hearted criminal. Given the opportunity to speak on his own behalf, the thief explains that he is innocent of the alleged crimes, and guilty only of running from political persecution. Cuchillo sums up the political landscape of the Zapata western: "I do know a law—the one that says most of the world is two parties: the masters and the poor peons. In my country, there was such a law—and no one ever know who wrote it, but we lived under it. Then one day we listen to [Mexican President Benito] Juarez and he say we should change it. Everybody should be nice and we shouldn't hate each other and the peons should be free.... We thought it would work for a while, but nothing really changed." After Cuchillo identifies himself as a disillusioned revolutionary, Corbett realizes that he has become an unwitting soldier in the Mexican president's secret army of counter-revolutionaries. In the final act, the hunter stands up for the dreamer, and Cuchillo keeps running.

"I did my revolution in the movies": Tomas Milián as Cuchillo in *Run, Man, Run* (1968, Columbia).

Sollima and Milián revived Cuchillo for a second outing in the picaresque *Run, Man, Run* (*Corri, uomo, corri*, 1968). This time, Cuchillo is on the trail of lost gold in Texas, followed closely by a greedy American sheriff, French assassins, Mexican bandits, two feisty women and a ragtag band of revolutionaries. When Cuchillo finds the gold, he faces a moral dilemma: Should he take the money and run, or join the revolution? The hero recognizes this as a defining moment. His life so far has been determined by circumstances beyond his control, but now he has an opportunity to choose his own destiny. "I'm a peaceful man at heart," he contemplates, "If I was born in another country, in another time ... the knife, I would have used it just to cut bread." Recognizing that he cannot change his circumstances, he decides to stop running and fight.

Milián continued his political crusade in *Tepepa* (1968), a film that pitted him against a fascist police chief played by Orson Welles. Tepepa's revolutionary ideals are defined in an early scene in which he converses with Mexican president Francisco Madero. Madero asks him to surrender his weapon after two years of fighting alongside Pancho Villa and his revolutionaries, but Tepepa is understandably hesitant:

> TEPEPA: I took this rifle to fight against the Army and now I have to give it back to the Army. Who won? The revolution or the Army?
> MADERO: The Revolution.
> TEPEPA: And the Army?

MADERO: The Army is at the service of the State.
TEPEPA: The State?
MADERO: The organization of all citizens.
TEPEPA: Rich and poor?
MADERO: Rich and poor.
TEPEPA: We have made a mistake, señor presidente, because everything is like it was before.
MADERO: No. The rich will be less rich and the poor, less poor.

The jaded soldier returns home to a town run by a Welles, and quickly becomes frustrated with the new normal. He vows to "find men, find weapons and fight again like before." The conventional war is over, but Tepepa aims to ignite a new war in the hearts and minds of the common people. Along the way, however, he becomes corrupted by his embrace of violence. In the end, the revolutionary persona that started out as an innocent dreamer becomes the rapist and murderer that he was accused of being. At this point, the spaghetti western rejects even the hope for revolutionary change.

Significantly, Italian filmmakers didn't just overhaul the western genre by making it more overtly political; they also made it more existential. Sergio Corbucci's *Django* (1966), another modification of Leone's *Fistful of Dollars* formula, begins with the image of a dark stranger wandering through a winter wasteland, dragging a coffin behind him through the mud. The image sets the tone of the film: this is no blue-sky western about a noble crusader. Played by Franco Nero, Django is an agent of death in a world that has moved on from war to something worse. Django says that he "fought for the North," but his demeanor suggests only defeat. At times, he acts heroically—rescuing a woman who is being tortured by racists—but he remains aware that he is merely playing a role. When the villains of the piece become cruel and bloodthirsty, Django becomes equally cold and brutal. When the time is right, he opens his coffin, hauls out a Gatling gun and kills everyone in sight.

Up to this point Corbucci's characters seem to exist in a godless universe. The tone changes when Django confronts his own death, and survives due to divine intervention. Afterward, the existential hero remains an agent of death—but he also becomes a democrat and a Catholic. Django makes it his mission to destroy the "Fanatics," a gang of bigoted fascists who are destroying Mexico. In the final act, the universe of Corbucci's film seems not to be lost to chaos, but governed by a vengeful Old Testament God. The avenger, with two crushed hands, prays for the strength to carry out this invisible God's will in a cemetery showdown. Playing directly to the common values of postwar Italy, the film became a commercial success and spawned dozens of imitations. *Texas, Adios*, a previously released film starring Franco Nero, was re-released as *Django 2*, while future genre stars Gianni Garko and Terence Hill adopted the moniker in *$10,000 for Django* (1967) and *Django, Prepare a Coffin* (1968).

Giulio Questi's *Django, Kill ... If You Live, Shoot!* (*Se sei vivo spara*, 1966) was perhaps the boldest film to claim the name. Moving from existentialism to gothic surrealism, the narrative suggests that the title character (played by Tomás Milián) is literally fighting his way through Hell. Questi plainly confessed that was not interested in making a western, only in expressing thoughts and feelings about the horrors of war: "I wanted to recount all of the things, the cruelty, the comradeship with friends, the death, all of the experiences I had of war, in combat, in the mountains."[19] Accordingly, his film revels in the darkest impulses of western civilization. After a disorienting barrage of sadomasochistic violence and blasphemy, it ends with a gruesome finale straight out of a horror movie.

Director Giulio Petroni's *Death Rides a Horse* (*Da uomo a uomo*, 1967) is equally apocalyptic, tearing its opening sequences out of the book of Revelation. Lee Van Cleef makes his first appearance during a late-night thunderstorm, as one of four horsemen of the apocalypse who rain death and destruction on a sleepy western town. The hero is a gunman named Bill Meceita, the only survivor of the horrific massacre. Meceita devotes his life to seeking revenge on the four horsemen and teams up with Van Cleef's character to hunt them, not realizing that Van Cleef is actually one of the four. Eventually a bond forms between the two hunters, not unlike the father/son bond in *For a Few Dollars More*, and generates sympathy for the devil. All the while, the story creeps toward an inevitable death-dealing confrontation between the two. With this film, horror is perfectly integrated into the western mythos.

Franco Nero, the original Django, in *The Mercenary* (1968, United Artists).

In 1968 the first wave of Italian westerns reached its high water mark, and Sergio Leone and Sergio Corbucci—the undisputed masters of the genre—made their most accomplished films. Leone intended *Once Upon a Time in the West* (*C'era una volta il West*, 1968) to be his ultimate achievement in the genre, and so his story unfolds in grand, almost operatic, style. The director had originally hoped to open the film by killing off the three actors from *The Good, the Bad and the Ugly*, an audacious promise to one-up his previous films, but Eastwood rejected the idea. Instead, Leone took aim at genre veterans Woody Strode, Jack Elam and Al Mulock—putting them against his new revenge hero. For that key role, Leone cast the actor he'd originally pursued for *A Fistful of Dollars*. Charles Bronson plays the laconic gunfighter called Harmonica, a man dead-set on avenging the murder of his parents. In the role of his nemesis Frank, Leone cast Henry Fonda, gleefully transforming "the face of America" into a portrait of a stone-cold psychopath. With these two polarizing figures in place, Leone built the rest of his story around stereotypes from the Hollywood western—a hooker with a heart of gold (played by Claudia Cardinale), a romantic bandit (Jason Robards) and a robber baron (Gabriele Ferzetti)—and set it in legendary Monument Valley, where John Ford made his most iconic westerns. Leone's plan was to create his own monomyth: a "kaleidoscopic view of all American westerns put together," "*my* version of the story of the birth of a nation."[20]

The big difference between *Once Upon a Time* and most prior westerns was the film's emphasis on Claudia Cardinale's character Jill McBain. Female characters had been

The rock against which the male characters test themselves: Claudia Cardinale as Jill McBain in *Once Upon a Time in the West* (1968, Paramount).

particularly rare in Leone's earlier films, and the director was very forthcoming about his reluctance to highlight women in his stories, saying: "Even in the greatest westerns, the woman is imposed on the action, as a star, and is generally destined to be 'had' by the male lead. But she does not exist *as a woman*. [...] She has no real character, no reality. She is a symbol. She is there without having any reason to be there, simply because one must have a woman, and because the hero must prove, in some way or another, that he has 'sex-appeal.'"[21]

In *Once Upon a Time in the West*, however, Jill McBain is the fixed point around which the entire film revolves. She has plenty of sex appeal, but she is also the rock against which the male characters test themselves. Harmonica defines himself as a hero by protecting her. Frank defines himself as a villain by murdering her husband and subsequently raping her. Robards's more ambiguous character Cheyenne lusts after her but eventually learns to respect and admire her. He finally realizes that, no matter how she is treated, Jill McBain will maintain her strength and independence; she refuses to accept the role of victim, and that makes her every bit as powerful as the Men of the West.... Maybe moreso, because unlike the gunslingers in the film she will actually survive to see the future of America. In the final scene, Cheyenne urges her to spend some time among the railroad workers who are literally building a road to the future, explaining that she will be for them a symbol of hope. In short, Leone's birth of a nation is not a virgin birth. Instead of proffering a puritanical, black-and-white vision of American history, the film suggests that recognizing and accepting hard, complicated truths about the past is the prerequisite for building a strong future.

In contrast, Sergio Corbucci's *The Great Silence* (*Il grande silenzio*, 1968) was decidedly pessimistic about the future. Like *Once Upon a Time in the West*, the film sets up a struggle between a lone avenger and a cold-hearted killer-for-hire. Jean-Louis Trintignant stars as Silence, a hero who's even more laconic than Eastwood's Man with No Name or Bronson's Harmonica. This is not a matter of temperament, but a physical necessity: the man who killed his father also cut out Silence's throat. Since then, he has worked as an assassin. His latest job brings him to a snow-blind community in the Utah Territory, where a woman has hired him to kill a fellow assassin named Loco (played with maniacal glee by Klaus Kinski).

Before Silence can finish the job, local politicians empower Loco to rid the territory of Mormon settlers, and Silence finds himself pitted against an entire gang of cutthroat bounty hunters. He narrowly escapes with his life, but the villain crushes his gun hand. Eager to finish the job, Loco holds the entire Mormon population hostage—promising to kill them all if Silence doesn't consent to a duel. As in *Django*, the hero enters his final battle with the odds stacked hopelessly against him. Unlike *Django*, *The Great Silence* offers no divine intervention. In the latter film, the hero and the innocents are slaughtered like cattle.

Some viewers have suggested that the final sequence in *The Great Silence* is based on the Mountain Meadows Massacre of 1857, the mass murder of a wagon train of eastern immigrants by a Mormon militia in southern Utah. Corbucci's widow claimed, however, that her husband drew his inspiration from the assassinations of Malcolm X in 1965 and Che Guevara in 1967.[22] Viewed in this light, the death of Silence implies that America's heroic western myth is so hopelessly at odds with the reality of modern American life that it cannot possibly survive.

After 1968 many Italian westerns veered increasingly toward horror. Robert Hossein's *Cemetery without Crosses* (*Une corde, un Colt...*, 1968), co-written by future horror icon Dario Argento, represents the bleakest kind of revenge western—one in which the cycle of violence goes on and on until everyone is dead and every last shred of hope and humanity has been eradicated. Antonio Margheriti's *Vengeance* (*Joko invoca Dio ... e muori*, 1968) promised the same level of savagery, opening with a God's eye view of a man being torn apart by five ropes. The film culminated with a showdown between a Byronic hero and a cackling villain in a Dracula cape. Margheriti's subsequent film, *Twice a Judas* (*Due volte giuda*, 1969), turned into a Gothic study of duality that would make Robert Louis Stevenson proud. In short order, the Italian horror-western reached its own dead end. At that point, filmmakers turned to comedy: Ringo, Django and the Man with No Name gave way to the likes of Sartana and Sabata (James Bonds of the Wild West), Bambino and Trinity (Bud Spencer and Terence Hill's comic personas in *They Call Me Trinity* and *Trinity Is Still My Name*).

Director Sergio Corbucci followed up *The Great Silence* with lighter fare. His film *Specialists* (*Gli specialisti*, 1969) follows a lone gunman named Hud to a small western town that is comically affected by lust, bigotry and dirty politics. In the end, a group of angry hippies literally strips the town bare—unveiling the citizens' collective guilt as well as scores of body parts that have clearly never seen the light of day. Hud manages to escape this Euro-western Woodstock, but he's mortally wounded and obviously confused. *Compañeros* (*Vamos a matar, compañeros*, 1970) is a more coherent, but equally humorous, story about a Swedish-American gun-runner caught up in the Mexican Revolution. One could read the film as a criticism of American foreign policy circa 1970, but *Compañeros* is too lighthearted for a very serious reading. The heart of the film is the comic interplay between Franco Nero and Tomas Milián, who team up against Jack Palance's one-handed, pot-smoking aristocrat.

Sergio Leone concluded his adventures in the West with an equally pale shadow of his earlier work. *Duck, You Sucker!* (*Giù la testa*, 1971) presents revolutionary ideals as a cruel joke, worthy only of a dry laugh. The film's bank robbing anti-hero Juan Miranda sums up: "The people who read books go to the people who can't read the books—the poor people—and say, 'We have to have a change.' So the poor people make the change. And then the people who read the books, they all sit around the big, polished tables and talk and talk and talk and eat and eat and eat. But what has happened to the poor people? They're dead! That's your revolution!" Although Miranda continues to fight, alongside an anarchic Irish bomber John H. Mallory, he no longer believes that it is possible to stimulate lasting social or political change. When the air clears on his revolution, all that remains is the ruins of peaceful, happy lives sacrificed for someone else's ideals. For screenwriter Sergio Donati, the film represented "the end of the illusions we had at the time of *The Big Gundown*"—a suggestion that the revolutionary ideals of the mid-1960s had already turned to bile.[23] In the United States that was very much the case, as Woodstock gave way to Altamont, the Manson family murders, news of the My Lai massacre, race riots and the continued escalation of the Vietnam War.

Within a few years, one of Italy's future masters of horror provided a fitting tombstone for the spaghetti western craze. Lucio Fulci's *Four of the Apocalypse* (*I quattro dell'apocalisse*, 1975) revolves around an unlikely group of outsiders who are attacked and tortured by a sadistic psychopath. In the role of the villain, Tomás Milián comes across like Charles Manson, violently destroying the hopes and dreams of the hippie generation. Italian filmmakers had taken America's myth as far as they could.

Chapter IX

Mud and Rags
(1967–1973)

> *"I wondered why it is that the western survives year after year after year. A good western will outdraw some of the other subjects. Perhaps one of the reasons, in addition to the excitement, the gun play, and the rest—which perhaps is part of it, but they can get that in other kinds of movie—but one of the reasons is, perhaps—and this may be a square observation—is that the good guys come out ahead in the westerns; the bad guys lose."*
> —Richard Nixon, press conference in Denver, Colorado, August 3, 1970

The years 1967 to 1973 were a time of overwhelming social unrest in the United States. As the Vietnam War escalated, American politics became more divisive and the counterculture movement became more aggressive. In 1967, antiwar rallies in New York, San Francisco and Washington, D.C., illustrated the disillusionment of a generation, and race riots in Newark and Detroit revealed the explosive anger behind that disillusionment. Things only got worse in 1968, when the Tet Offensive suggested that the United States could actually lose the war, and assassins cut short the lives of Martin Luther King, Jr., and Robert Kennedy. In the midst of the chaos, conservative stalwart Richard Nixon was elected president on vague promises to end the war and rein in the social anarchy at home. He accomplished neither goal during his first term, and ran again on essentially the same platform in 1972. Not long after his reelection, the U.S. withdrew from Vietnam, and the Watergate scandal prompted Nixon to resign.

The result of all this turmoil was a demoralized nation, including a new Hollywood that could no longer embrace the old western myth of American exceptionalism. During these years, many filmmakers tried to refashion the genre to fit the tenor of the times. Most westerns suggested that the traditional lone gunslinger was outmatched against America's businessmen and bureaucrats, corporate capitalists and conscience-free criminals. As a result, American heroes had to rebel against all forms of authority and reject all institutions in order to avoid being overrun by cutthroat opportunists. In this milieu, the hero was usually also a victim or a victimizer. As a result, the iconic figure became more of an outsider than ever before, and westerns became social protest documents rather than celebrations of American values and traditions.

At crucial points along the way, there were signs that the genre might not survive the times at all. The influence of Italian westerns began transforming Hollywood westerns into overt horror films and comedies. One of the first films to illustrate the tendency was director Burt Kennedy's *Welcome to Hard Times* (1967), a weirdly metaphysical western starring Henry Fonda as an over-the-hill sheriff whose town gets burned to the ground by a psychopathic (or possibly demonic) gunslinger. Fonda and his surrogate family patiently rebuild the town, only to be attacked again. When the hero finally kills the psycho to protect his family, his actions seem desperate and ugly rather than heroic. The final scene, in which a stray bullet from the hero's gun kills his surrogate son, drives home a hard message: Violence can only destroy life; it cannot restore or redeem life. Kennedy followed up this note of defeat with *Support Your Local Sheriff* (1969), a film that mostly poked fun at western clichés.

Clint Eastwood also carried on the spaghetti western tradition in his first American western. A gruesome variation on *The Ox-Bow Incident*, *Hang 'Em High* (1968) begins with a scene in which a vigilante mob hangs a jaded ex-lawman named Jed Cooper (Eastwood). Cooper manages to survive (or does he?—there are some hints that he's literally "back from hell"), but he's a changed man. After he recovers, he resolves to bring the mob leaders to justice by any means necessary, and the film begins to ponder the nature of true justice: *Should a hero put his faith in the letter of the law or adhere to a more Old Testament morality?* Eastwood's vigilante ultimately decides to play by the rules and help create a state "where no one man calls himself the law"—but only *after* he's had his revenge. Despite Cooper's resolve, we can safely imagine that Eastwood will remain haunted by his propensity for violence. This is his new reality—perhaps his purgatory—as demonstrated by *Dirty Harry* (1971) and *High Plains Drifter* (1973).

At this point in his career, some viewers criticized Eastwood for making hyper-violent European westerns rather than traditional American westerns. The actor stuck to his guns, saying, "I am not an advocate of violence, but on the other hand, if it is one of the narrative elements in the story, I am not as upset by it as other people are. The world is a violent place—no one can escape that. In films, when it is justified, violence acts as a sort of release."[1] In his view, hyper-violent westerns simply mirrored reality in contemporary America—a hyper-violent society plagued by injustice. Although the antiheroes in his films cannot restore moral balance to an unjust world, he argued, that doesn't mean they should accept injustice. Their violent rebellion against such a reality makes them, in a limited sense, heroic—and makes the films genuinely cathartic.

In this regard, Eastwood's early westerns stand apart from the more elegiac Hollywood westerns of the day, which offered no such escape from bleak emotional landscapes. In writer/director Tom Gries's *Will Penny* (1967), Charlton Heston plays an old-fashioned frontiersman trying to settle down and lead a domesticated life. When a sadistic preacher—a villain worthy of a slasher movie (and aptly played by Donald Pleasance)—tortures his family, the demoralized hero abandons all hope for the future. For Heston, the narrative represented a cold, hard truth: "Old Will wasn't being bitter about life, but noting that it goes by; and things don't always turn out the way we thought they would."[2] For this old hero, there is nothing left to do except die.

John Sturges tapped into the defeatist spirit of the times by offering a dark variation on his earlier western *Gunfight at the O.K. Corral*. In *Hour of the Gun* (1967), Wyatt Earp is neither a hero nor a rebel. He is simply a self-serving son of a bitch. After cowboys gun down his brothers Virgil and Morg, the infamous lawman hunts down the killers and executes them in cold blood. After he's had his revenge, he turns down a new marshaling job, saying, "I'm through with the law." Actor James Garner, who played Earp in the film, explained that he saw the character as a ruthless vigilante, pure and simple: "He was a guy taken with his own power, who nobody could defy. He had no qualms about

Jason Robards (left) as Doc Holliday and James Garner as self-serving vigilante Wyatt Earp in *Hour of the Gun* (1967, United Artists).

shooting those boys."[3] The actor and the filmmaker both insisted that this perspective was historically accurate. Regardless, the film was a commercial failure. Years later, Sturges reflected: "I thought the reality of the thing would catch people, who would say, 'Gee, that's the way it was? That's fascinating.' Not so. I got [preview] cards that said of all the stories told about Earp and Holliday, this was the dullest. They considered them fictional characters. They couldn't have cared less that that's the way it really was."[4] *Hour of the Gun* reinforced the lesson of *The Man Who Shot Liberty Valance*: "When the legend becomes fact, print the legend."

American moviegoers may not have been eager to see their national myths debunked, but Hollywood filmmakers continued to debunk them. Writer Elmore Leonard's *Hombre* (1967) plays out like a pessimistic variation on *Stagecoach*, with Paul Newman starring as the social outcast (a white man raised by Apaches) who gets shunned by his fellow travelers. In the end, the outsider does his part to save the white community, but at the cost of his life. Whereas John Wayne's outlaw in *Stagecoach* was saved from the "blessings of civilization," the outcast hero in *Hombre* gets overrun and crushed. Times had changed.

Custer of the West (1967) offers an equally dark revision of a classic Hollywood western. In 1941, *They Died with Their Boots On* presented George Armstrong Custer as a principled romantic committed to saving lives—be they white or Indian. *Custer of the West* presents him as an equally principled romantic, but one committed only to the art of war. When interrogated by one of the natives on the subject of Indian rights, Custer replies: "I'm a soldier. The only rights that concern me are the rights of my soldiers. The only duty that concerns me is the duty of my command. The fact that we seem to be pushing you clear off the earth is not my responsibility." The American icon goes on to say that, for him, the only rule of life is survival of the fittest. Fittingly, when the U.S. military begins replacing the cavalry with armored train cars, Custer becomes a victim of his own ideology. Like an anachronistic gunslinger riding off into the last sunset, this man of war leads his soldiers into battle against hopeless odds at Little Big Horn—a vain act of protest against the passage of time. Like *Hour of the Gun*, *Custer of the West* pledged its allegiance to mythic revisionism. In New Hollywood's distinctly liberal western, men of the West—even those who became legends—are rarely heroes.

At the opposite end of the political spectrum, living legend John Wayne redoubled his commitment to the old myths. The conservative icon intended his 1968 war movie *The Greet Berets* to be a rallying cry for the war in Vietnam. His son and producer Michael Wayne described the film as a simple "cowboys and Indians" narrative, explaining, "The Americans are the good guys and the Viet Cong are the bad guys. It's as simple as that."[5] To the elder Wayne, real world politics were equally black-and-white, and he couldn't understand how his fellow Americans could see things any other way. Maligning liberal politicians who spoke out against the Vietnam War, he complained, "All they're doing is helping the Reds and hurting their own country."[6] Wayne's widow Pilar remembered his exasperation:

> Duke felt we had every right to be fighting in Asia. His only regret was that we refused to commit ourselves to the war 100 percent. He thought we owed total commitment to the men of our armed forces, men who were dying while their countrymen debated the rightness of their deaths. Duke wanted action, not debate. He was a firm believer in the Domino theory, convinced that all Southeast Asia would eventually fall under communist domination if Vietnam toppled. "Nobody enjoys the damn war," he said. "But it happens to be necessary. Besides," he added, "we gave our word."[7]

Wayne, however, was in the minority—at least in Hollywood. The year 1969 was the turning point in the public debate over Vietnam. The draft lottery brought the politics of war into every home, escalating the tension. Around the same time, the New Hollywood generation effectively inherited the film industry, and with it the western genre. Although John Wayne won a long-overdue Oscar for his performance as surly U.S. Marshal Rooster Cogburn in *True Grit* (perhaps because the film carefully avoided any kind of political message), counterculture films like *Butch Cassidy and the Sundance Kid* and *Midnight Cowboy* (a film that had the nerve to call John Wayne a fag) dominated the awards season and the box office, while *Easy Rider* made the biggest impact on pop culture. Paramount's innocuous musical-western *Paint Your Wagon* earned more money than Sam Peckinpah's irreverent anti-western *The Wild Bunch*, but it was nevertheless a commercial failure. The former represented the losing gambit of major studios to draw audiences with expensive epics. The latter inspired westerns and action films for decades to come.

Peckinpah's film began with a script by Walon Green, who shared the filmmaker's ideas about what a western should be. "I wrote it," Green said, "thinking that I would like to see a western that was as mean and ugly and brutal as the times, and the only nobility in men was their dedication to each other."[8] Just as Peckinpah's *Ride the High Country* had imported Randolph Scott and Joel McCrea into world they no longer understood, *The Wild Bunch* depicted genre stalwarts William Holden, Ernest Borgnine, Warren Oates, Ben Johnson and Robert Ryan as a dying breed of men facing the end of western civilization as they know it.

Holden plays Pike Bishop, the leader of a motley crew of outlaws, who realizes that times are changing. When he and his bande à part arrive in Mexico, he advises the gang, "We gotta start thinking beyond our guns—those days are closing fast." His words prove prophetic. After the gang steals a cache of guns for a group of revolutionaries, they end

Dour-faced death dealers (from left): Ben Johnson, Warren Oates, William Holden and Ernest Borgnine are *The Wild Bunch* (1969, Warner Bros./Seven Arts).

up at war with both the revolutionaries and the Mexican army. Under the circumstances, the rogue gunslingers don't stand a chance of survival—but that doesn't mean they're ready to surrender. Peckinpah's heroes have more in common with Clint Eastwood's spaghetti westerners than with Will Penny. Rebels to the end, they go out in a blaze of glory.

In 1969, the final act of *The Wild Bunch* was one of the bloodiest affairs in the history of cinema, provoking impassioned responses from many critics and viewers who felt that the film was shamelessly exploitive. Like Eastwood, however, Peckinpah claimed that his intention was to use cinematic violence as a way to protest real-world violence. "Actually it's an anti-violence film," the director insisted, "because I use violence as it is. It's ugly, brutalizing, and bloody fucking awful. It's not fun and games and cowboys and Indians, it's a terrible, ugly thing."[9] In contrast to the films of Sergio Leone, which spent most of their time building suspense and then doled out the violence in short, quick bursts, *The Wild Bunch* depicts acts of violence in painstaking slow-motion—forcing the viewer to dwell on the brutality. Peckinpah reflects: "If we don't recognize violence, that we are violent people—we all are, everyone of us standing around here—we're dead. We really and truly are. We're going to be on some beach. You know, we're going to drop bombs on each other."[10] Viewed in this context, the final scene approximates a nuclear war, reducing the familiar, reassuring world of western heroes to ashes.

For audiences already overwhelmed by visions of violence, *Butch Cassidy and the Sundance Kid* offered a more lighthearted dirge, filtering the same themes of chaos and loss through a warm blanket of humor and nostalgia. Like Pike Bishop and company, Butch and Sundance are legendary outlaws who flee south of the border only to find themselves outnumbered and outgunned by local authorities. Unlike the dour-faced death-dealers of Peckinpah's film, however, Paul Newman's Butch and Robert Redford's Sundance come across like characters in a fairy tale, blessed by some kind of divine luck. They are not devoted to any moral code or political cause, only to a simple philosophy of living for the moment. Screenwriter William Goldman remembers, "The original thing that moved me was the story of these two guys whom I liked, but they were pretty much aimless."[11] As the story unfolded, the screenwriter realized that his story wasn't really a western. In fact, he didn't know what genre he was writing in. "Not only did it not have enough violence to be considered an action film," he recalls, "it also wasn't funny enough to be a comedy."[12] Later, director George Roy Hill recognized the story as a character study about two individuals who simply chose to be outlaws "as others decided to be lawyers and dentists."[13] In that respect, *Butch Cassidy and the Sundance Kid* was a western by accident.

In another respect, however, the western milieu gave the film a cultural resonance that it would not have had otherwise. What *Butch Cassidy* and *The Wild Bunch* have in common is an overwhelming sense of melancholy that is implicitly related to both the closing of the western frontier and the end of the 1960s. In the end, the heroes of both films run out of time and space. For Goldman, the story of Butch and Sundance represented a longing—and perhaps a successful attempt—to recover the past: "Butch and Sundance did what Gatsby only dreamed of doing: They repeated the past. As famous as they were in the States, they were bigger legends in South America: *bandidos Yanquis*. And probably that fact—recapturing the past—is what I found so moving about the narrative. We all wish for it; they made it happen."[14] At the same time, the ending—a freeze frame that immortalizes Butch and Sundance in their final moment together, instead of showing their demise—suggested to Goldman's mind something unattainable:

Characters in a fairy tale: Robert Redford (left), Katherine Ross, and Paul Newman in *Butch Cassidy & the Sundance Kid* (1969, 20th Century-Fox).

I believed [in 1969] that it was not possible for two people to truly know each other. No matter how close the husband and wife, the father and son, the lover and beloved, we are locked inside ourselves. And here I had two friends, who lived through decades together, who traveled tens of thousands of miles, only to die bloody in a country where no one knew their names, where they barely spoke the language—it seemed a wonderful vehicle to say something about our lack of knowledge, about our hopeless and terrible and, alas, enduring, permanent loneliness.[15]

As a result, *Butch Cassidy and the Sundance Kid* is neither an optimistic nor a defeatist western; it is a product of America in a liminal phase—suspended in a timeless moment between the radical Sixties and the cynical Seventies.

The hidden western *Easy Rider* is even more firmly grounded in 1969, shedding the historical milieu in favor of a journey through modern America. Actor Peter Fonda, son of Henry Fonda, remembers that the idea for the film came to him while he was ruminating on his role in director Roger Corman's biker movie *The Wild Angels* (1966): "I was a little bit loaded, and I looked at … a photograph from *The Wild Angels* of me and Bruce Dern on a chop. Suddenly I thought, that's it, that's the modern western; two cats just riding across the country."[16] Fonda continued to develop the idea, conceptualizing *Easy Rider* as a variation on *The Searchers*. In his 1998 memoir, he wrote: "It would be about the Duke and Jeffrey Hunter looking for Natalie Wood. I would be the Duke and [Dennis] Hopper would be my Ward Bond; America would be our Natalie Wood. And after a long journey to the East across John Ford's America, what would become of us? We would be blasted to bits by narrow-minded redneck poachers at dawn, just outside of Heaven, Florida."[17]

Screenwriter Terry Southern proclaimed the brutal finale of the story to be a political message, saying, "In my mind, the ending was to be an indictment of blue-collar America, the people I thought were responsible for the Vietnam War."[18] Fonda's co-star Dennis Hopper, who directed the film, concurred, believing that the film—which he personally saw as a modern-day tale of Wyatt Earp and Billy the Kid—would reflect the death of the American Dream: "When we were making the movie, we could feel the whole country burning up—Negroes, hippies, students. I meant to work this feeling into the symbols in the movie, like Captain America's Great Chrome Bike—that beautiful machine covered with stars and stripes with all the money in the gas tank is America—and that at any moment we can be shot off it—BOOM—explosion—that's the end."[19]

In Hopper's mind, the film would not only be an indictment of "blue-collar America," but also of the hippie generation. The director later pointed out that the two riders start their journey with a major misstep: They smuggle drugs for easy money, thus destroying the purity of their search. "They're sick too," the filmmaker explained, "just like the establishment. They won't take responsibility for what they see around them: They have wrong goals, false values."[20] At a pivotal point in the narrative, Fonda's character realizes this and delivers the famous self-indictment of his generation: "We blew it."

By putting an epitaph on the Sixties, *Easy Rider* helped to clear a path for a generation of young, iconoclastic filmmakers. Hopper was, for the moment, at the forefront of his generation, and thoroughly determined to keep dismantling old Hollywood. He reputedly aimed his second film directly at John Wayne.[21] Hopper had acted alongside Wayne in *The Sons of Katie Elder* and again in *True Grit*. In *Katie Elder*, Wayne's character brutalized Hopper's sniveling youth so embarrassingly that Hopper's own father shot the boy dead. In *True Grit*, Wayne refused Hopper's "rights of the accused," and cruelly tortured him to get information. In the younger actor's mind, the lionization of this tyrannical cowboy was evidence of a warped value system in America. With that in mind, he conceived *The Last Movie* (1970) as an indictment of "lousy westerns" that perpetuate "a tragic legend of greed and violence." Like *Easy Rider*, it would be "a story about America and how it's destroying itself."[22]

In the film, Hopper plays a professional stuntman who travels to Peru for a film shoot. When the shoot is over, he stays and plans another film—a violent western. The

Death of the American Dream: Dennis Hopper (left), Peter Fonda and Jack Nicholson in *Easy Rider* (1969, Columbia).

latter film introduces the innocent native Peruvians to American rituals of violence. When it comes time for the stuntman to die within the film, the natives—misunderstanding the illusory nature of these rituals—plan to kill him for real. Somewhere along the way, this meta-fictional conflict devolved into a chaotic mishmash of improvised scenes and impressionistic montages. Actor Tomas Milián remembered how Hopper lost his focus: "The real movie, nobody shot it. The real movie was what was going on while we were doing that movie."[23] When the director returned from Peru, he struggled to assemble his footage into a coherent narrative. Then, while he was editing the film, he watched Alejandro Jodorowsky's acid western *El Topo* (1970) and decided to completely abandon the idea of creating a coherent narrative.[24]

According to Jodoroswky, any attempt to synopsize his film *El Topo* would be missing the point. The "story" exists entirely in symbols, drawn from influences as varied as Sergio Leone, Luis Buñuel, Jean-Luc Godard, Buster Keaton, Jungian psychology and Sufi mysticism. On some level, however, *El Topo* is intended as a comment on the classic Hollywood western, as the filmmaker explained in his dissection of a scene involving two amputees: "The two men: the one with no arms, and the other with no legs. I designed their costume from one I saw in the *Encyclopedia of Film*: a John Wayne costume. It was one costume, which I cut into two parts. I put the upper half on the man with no legs and the pants on the man with no arms. Two cripples make one John Wayne."[25]

Of course, films like *El Topo* and *The Last Movie* weren't aimed at the mainstream western audience. Following the success of *Easy Rider*, Peter Fonda attempted a much more traditional western. In *The Hired Hand* (1971), the actor/director plays a gunslinger who gives up a life of crime to return to his family. The only problem: His wife doesn't want him back and his daughter believes he's dead. The penitent man agrees to work on his own ranch as an anonymous hired hand—a decision that enhances his solitude and sense of self-alienation. The film recalls the complex ambiguity of *The Gunfighter* and captures the loneliness of the West just as effectively as *Butch Cassidy and the Sundance Kid*, but unfortunately Fonda was paying subtle tribute to a form that had been rendered (at least temporarily) passé.

The most popular New Hollywood westerns were comparatively audacious and often overtly political. Director Ralph Nelson's *Soldier Blue* (1970) was a fiery indictment of American policies, foreign and domestic, past and present. Ostensibly based on the Sand Creek Massacre of 1864, in which a U.S. Cavalry unit attacked a peaceful Cheyenne village and murdered dozens of innocents, the film also echoed the horrors of the My Lai Massacre of 1968, in which a U.S. Army company attacked a village in South Vietnam and murdered hundreds of unarmed men, women and children. Nelson, a World War II veteran disgusted by reports of the war in Vietnam, made the film to decry the obscenity and hypocrisy of war itself. He reflected, "We like to think of our soldiers as epitomes of grown-up Boy Scouts incapable of evil. [But] in *Soldier Blue*, I have tried to show the true face of war ... how it changes normally peaceful men into savage beasts."[26]

Soldier Blue revolves mostly around a young white woman named Cresta Lee, played by Candice Bergen, who is being transported by the U.S. cavalry back to "civilization." Although taken hostage by Cheyenne warriors two years earlier, Cresta sympathizes with the Cheyenne people more than with the whites. She bluntly tells one of the Army soldiers, "I am not a Cheyenne, but I'd rather be one than any runt-butt soldier of any bloodthirsty army you can name." Realizing her loyalty lies with the Indians, the company commander responds, like John Wayne chastising Vietnam protesters, "When I see young people today behaving like that, I can't help wondering what this goddamn country is coming to."

Eventually, Bergen's character tries to warn the Cheyenne people of an impending cavalry attack—but her warning comes too late. The film culminates with an epic vision of death and destruction: a village razed; women and children slaughtered; innocents defiled, dismembered, even crucified. The filmmakers showed the brutality of war in all its hideous glory. Bergen remembers:

> There was a "prosthetics truck" on the set specifically for the bloody battle scenes, the inside stocked with artificial limbs and every conceivable extremity. Wooden legs swung from the top of the truck and arms were stacked along the sides. Heads stared from stands in wispy dark wigs, headbands and Indian braids, their necks severed clean, arteries dangling, ready for decapitation by the cavalry. Rubber breasts lay neatly in drawers, fitted with blood bags that would burst when lobbed off by the soldiers' bayonets; and some artificial legs were wired electronically, specially rigged to simulate spasm when run over and severed by wagon wheels. Paraplegics and amputees were bused in from Mexico City for the massacre scene—men and women missing arms and legs, who were fitted with the prosthetic devices and instructed to watch in horror as the limbs were hacked from their bodies, spurting blood and twitching in the dust.[27]

Bergen—a blonde-haired, blue-eyed Beverly Hills "brat" who was active in the anti-war movement, the Black Power movement, and the feminist movement—remembers *Soldier Blue* as "a movie whose heart, if nothing else, was in the right place."[28]

Arthur Penn remembered that it wasn't until after the success of *Soldier Blue* that he was able to get the financing for his own politically-minded anti-western *Little Big Man* (1970).²⁹ Based on a novel by Thomas Berger, and taking additional cues from recent revisionist histories like Vine Deloria, Jr.'s *Custer Died for Your Sins* (published in 1969) and Dee Brown's *Bury My Heart at Wounded Knee* (published in 1970), *Little Big Man* urged audiences to question their assumptions about America's past. In the film, Dustin Hoffman plays the self-proclaimed "sole white survivor" of the Battle of Little Big Horn. Like James Stewart in *The Man Who Shot Liberty Valance*, he narrates his own alternative version of the history of the West—transforming America's story into a tragic comedy. The film playfully satirizes Puritan ethics, consumerism, and the popular mythos of the wild, wild West, before landing its picaresque hero in the middle of Custer's last stand. Hoffman's Little Big Man wryly reflects on it all: "If it wasn't the Injuns trying to kill me for a white, it was the whites trying to kill me for an Injun." He concludes, "The world was too ridiculous even to bother livin' in it."

In the end, Little Big Man lives to see the near-genocide of the Cheyenne people and offers a timely reflection on the real-life effects of Manifest Destiny and imperialist philosophy. In a 1971 interview, Penn summed up: "Today, as our nation is going through a period of great crisis, there is a tendency to look inward. With the war in Vietnam, racial intolerance, and social disparity, America in the seventies is tormented by conflicts of conscience. It seems that nothing has changed in all these years. Cinema, at least a certain kind of responsible cinema, is facing this reality again, a reality that holds up a mirror to humanity."³⁰

Little Big Man goes a step further than *Soldier Blue*, not only by holding up a mirror to past and present injustice but also suggesting a road to the future. The filmmaker points to the Cheyenne way of life as a solution to America's cycle of violence and its basic philosophy of cultural expansion and dominance:

> They believed that the world provided for them and they paid back the world in kind. It worked both ways, a notion that was very important to them. The old man talks about the cycle of earth and water, and at the end he says to the spirits, "Thank you for turning me into a warrior. Thank you for my victory and also for defeat. Thank you for giving me sight and thank you for making me blind." He accepts the paradox. He might appear too passive in our eyes but we could really benefit from some of that passivity right now. It would mean some tranquility and some time for reflection rather than us continuing to pollute the world with our rampant consumption.³¹

Director Robert Altman's *McCabe and Mrs. Miller* (1971) charts similar territory with its bleak commentary on violence and entrepreneurialism in America. In the film, Warren Beatty's McCabe, a professional gambler and amateur gunfighter, makes a name for himself in a mud-and-rags frontier town by opening a saloon and whorehouse. When corporate vultures try to buy him out, however, the none-too-bright entrepreneur ends up on the dark side of the American Dream. In Altman's West, you see, the business of America is business: sex is business, religion is business, law and order is business. In all of these businesses, the value of human life is relatively low—so low that, in the final reel of the film, the climactic confrontation between McCabe and corporate America is decidedly anti-climactic. There is no grand duel at high noon, only a desperate game of cat-and-mouse resulting in an undignified death. The whole struggle is met with indifference by the other characters in the film.

Altman called *McCabe and Mrs. Miller* an "anti-western," because it "turns a number of western conventions on their sides, including male dominance and the heroic standoff; gunplay is a solution only after reputation, wit and nonviolent coercion fail; and law and

Warren Beatty rides into the mud-and-rags settlement of Presbyterian Church in *McCabe and Mrs. Miller* (1971, Warner Bros.).

order do not always prevail."³² Most of the Hollywood westerns produced around the same time remained equally defiant. *Doc* (1971) transformed Doc Holliday into an idealist, only so that power-hungry Wyatt Earp could corrupt and destroy him at "the ass-end of the West." *The Great Northfield Minnesota Raid* (1972) debunked the Robin Hood myth of Jesse James, presenting the iconic westerner as a crude, bigoted gangster with no sense of loyalty to his friends. *Dirty Little Billy* (1972) depicted Billy the Kid as a mentally retarded psychopath. *The Culpepper Cattle Co.* (1972) chronicled the life of an anonymous romantic cowboy who foolishly fights for a noble-but-already-lost cause. *Bad Company* (1972) followed another romantic youth, whose experiences in the West transform him from a Christian pacifist into an uncaring thief and murderer. *Ulzana's Raid* (1972), starring Burt Lancaster as an Indian-hating cavalryman, tops them all with a veritable buffet of gruesome wartime atrocities, all committed in the name of Manifest Destiny.

Even John Wayne couldn't entirely escape the cinematic scalping of the genre. In director Mark Rydell's *The Cowboys* (1971), Wayne plays a stiff-necked old rancher who gets fatally shot in the back. It was the first time Wayne had been killed onscreen in his favorite genre, and his death leads to even more dire consequences when a group of prepubescent trail hands decide to avenge him. According to Wayne's costumer Luster Bayless, "Duke liked Mark but the two had a different opinion on how the ending should be. Duke didn't believe the boys should take the law into their own hands."³³ This time, Wayne lost.

Nineteen seventy-two was the final year that westerns made up a significant portion of Hollywood's output. Filmmakers continued to sound the last hurrah by alternating notes of melancholy and nostalgia. Writer John Milius conceived *Jeremiah Johnson* (1972) as a minimalist character study with a simple message: mountain man as endangered species. Actor Robert Redford responded to the story because it stripped the western formula down to its barest essence: a man alone, trying to survive a literal and metaphorical "long winter." The film offers a vision of human life at its most primal and its most unencumbered. For director Sydney Pollack, it was the story of a spiritual journey from civilization to wilderness and (inevitably) back again: "I was striving for a sense of mysticism. There is a lot of dialogue in the film with innuendo and mysticism. The other mountain men survive because they do not get involved. Jeremiah's problem was his humaneness in an inhuman atmosphere. What destroyed Jeremiah was the set of values we uphold. He could not escape them."[34]

Milius also wrote the original screenplay for director John Huston's *The Life and Times of Judge Roy Bean* (1972), a film that replaces melancholy with whimsy. Huston's goal was not to produce a historically accurate biopic but rather a Quixotic romance— to print the legend and playfully acknowledge it as such. The director concedes that he "departed from the historical facts and made Bean more of a scalawag than he really was," but insists he had to do so in order to capture the grand spirit of the film—and perhaps the spirit of the western genre.[35] "It's a big picture," he says. "I don't mean just physically. It has a big spirit. The wind blows through it. Adown the corridors of time."[36]

Following his cathartic outburst in *The Wild Bunch*, director Sam Peckinpah was in a similarly rhapsodic state of mind. With his films *The Ballad of Cable Hogue* (1970) and *Pat Garrett and Billy the Kid* (1973), the filmmaker continued to champion the individualism of restless loners and losers. *The Ballad of Cable Hogue*, about a tough old romantic entrepreneur, reveals Peckinpah's ideal conception of the men of the West: savvy, determined opportunists who will do whatever it takes to win the day. The film is also a eulogy for this rare breed of men. In the end, the nineteenth century westerner played by wily Jason Robards is literally overrun by twentieth century technology. Peckinpah asserted that he'd taken his favorite theme as far as he could: "That's a thing that ends with me in *Cable Hogue*. I'll never go back to that. Men who lived out of their time, etcetera, I've played that out."[37]

A few years later, he made one final film in the genre. *Pat Garrett and Billy the Kid* concludes a western narrative that began with Arthur Penn's *The Left-Handed Gun*. In Penn's film, Billy the Kid represents the rebellious-but-aimless baby boomer generation at the end of the 1950s. In Peckinpah's film, the outlaw represents the same generation after the Vietnam War. Billy's nemesis, sheriff Pat Garrett, embodies the older generation of "sell-outs" who are "trying to put a fence around this country." Screenwriter Rudy Wurlitzer explains: "The film is kind of a discussion of what the myth of the frontier means about freedom. Personal freedom as opposed to collective choices: that's another way of looking at the film. Garrett identified with the collective reality and Billy rejected it. So in a way Billy becomes anachronistic. And he has got to be got out of the way."[38] Viewed within this context, the legend of Billy the Kid takes on new meaning. Not only is the traditional heroic westerner a relic of the past—so is the hippie generation. Film critic Jim Kitses reads the film as a statement that "America's youthful protesters were like the West's last heroes, at the mercy of corrupt law and ruthless institutions, and the fate of Billy the Kid and his boyish bunch provided a mythic parallel for the victimization of an idealistic counter-culture in its struggle against the government and its Vietnam policy."[39]

Within the space of a few short years, the traditional Hollywood western hero had been debunked, converted, and effectively killed. Western filmmakers were apparently demoralized, and film historian James Hoberman reports that the subsequent demise of the genre was swift and dramatic: "Four westerns were released in 1973, two in 1974, five in 1975, seven for the Bicentennial, two in 1977, three in 1978, and a total of three between 1979 and 1984."[40] For the time being, Hollywood had hung up its spurs.

CHAPTER X

Death Wish
(1971–1980)

> *"As we begin our third century, there is still so much to be done. We must increase the independence of the individual and the opportunity of all Americans to attain their full potential. We must ensure each citizen's right to privacy. We must create a more beautiful America, making human works conform to the harmony of nature. We must develop a safer society, so ordered that happiness may be pursued without fear of crime or manmade hazards. We must build a more stable international order, politically, economically, and legally. We must match the great breakthroughs of the past century by improving health and conquering disease. We must continue to unlock the secrets of the universe beyond our planet as well as within ourselves. We must work to enrich the quality of American life at work, at play, and in our homes. It is right that Americans are always improving. It is not only right, it is necessary. From need comes action."*
> —Gerald Ford, remarks at Bicentennial Celebration, July 4, 1976

In a 1967 essay about the heightened realism of recent western films, author/screenwriter Larry McMurtry prophesied the decline of the genre by noting that "applying an anti-romantic technique to an essentially romantic subject" was "a sort of alchemical reverse English [...] deliberately turning gold into lead."[1] Hollywood learned this lesson the hard way. When filmmakers replaced romantic celebrations of Manifest Destiny with polemics about imperialist aggression, many moviegoers abandoned the genre. The genre, however, did not simply disappear; it mutated into other forms. McMurtry noted that the cinematic westerner was already being replaced by "more modern figures" like detectives and secret agents, and speculated that audiences could eventually "expect to see the conquest of space (if we really conquer it) to take over the place in the American mythos now held by the winning of the West."[2] By the early 1980s, science fiction had indeed filled the void created by the disappearance of the western. In the meantime, Hollywood's transmuted lead filled the guns of urban crime pictures and horror films. Like the revisionist westerns of the day, these action/horror hybrids eschewed romanticism for more critical reflections on the relationship between violence and order in contemporary America. Film historian Richard Slotkin summed up:

> What makes the urban vigilante genre different from the westerns is its "post–Frontier" setting. Its world is urbanized, and its possibilities for progress and redemption are constricted by vastly ramified corporate conspiracies and by monstrous accumulations of wealth, power, and corruption. Its heroes draw energy from the same rage that drives the paranoids, psychopaths, mass murderers, and terrorists of the mean streets, and their victories are almost never socially redemptive in the western mode. In these respects, the world of the urban gunfighter is cognate to that of the horror and "slasher" film.[3]

According to U.S. Department of Justice statistics, the violent crime rate jumped 132 percent between 1960 and 1970, and continued to climb dramatically in subsequent years. In response, action films like *Dirty Harry* (1971) and *Death Wish* (1974) depicted would-be western heroes Clint Eastwood and Charles Bronson rebelling against a broken justice system, while savage thrillers like Sam Peckinpah's *Straw Dogs* (1971) and Wes Craven's *The Hills Have Eyes* (1977) showed ordinary men and women fighting to maintain their humanity in an inhumane world. In Craven's mind, all of these films looked beyond the traditional western myth, exposing failure and frustration at the heart of the contemporary American experience. He explained:

> I don't think anybody buys the John Wayne image of how we confront violence, both collectively and in the individual. We can't kid ourselves that Lt. Calley [the U.S. Army officer who ordered the My Lai massacre in Vietnam] was some sort of monster; he was the most ordinary of guys. [...] He was just thrust into a reality that the myth did not serve. Before Vietnam the image of war was the front line, which is the good guys vs. bad guys myth that fell apart. There is no longer any such myth when you see civilization being killed all around you and this is being transmitted regularly by the media. The only way to survive this is by an enormous cynicism unless you are ready to confront the myth.[4]

That's exactly what many action and horror films did in the 1970s.

Dirty Harry was not Eastwood's first attempt to confront western mythology in an urban setting. In 1969 he collaborated with director Don Siegel on *Coogan's Bluff*, a film about a testosterone-driven Arizona lawman chasing a fugitive through the streets of New York. The director recalled: "In Arizona, when hunting his two-legged prey by means of scent, 10/10 vision—and that includes girls as well as malefactors—Coogan used western lore and knowledge. But in New York City he can only see across the street, his vision blocked by huge skyscrapers. He is assailed by a thousand scents. He is indeed a fish out of water."[5] The upshot of the film is that this fish can still swim upstream, water or no. The filmmaker and the star both understood that, although audiences may have grown tired of the western, they had not grown tired of watching larger-than-life heroes. Eastwood explained: "A superhuman character who has all the answers is double cool, exists on his own without society or the help of society's police forces. A guy sits in the audience, he's twenty-five years old, and he's scared stiff about what he's going to do with his life. He wanted to have that self-sufficient thing he sees up there on the screen."[6] Much of Clint Eastwood's subsequent career has in fact revolved around his ability to maintain that rugged individualism and self-sufficiency within a society that offers fewer and fewer opportunities for true independence and self-determination.

In *Dirty Harry* Eastwood plays a San Francisco detective who is even more independent, displaying a none-too-subtle contempt for authority and bureaucracy. Disgusted with a legal system that seems to value killer's rights above victim's rights, Harry Callahan becomes a modern-day Ethan Edwards—a man driven by anger and his own ideas about justice. (At one point, Eastwood even echoes John Wayne's famous line from *The Searchers*: "That'll be the day.") His pursuit of a psychopathic killer nicknamed Scorpio culminates with a showdown that is distinctly different from a cliché western movie finale. Instead of meeting the hero in a fair fight, the villain uses an innocent child as a human shield. Instead of treating violence as a last resort, the hero goads the villain ("Well, do ya, *punk*?!") into committing suicide-by-cop. In this defining moment, Callahan shows that he has more faith in vigilante justice than in the law. Accordingly, he throws away his badge like Gary Cooper in *High Noon*.

According to director Don Siegel, Eastwood refused to perform this final act until

Siegel convinced him that it did not mean that Harry Callahan was quitting his job, only that he was symbolically "rejecting the stupidity of a system of administration, marked by officialdom and red tape."[7] Harry was making a statement of protest, not shirking his civic responsibilities. Critics like Pauline Kael, however, popularized a wary reading of the film as a right-wing fantasy that wholeheartedly endorsed vigilante justice. Kael concluded, "*Dirty Harry* is obviously just a genre movie, but this action genre has always had a fascist potential, and it has finally surfaced."[8] The public debate continued for years.

Burt Lancaster responded with a coded warning about the dangers of vigilantism in *Lawman* (1971). In the film, Lancaster plays Maddox, a town marshal on the trail of five rowdy cowboys who accidentally killed a man. Intent on bringing them to justice, Maddox tracks them to a town where they fall under the protection of a powerful rancher and a cynical local lawman. The rancher tries to make amends with the murdered man's family, while the local lawman encourages Maddox not to pursue the matter further. Maddox tells the rancher that he will accept nothing less than the unconditional surrender of the five men. He then self-righteously tells the local

Fascist potential? Clint Eastwood is *Dirty Harry* (1971, Warner Bros.).

lawman, "Without the rules, you're nothing." For Maddox, this is an absolute truth. His uncompromising sense of justice—an eye for an eye—allows no room for compassion, mercy or forgiveness. In the end, he guns down all five cowboys, shooting the last one in the back as the man tries to run away. No viewer could possibly mistake this cold-blooded murder for justice. When Maddox rides off into the sunset, we see him for what he really is: a killer with a badge. *Lawman* screenwriter Gerald Wilson summed up: "The point is, law-and-order, if it's applied narrowly and without imagination, becomes a destructive force."[9]

Ironically, *Lawman* director Michael Winner went on to make a film that seemed to endorse vigilante violence more pointedly than *Dirty Harry*. *Death Wish* was based on a 1972 novel by Brian Garfield, about a middle-aged accountant who begins to question his liberal values after muggers murder his wife and terrorize his daughter. Before long, the former bleeding-heart liberal becomes a one-man death squad committed to "cleaning up" the city streets. Garfield offers a criminal profile that sums up the vigilante's philosophy and the essential appeal of his story:

> There's a large reservoir of aggression in all of us. We hate crime, yet we don't *do* anything about it. We begin to feel that we're not merely decent people, we're so decent that we're immobilized. That's why a man like this captures our imagination so vividly—he's acting out fantasies we've all shared. He's not the only one acting out, of course—we've seen how a great many groups who claim to be for or against something find it necessary to take the law into their own hands. Terrorism has become a legitimized political tool. In that respect the only unusual thing about this fellow is that he's doing it as a one-man operation. If it were an organized effort like the Jewish Defense League or the Black Panthers we'd find it far less fascinating. It's the lone-wolf aspect of it that appeals to the American sensibility. One rugged individualist out there battling the forces of evil—it fits right into our mythology, you see.[10]

Director Michael Winner obviously recognized the appeal of the lone wolf mythology and also realized that western hero Charles Bronson would be perfect for the role.

In the film, Bronson's Paul Kersey realizes his calling as a vigilante during a visit to the Old Tucson movie studio in Arizona. Strolling the dusty streets where classic westerns like *Winchester '73, Gunfight at the O.K. Corral* and *Rio Bravo* were shot, Kersey contemplates the differences between modern-day New York and the Old West. A friend argues that there was more order and safety in the historic Dodge City or Tombstone, because good men like Wyatt Earp were able to act as judge, jury and executioner. Even today, the man insists, the West remains safer than New York—because everyone out west owns a gun. Kersey buys the argument and returns home with that western vision of law and order. Enacting "the old American social custom of self-defense," he guns down a group of street thugs. To his surprise, the press promptly declares him a hero. Later, when he starts targeting criminal "types" and luring them to their deaths, even the New York police refuse to treat him like a criminal. Instead of arresting him, a detective advises Kersey to get out of town by sundown. The film thus concludes that civilized people can't condone a vigilante's actions, but it also suggests that they will not condemn him.

Bronson claimed that the message of the film was "that violence is senseless because it only begets more violence," but *Death Wish* nevertheless inspired a rash of action films about hyper-masculine individuals taking the law into their own hands. The actor continued his noble crusade in *Mr. Majestyk* (1974), a film that was originally written by Elmore Leonard for Clint Eastwood, who wanted something "just like *Dirty Harry*, only different."[11] Meanwhile, Eastwood returned to the role of Dirty Harry in *Magnum Force* (1973). In the latter film, members of a vigilante death squad try to recruit the now-famous rogue detective. The hero responds, coolly, "I'm afraid you've misjudged me." Harry maintains that he still hates "the goddamn system," but adds: "Until someone comes along with some changes that make sense, I'll stick with it." Screenwriter John Milius summed up the film's moral message as a counterpoint to the misconstrued sentiments of the original film (and its many imitators): "*Magnum Force* is the flip side of *Dirty Harry*. In other words, if you can go beyond the law, how far can you go? To me, one answers the moral question that the other brings up. It's not just a sequel."[12] In short, the urban vigilante film restores the moral code of the classic western.

Regardless of this retraction, Eastwood did not become a traditional hero overnight. Director Don Siegel said that the actor had "an absolute fixation on [being] an antihero. It's his credo in life and in all the films that he's done so far."[13] That credo defined Eastwood's directorial debut *High Plains Drifter* (1973), a film that begins with the ghostly image of a pale rider crossing a nightmarish landscape. When the rider arrives in the desolate town of Lago, he promptly kills three men and rapes a woman. After that, no one dares to cross him. Instead, the cowardly locals offer the sadistic stranger anything he wants in exchange for protection from other outsiders. He agrees to stay on, but his protection costs the townsfolk everything they have.

Eastwood says his original idea for the film was to create a supernatural sequel to *High Noon*: "The starting point was: 'What would have happened if the sheriff in *High Noon* had been killed? What would have happened afterwards?'"[14] A dream sequence in the finished film suggests that someone who looks very much like Eastwood's character once served as the marshal of Lago, until he was whipped and hanged by a lynch mob while the citizens looked on. Before he died, the marshal cursed the town. Now, Eastwood's pale rider is fulfilling that curse. He deals death at every turn, and literally paints the town red. When Lago lies in hellish ruins, one of the survivors begs to know the drifter's identity, but the film offers no definitive answer. Eastwood remembered: "It was written as the brother [of the hanged marshal] in the original treatment and in the script, but I took out references to the brother because I felt that I wanted to present it as an apparition or a ghost."[15] As a result, *High Plains Drifter* seems like a horror film as much as a western. In Eastwood's mind, this was the only type of western he could make honestly in 1973. He explained: "My westerns are the way they are because of the point in history where I picked up. John Wayne once wrote me a letter and he wasn't very pleased about *High Plains Drifter*. He said that isn't what the West was all about, that isn't the American people who settled this country. I said: 'You're absolutely right.'"[16] Instead *High Plains Drifter* is a reflection of American life in the wake of the Vietnam War—a moment of karmic reckoning and cultural despair. It suggested, like so many American horror films of the period, that the nation's hyper-violent culture was achieving cataclysmic (if not apocalyptic) dimensions.

Enacting the old American social custom of self-defense: Charles Bronson in *Death Wish* (1974, Paramount).

In all fairness to John Wayne, such films raised the question of what defined a modern western in the 1970s. Was it simply a film set in the historic American West? If so, then *Dirty Harry* and *Death Wish* would not qualify, in spite of their traditional western themes and motifs. Was it a film that embodied conservative ideas about American values? If so, then films like *Soldier Blue*—which some critics deemed "un–American"— would not make the cut, in spite of their historical setting and traditional western-movie plots. Perhaps the common element was an emphasis on white male heroes? But that too was gradually changing, as women and minorities took leading roles.

Actress Candice Bergen followed up the politically-charged *Soldier Blue* with a co starring role in *The Hunting Party* (1971), a dark and disturbing western about a woman caught between an abusive husband and a boorish rapist. The film aggressively illustrated that the battered woman was merely a second-class citizen in a man's world. After the rough treatment she received onscreen, Bergen said she "fantasized a movie where the women do the raping and plundering for a change, and even wrote a treatment for a women's western about a clandestine female gang that ended with the comely leader spraying the ground around the bruised and beaten bully with bullets, commanding him to 'Dance!' till he begs for mercy."[17] Actress Raquel Welch came close to realizing that fantasy in the British western *Hannie Caulder* (1971), about a woman who seeks revenge against three men who raped her and murdered her husband. During the course of this heroine's journey, Hannie learns the ways of the West from a drifting bounty hunter and a master gunsmith. Unfortunately, director Burt Kennedy couldn't take the feminist narrative seriously, so he crafted a mostly tongue-in-cheek western which he later dismissed as "*A Titful of Dollars*."[18]

Lust in the dust: Raquel Welch is *Hannie Caulder* (1971, Paramount).

Black cowboys fared a bit better, if only because black filmmakers told their stories. *The Scalphunters* (1968), a western variation on Stanley Kramer's *The Defiant Ones*, and *Skin Game* (1971), a comic buddy movie, helped to pave the way for Sidney Poitier's *Buck and the Preacher* (1971), the first film of its kind. The film revolves around a party of former slaves headed West after the Civil War, led by Poitier's cowboy and Harry Belafonte's clergyman. Along the way, they fight off bounty hunters, become outlaws, and forge an alliance with Native Americans that gives them hope for the future. Poitier reflected: "Harry and I wanted black people and minorities in general to find in *Buck and the Preacher* a certain substance, a certain nourishment, a certain complement of self. We wanted black people to see the film and be proud of themselves, be proud of their history."[19]

In the following years, black cowboys had a brief day in the sun—due to the popularity of urban action films like *Shaft* (1971) and *Superfly* (1972), which introduced black heroes to a new generation of moviegoers. *Superfly* actor Ron O'Neal remembered: "We were trying to emulate what we saw white films achieving—what white movie stars we admired were doing. Charles Bronson, Clint Eastwood, Burt Reynolds. Not John Wayne. Although I happen to like John Wayne, we weren't trying to do John Wayne's thing."[20] O'Neal steered clear of Wayne's world, but several of his contemporaries made valiant attempts to conquer the West. Fred "The Hammer" Williamson starred in *The Legend of Nigger Charley* (1972), a supposedly true story about a pair of runaway slaves who head West, while Richard Roundtree made *Charley One-Eye* (1973), a British western about an alliance between a runaway slave and a runaway Indian. Both films were bolder than *Buck and the Preacher*, thriving on scenes of overt violence that were clearly intended to upset the status quo in America.

By mid-decade, however, many of these new variations on old western stories had played themselves out. 1974 and 1975 were particularly grim years for the genre. Charles Bronson failed to generate much enthusiasm with the historical adventure *Breakheart Pass* (1975) or the western-comedy *From Noon Till Three* (1975). Kirk Douglas echoed the country's cultural malaise with the dour Watergate western *Posse* (1975), while John Wayne merely repeated himself in *Rooster Cogburn* (1975). *The Spikes Gang* (1974) proved to be a lackluster sequel to *Bad Company*, and Richard Brooks' *Bite the Bullet* (1975) failed to recapture the fighting spirit of *The Professionals*. Arguably the most memorable westerns of the day were *Blazing Saddles* (1974) and *Hearts of the West* (1975), two films that playfully mocked the genre. On the occasion of America's bicentennial anniversary, only a few dedicated westerners were still at large in Hollywood. With a handful of star vehicles they attempted to recapture the essential spirit of the genre.

The first western film to hit theaters in the summer of 1976 seemed like a sure bet. The driving force behind *The Missouri Breaks* was Jack Nicholson, the brightest star of the New Hollywood generation and a lifelong devotee of westerns. After an early cowboy role in *The Broken Land* (1962), Nicholson had starred in a pair of minor but memorable westerns for producer Roger Corman and director Monte Hellman. The actor recalled, "Roger wanted some good tomahawk numbers with plenty of ketchup, but Monte and I were into these films on another level."[21] Nicholson himself wrote the script for *Ride the Whirlwind* (1965), an existential film about a trio of drifters who are mistaken for outlaws and then must become outlaws in order to survive. The film was shot back-to-back with *The Shooting* (1965), which screenwriter Carole Eastman conceived in similar terms: "Roy Rogers meets *Last Year at Marienbad*."[22] The two films were relatively obscure until Nicholson scored his breakout role in *Easy Rider* and began his ascent to fame. In 1975, the actor earned an Oscar for his performance in *One Flew Over the Cuckoo's Nest*—a film that at least one critic has called an "allegorical western" about how "the white man is destined to live in a world of his own creation which must ultimately deny him his liberty, whereas the Native American lives in the world of Nature and can only be destroyed if he remains in the white man's world."[23]

Nicholson was apparently determined to keep making westerns, in spite of Hollywood's growing aversion to them. For several years, he dreamed of adapting Don Barry's 1971 western novel *Moontrap*, with Marlon Brando in the lead role.[24] After he failed to secure financing for that project, producer Elliott Kastner offered an alternative: to costar with Brando in an epic adaptation of Thomas McGuane's novel *The Missouri Breaks*.

Marlon Brando and Jack Nicholson match wits and egos in *The Missouri Breaks* (United Artists, 1976).

With the two heavyweight actors attached, and acclaimed director Arthur Penn at the helm, McGuane's story about a Montana range war quickly turned into a battle of wills. McGuane himself later suggested that Nicholson saw the film as "*mano a mano* with the other big guy on the hill."[25] That wasn't necessarily a bad recipe for a western—but Brando had his own ideas. At every turn, the legendary Method actor upstaged the young upstart by playing his coldblooded killer as a cross-dressing Indian with an Irish brogue. Brando reportedly told Penn, "[My] character has no psychological spine, so I can do anything I want ... move like an eel dipped in Vaseline. I'm here, I'm there, I'm all over the place."[26] Frustrated, Nicholson demanded a rewrite that unceremoniously eliminated his nemesis before the climax of the film. The result was a freakishly entertaining western with no narrative spine.

The Last Hard Men was a more predictable *mano a mano* western, pitting hardnosed hero Charlton Heston against perennial tough guy James Coburn. Building on a novel by Brian Garfield, veteran western filmmaker Andrew V. McLaglen crafted a throwback to dualistic westerns like *Vera Cruz* and *Last Train from Gun Hill*. Like Howard Hawks's later westerns with John Wayne, the film flaunts its conservative bias. In fact, *The Last Hard Men* plays out like a personal mission statement from Charlton Heston, a newly minted neoconservative who saw America's future in terms of a return to the past. In his role as Sam Burgade, the old-fashioned, no-nonsense lawman who comes out of retirement to hunt down an old nemesis, the actor sums up: "I quit the law because

I thought it was over—what I knew how to do. Too much was changing. Modern times. I liked the world the way it was. Now it's coming back. Running back." Years later, in his 1997 autobiography, he reflected similarly:

> In our time, great men are an endangered species. Indeed, in the minds of many, they are less than that; they are mythic creatures who never really existed, like the unicorn. It's even been suggested that greatness in itself is somehow undemocratic. We live, after all, in the century of the common man. True enough, but I believe in the uncommon man, maybe because I've played so many of them. Great men are suspect today, perhaps because we don't happen to have any of them around. We have good men, gifted men, God knows we have plenty of *famous* men, but that's not the same thing.[27]

This assessment could have easily been directed at the two avowedly liberal stars of *The Missouri Breaks*.

Just as *The Last Hard Men* was a testament to the existence of the "great men" of the American West, Robert Altman's *Buffalo Bill and the Indians, or Sitting Bull's History Lesson* was a satire about such mythologizing. In the film, Paul Newman played Buffalo Bill Cody not as a real-life hero but as "the first movie star, in one sense, the first totally manufactured hero."[28] Surrounded by cynics and hustlers who sell a simple-minded version of American history to a simple-minded public, the Indian scout-turned-stage performer comes across as a self-righteous buffoon. Altman's film contrasts Cody with Sioux chief Sitting Bull, who (like Will Sampson's Chief Bromden character in *One Flew Over the Cuckoo's Nest*) maintains a quiet dignity thanks to his detachment from the sound and fury of the white man's world. The film was incisive, but not much fun. Perhaps for that reason it was a commercial misfire on America's birthday.

The most significant pair of westerns released in 1976 appeared almost like a coordinated coda to Hollywood's decades-long romance with the genre. With *The Outlaw Josey Wales*, Clint Eastwood finally made a traditional western, more American than Italian in spirit. In it, Eastwood plays a Southern farmer whose wife and son are killed by Union raiders—an event that turns him into a vengeful outlaw who continues to fight the Civil War after its formal conclusion. Pursued by regulators and bounty hunters, he flees to Texas, leaving multiple bodies in his wake. Unlike Eastwood's character in *High Plains Drifter*, however, Wales demonstrates a capacity for change. Realizing the futility of violence, he seeks peace with a Comanche war chief, saying: "Dying ain't so hard for men like you and me. It's living that's hard, when all you care about's been butchered or raped. Governments don't live together. People live together. With governments, you don't always get a fair word or a fair fight. Well, I've come here to give you either one or to get either one from you. [...] And I'm saying that men can live together without butchering each other."

It was, in a sense, a rare pro-life western. Eastwood reflected, "At the time I felt [...] that mankind has to find a better solution than just battling themselves into the ground [or else] there'll be no one left, eventually."[29] Josey manages to make peace with both the natives and himself, and his new beginning suggests hope for a war-torn country—a future in which Americans move beyond the *mano a mano* style of conflict resolution.

John Wayne's *The Shootist* was an even more melancholy reflection on America's (and Hollywood's) fading mythology. At the start of the 1970s, Wayne remained a highly bankable star and continued to make chest-beating westerns like *Chisum* (1970), *Rio Lobo* (1970), *Big Jake* (1971), *The Train Robbers* (1973) and *Cahill: U.S. Marshal* (1973). By mid-decade, however, the sexagenarian was finally losing ground to younger stars. When he failed to make a successful leap to modern-day actions movies (with *McQ* and *Brannigan*),

John Wayne goes down fighting in his final film, *The Shootist* (1976, Paramount).

he considered bringing an end to his fifty-year career. In *The Shootist*, he played a terminally-ill gunslinger named J.B. Brooks, who arrives in the sleepy town of Carson City, Nevada, to die in peace. Instead, he is drawn into one last battle. Over the course of the film, he also manages to teach a fatherless young man that "there's more to being a man than handling a gun." Wayne's widow later claimed that delivering this swan song was "the most difficult experience of Duke's long career." She remembered: "He had severe difficulty breathing and used oxygen constantly. His voice was going, and he couldn't imagine a more useless creature than an actor without a voice. Riding, walking, just sitting and talking tired him. His body was failing and there didn't seem to be a thing he could do about it."[30] In spite of it all, America's most iconic actor projected both warmth and strength onscreen.

In spite of his difficulties on *The Shootist*, he also continued to develop film projects. Among the prospects was a western called *Blood River*, written by a young filmmaker named John Carpenter, who recalled: "I knew how to write for J.W., as his sons called him. I really cared about the Wayne family. They were nice 'dogs' and they really treated me nice. I was completely out of place—I had long hair—but they completely accepted me."[31] Carpenter didn't get a chance to make *Blood River*, but he did go on to write and direct a hidden western that paid homage to one of Wayne's best-known films. *Assault on Precinct 13* (1976) combined story elements of Howard Hawks's *Rio Bravo* and George

Romero's *Night of the Living Dead* (1968), revolving around a group of unlikely heroes who get trapped in an abandoned Los Angeles police station, surrounded by a gang of unseen snipers. The three main characters—a tough cop, a sly criminal, and a stoic female secretary—are distinctly "Hawksian" characters. Carpenter says he imagined John Wayne and Charles Bronson in the first two roles, and named the third after screenwriter Leigh Brackett, who created "tough, direct" female characters for Hawks's films.[32] Although he certainly didn't share John Wayne's politics, Carpenter had no desire to create a revisionist western that confronted the myth within a modern context. Instead he made a traditional Hollywood western disguised as a contemporary action movie.

Filmmaker Wes Craven did the opposite, infusing the pessimistic spirit of the modern American horror film onto a western landscape in *The Hills Have Eyes* (1977). The filmmaker said that he initially conceived his film as a futuristic version of *The Grapes of Wrath*, building around a New York family moving west to escape the effects of pollution.[33] The finished film dispensed with this backstory, getting more directly to the conflict between the middle-class American family and a "tribe" of cannibals. In essence, *The Hills Have Eyes* is a dystopian western about pioneers and Indians. At the end of this western, however, the pioneers prove to be every bit as savage as the "savages."

Taken together, *Assault on Precinct 13* and *The Hills Have Eyes* illustrate the limitations of the 1970s western, which existed in two basic forms: nostalgia and anti-myth. With so little flexibility, most filmmakers abandoned the genre. After 1977, there were very few attempts to make conventional westerns. Jack Nicholson stubbornly persisted with the offbeat western comedy *Goin' South* (1978), but he struggled in vain to raise financing for an adaptation of novelist Richard Brautigan's gothic western *The Hawkline Monster*. Charles Bronson, apparently intrigued by the notion of monstrous westerns, played Wild Bill Hickok in *The White Buffalo* (1977), but this surreal variation on *Jaws* only confounded audiences. Joe Don Baker, who had risen to fame as Tennessee's answer to Dirty Harry in *Walking Tall* (1973), had a similar encounter with the weird West in *The Shadow of Chikara* (1978), but this vaguely mystical horror-western was another failed experiment. Clint Eastwood kept playing it tough in *The Enforcer* (1976) and *The Gauntlet* (1977), but even he couldn't take himself seriously all the time, as demonstrated by *Every Which Way but Loose* (1978), a film that paired him with a pet orangutan named Clyde. On the verge of a new decade, the Hollywood western was a desert full of sun-bleached bones. Only one film pointed a way forward—but it was overshadowed by the biggest fiasco of the New Hollywood era.

In the early 1970s, writer/director Michael Cimino had conceived *Heaven's Gate* (1980) as a film that would completely transcend the western genre. Producer Steven Bach remembers: "[It] seemed to correct a sentimental and simplistic image of America's open embrace of those tired, poor, huddled masses of patriotic legend; in a way it seemed a sort of counterpart to *The Godfather*, which had transformed an equally familiar genre in dealing with the immigrant classes in urban settings."[34] Over the course of the decade, Bach's studio eagerly tried to secure a star for the film. They approached Steve McQueen, Robert Redford, Paul Newman, Clint Eastwood, even John Wayne, but the project remained mired in development hell. By the time *Heaven's Gate* finally went into production in 1978, with Kris Kristofferson and Christopher Walken in the lead roles, the filmmakers were treating it as a groundbreaking historical epic on par with David Lean's *Lawrence of Arabia*. Production costs ballooned from an initial estimate of $7.5 million to a whopping $44 million, making it one of the most expensive movies ever produced at the time. The initial director's cut, according to Bach, was "five and a half hours of staggering self-indulgence."[35] In its truncated form, what should have been a complex and moving study of America's frontier days became a disjointed and demoralizing dirge for the American Dream—and, by extension, for western films.

One of the biggest problems was the fact that Cimino's film, written for 1971 America, did not get produced and released until 1980. Just as the spirit of the country had changed profoundly over the course of the 1960s, so things had changed again over the course of the 1970s, as many Americans adopted more conservative views. In 1980, the year that Ronald Reagan became president based on a promise to restore American pride and prestige, no one was particularly interested in an epic exposé of the nation's dark historical secrets. Moviegoers wanted morning in America, not mourning in America.

Unfortunately, *Heaven's Gate* all but eclipsed a more successful western that was released around the same time by the same studio—a film that managed to chart the middle-ground between revisionism and romanticism. *The Long Riders* (1980) was a simple retelling of the true story of the James/Younger gang, but it stood apart from the other westerns of the 1970s because of the filmmaker's dedication to the *purity* of the genre. Just as John Carpenter was a student of Howard Hawks and John Wayne, Walter Hill was a devotee of Raoul Walsh and Anthony Mann and a protégé of John Huston and Sam Peckinpah. Like his predecessors, Hill believed that westerns should express more than the politics of the age in which they are made. He thought they should primarily express "Homeric virtues" like loyalty and courage, as he explained: "The quality of courage, I think is *vers dramatic*. I'm interested in that kind of drama. They are a little out of step and a little out of fashion these days, but audiences like them. They are as old as the literature we know, and they certainly have had a large place in the history of the cinema. It's the old story: one person's stereotype is another's archetype. I think it's fairly clear what side of the line I'm on."[36]

The Long Riders is a timeless western about a certain type of man. It doesn't blindly celebrate, angrily vilify or sentimentally eulogize the type; it simply tells his story via a narrative that is episodic and character-based rather than nostalgic or didactic. Hill says, "There's a line from a Jean-Luc Godard film: 'The jokes are funny but the bullets are real.' That's really what this movie is about. These were big, reckless, high-spirited guys that were unaware of the ripples they caused [in American history]."[37] With an exceptional cast of charismatic actors including James and Stacy Keach (as the James boys), David, Keith and Robert Carradine (as the Younger brothers), Dennis and Randy Quaid (as the Millers), and Christopher and Nicholas Guest (as the Fords), *The Long Riders* should have made equally big ripples. Instead it was a full decade before Hollywood filmmakers made a serious return to the Old West. In the meantime, filmmakers explored a new frontier.

CHAPTER XI

Back to the Future
(1977–1988)

> *The choices this year are not just between two different personalities or between two political parties. They're between two different visions of the future, two fundamentally different ways of governing—their government of pessimism, fear and limits, and ours of hope, confidence and growth. Their government sees people only as members of groups; ours serves all the people of America as individuals. Theirs lives in the past, seeking to apply the old and failed policies to an era that has passed them by. Ours learns from the past and strives to change by boldly charting a new course for the future. Theirs lives by promises: the bigger, the better. We offer proven, workable answers. Our opponents began this campaign hoping that America has a poor memory. Well, let's take them on a little stroll down memory lane...*
> —Ronald Reagan, accepting the presidential nomination
> at the Republican National Convention, August 23, 1984

In 1980, actor-turned-politician Ronald Reagan promised American voters a return to a romanticized past—before Watergate, before Vietnam, before the assassination of John F. Kennedy. He believed that his predecessor Jimmy Carter had dangerously tipped the balance of power in favor of the Soviets and, worse still, had caused America to "lose faith in itself." His plan for the future was simple: "We had to recapture our dreams, our pride in ourselves and our country, and regain that unique sense of destiny and optimism that had always made America different from any other country in the world. [...] I believed [...] that America's greatest years were ahead of it, that we had to look at the things that had made it the greatest, richest, and most progressive country on earth in the first place, decide what had gone wrong, and then put it back on course."[1]

The incoming president delivered on his promise by recreating the political atmosphere of the 1950s—reasserting the nation's role as "spiritual leader of the Free World" and re-escalating the Cold War with communist Russia.[2] Drawing his rhetoric from the clichés of Hollywood westerns, Reagan depicted the half-century standoff with the Soviets in decidedly cinematic terms: "It was like having two westerners standing in a saloon aiming their guns at each other's head—permanently."[3] His solution was to increase the size of America's gun and defeat the Soviet Union through intimidation, thereby establishing "peace through strength." The former screen cowboy clearly had faith that, just as Union and Confederate soldiers had joined forces to defeat the savage Apaches in his 1951 western *The Last Outpost*, Democrats and Republicans would unite behind him in his crusade to destroy "the evil empire."

Reagan's policies renewed the fighting spirit of many American citizens, and had a similar effect on Hollywood's mythmakers, who resurrected themes of the classic western film within a new genre. Since the early 1970s, the popularity of science fiction had been on the rise. Films like *The Andromeda Strain* (1971), *The Omega Man* (1971), *Silent Running* (1972) and *Westworld* (1973) offered bleak visions of the future, but—unlike the westerns of the same period—they quickly gave way to more invigorating frontier stories that harkened back to the laudatory historical dramas of the 1930s to 1950s. Film historian Fred Erisman observes that the "space western" grew quite naturally in alien soil:

> Science fiction, by its very nature, deals with issues of technological, ethnic, and social change, often in the context of a hostile and undeveloped environment. It explores the social consequences of technological advances, and its speculation about alien contact and the possibilities of the human mind raises fundamental questions about human ethnicity and what, exactly, being human means. It deals, in short, with the very stuff of the western myth, and deals with it in ways that attest to the myth's inherent vitality.[4]

Gene Roddenberry famously conceived his *Star Trek* series, about a future generation of mixed-species pioneers exploring "the final frontier," as "*Wagon Train* to the Stars." At times, the derivation of the series was particularly obvious: the TV episode "Spectre of the Gun" transplanted the 23rd century heroes into a simulacrum of the Old West, while the feature film *Star Trek II: The Wrath of Khan* (1982) played out like a classic revenge western with imperialistic overtones. George Lucas's *Star Wars* (1977) was also inspired by the westerns of yesteryear. The filmmaker remembered: "The western was the last American mythological genre, and there had not been anything since then. I wanted to take all the old myths and put them into a new format that young people could relate to."[5] His film pitted a small group of rebels, including a gun-slinging anti-hero named Han Solo, against a powerful evil empire, led by man-in-black Darth Vader. In some respects, the story echoes the war between President Kennedy's "Magnificent Seven" and the Soviet Union. Lucas's initial film, of course, was made several years before Reagan re-escalated that war and applied the term "evil empire" to America's longstanding political nemesis (as well as several years before Reagan introduced his space-defense initiative, which the press dubbed "Star Wars"). Nevertheless, the straightforward white hat/black hat mythology of *Star Wars* resonated strongly at a time when Americans were yearning for a less complicated geopolitical worldview. Lucas, like Reagan, delivered the satisfying illusion of a simpler world.

Due to the overwhelming popularity of the *Star Trek* and *Star Wars* series, as well as early imitations like *Space: 1999* (1975–1977) and *Battlestar Galactica* (1978–1979), many Hollywood filmmakers started exploring the "space western" idea—with mixed results. Independent producer Alan Ladd, Jr., who had greenlighted *Star Wars* during his tenure as president of 20th Century–Fox studios, put his faith in *Outland* (1981), a film conceived by writer/director Peter Hyams as an "adult" space opera. Hyams explained:

> I have two children—boys 11½ and 13—who are absolute freaks on the kind of *Star Wars* movies that there are. I wanted to make a movie that appealed to them, but that would also appeal to me. There seemed to be a dichotomy. A lot of the movies that were set in the future were kids' movies. I wondered why they didn't cross over. I began to realize that it would be interesting to make a movie that was set in the future, that used the future as a location—rather than the sole subject of the movie.[6]

In the same way that filmmakers like John Ford and Howard Hawks had transformed simple "horse operas" into sophisticated "adult westerns," so Hyams sought to make a space opera for grownups.

In *Outland*, Sean Connery stars as William O'Niel, a federal marshal assigned to keep the peace in a rugged mining colony on Jupiter's moon Io. When O'Niel learns that the colony leader is sacrificing human lives for higher profits, he becomes a target for assassination. Critics immediately recognized the story as "*High Noon* in space." Unlike Gary Cooper in *High Noon*, however, the hero isn't surprised when community members turn their backs on him in his time of need. In Hyam's view, the response is completely natural for settlers in a frontier environment, "who are there to make as much money as they can—and not for reasons of altruism or adventure." The filmmaker concluded: "I just don't think they are heroes. I think they are people who are doing a lot of menial work for a lot of money compressed together under awful conditions."⁷ As a result, *Outland* becomes a nightmare vision of unregulated capitalism. In comparison to the *Star Trek* or *Star Wars*, this film's vision of the "final frontier" is gritty and bleak, its darkness alleviated only by the actions of one exceptional man (and his Grace Kelly, of course).

Space cowboy Sean Connery in *Outland* (1981, Warner Bros.).

John Carpenter's *Escape from New York* (1981) was a similarly dystopian western, but without the conventional hero. Carpenter said he originally conceived the story for his film in 1974, after watching *Death Wish*: "I didn't agree with the philosophy of it, taking the law into one's hands, but the film came across with the sense of New York as a kind of jungle, and I wanted to make an SF film along those lines."⁸ *Escape* takes place in a seemingly post-apocalyptic America, where crime is epidemic and a despotic president has converted the island of Manhattan into a maximum-security prison. When revolutionaries take the president hostage behind prison walls, the only hope for the future of the not-so-free world is super-criminal Snake Plissken. Actor Kurt Russell, who imbued Snake with the quiet ferocity of Clint Eastwood (a particularly appropriate demeanor in scenes where he plays opposite Lee Van Cleef), summed up his character as "a person who says and does *absolutely* what he wants." He is, in short, the only truly *free* man left in America—and determined to stay that way. Viewed within that context, he is a hero. Russell concluded, "I think the audience will pull for him because he's trying to accomplish something."⁹ Carpenter concurred: "[I] define a hero a little differently. He is a character with a singleness of purpose. Whatever his single purpose is, whether it's dark or light or positive, that's where your hero is. You're not interested in somebody who has fifteen agendas. It's not interesting dramatically. Singleness of vision, singleness of purpose, that's what defines a hero. He could be a killer or not a good role model, but it's still a hero."¹⁰ Obviously, Snake is a different kind of hero for a very different world. Because Carpenter's future America is a fascist regime—where the basic rights to life, liberty and the pursuit of happiness have been curtailed—the hero becomes an anarchist who damns the U.S. government and hastens World War III in support of his own individualistic ideals. *Escape from New York* emerges as a Zapata western for the Reagan era.

In terms of their aesthetic and themes, *Outland* and *Escape from New York* had more in common with outré science fiction films like *Alien* (1979), *Blade Runner* (1982) and *The Terminator* (1984) than with the usual western hybrids of the 1980s, which adopted the more lighthearted tone of popular pastiches. Producer Roger Corman conceived his film *Battle Beyond the Stars* (1982) as a family-friendly version of "*The Magnificent Seven* in space," and *Space Raiders* (1983) as a cartoonish version of "*The Wild Bunch* in space." Other juvenile space operas like *Timerider: The Adventure of Lyle Swann* (1982), *Spacehunter: Adventures in the Forbidden Zone* (1983), and *The Last Starfighter* (1984) perpetuated the trend, practically repeating *The Legend of the Lone Ranger* (1981) for the space camp generation.

As Hollywood continued to explore the final frontier, President Reagan became a strong and vocal supporter of NASA's space exploration program, recognizing it as an apt symbol of a hopeful future—in large part because it was an evocative reminder of an idealized past. In the late 1950s and early 1960s, the first American astronauts had helped Uncle Sam fight a publicity war against communism. The Russians beat NASA into space, but a patriotic nation nevertheless rallied behind the Mercury Program astronauts—especially charismatic ex–Marine Col. John Glenn—as they visited the moon. Journalist Tom Wolfe recounted the story of the Mercury Seven in his 1979 book *The Right Stuff*, and Hollywood filmmakers quickly saw an opportunity to rally moviegoers behind a modern-day myth.

Screenwriter William Goldman initially envisioned a film adaptation of *The Right Stuff* as a patriotic rallying cry akin to Reagan's presidential campaign. He wrote:

> I wanted to "say" something positive about America. Not patriotic in the John Wayne sense, but patriotic none the less—because the hostages had just been seized in Iran. [...] The message Carter was sending from the White House was this: "The world is too much now—one man can't do more than I'm doing." [...] As the hostage crisis dragged on—as Carter began wrapping himself in the flag and running for reelection, hiding in the Rose Garden—I became increasingly obsessed with what *The Right Stuff* represented.[11]

While Goldman imagined *The Right Stuff* as a traditional western, however, director Philip Kaufman wanted to make a revisionist western—something like his earlier film *The Great Northfield Minnesota Raid*, which depicted Jesse James and company as decidedly *un-heroic* icons. According to Goldman, Kaufmann "felt the astronauts, rather than being heroic, were really minor leagers, mechanical men of no particular quality, not great pilots at all, simply the products of hype." Frustrated, Goldman abandoned the project, believing that "what Phil wanted to say was that America was going down the tubes. That it *had* been great once, but those days were gone, and wasn't that a shame."[12]

In the end, Kaufman's vision turned out to be more faithful to the scope and spirit of Tom Wolfe's source novel, which also focused on the lives of the military test pilots who preceded the Mercury Seven. Kaufman remembered: "Goldman began with the selection of the astronauts, and ended with John Glenn's flight. For me, the meaning of *The Right Stuff* was embodied in [military test pilot Chuck] Yeager, the early test flights at Edwards Air Force Base, and the relationship the astronauts had to those pilots."[13] As soon as the project migrated from United Artists to Alan Ladd, Jr.'s production company, Kaufman re-wrote Goldman's script to include Yeager and his peers, presenting them as

"Existential bravery": Sam Shepherd and Barbara Hershey as Chuck and Glennis Yeager in *The Right Stuff* (1983, Warner Bros.).

the missing link between the cowboys of the Old West and NASA's space cowboys. His main goal, he explained, was to capture the heroism of the World War II generation:

> There was something about the quality of men then that I remember. You think of John Garfield, Bogart. A quality that seems to be missing now. For me, it came from a way of talking, a way of walking, and a way of looking. We later came to call it laid-back, but it was a style that had something to do with bravery. The astronauts dealt more in heroism—for the public eye. Heroism is something you do for others, but bravery is done alone, for yourself. There is a kind of existential bravery that I felt Yeager had, pushing the rock, the Sisyphus thing, through the sound barrier.[14]

By building *The Right Stuff* around the connection between Yeager and Glenn, Kaufman gave the historical drama its mythic resonance. The film became a variation on transitional westerns like *The Tin Star* and *Warlock*, in which a young upstart supplants a revered older cowboy. Despite Goldman's fears that Kaufman wanted to lambast the younger generation, *The Right Stuff* presented the Mercury Seven as representatives of a different type of hero. In a crucial scene, Yeager's hero-beyond-reproach stands up for the astronauts, telling an outspoken critic that "it takes a special kind of man to volunteer for a suicide mission, *especially* one that's on TV." The line embodies Tom Wolfe's reason for writing *The Right Stuff* in the first place; he couldn't help wondering "why men were willing—willing?—*delighted!*—to take on such odds in this, an era literary people had long since characterized as the age of the anti-hero."[15] *The Right Stuff*, like the great classic westerns, explains: True heroism is timeless.

The 1983 film established several Hollywood actors—including Ed Harris, Scott Glenn, Dennis Quaid, Sam Shepard and Lance Henriksen—as leaders of a new generation of cinematic cowboys, but the nuances of Kaufman's storytelling were lost on viewers who merely wanted patriotic pablum. Even the real John Glenn was unimpressed, dismissing the film as "*Laurel and Hardy Go to Space*," and blaming it for his failure to win the Democratic presidential nomination in 1984.[16] Soon after, conservative cowboy Ronald Reagan was re-elected, and his gung-ho brand of patriotism achieved critical mass in Hollywood.

The differences between Reagan's tenuous first term and his triumphant second term in office can be measured by the difference between two popular action movies: 1982's *First Blood* and 1985's *Rambo: First Blood Part II*. The first film was an adaptation of David Morrell's 1972 novel about a Vietnam vet who returns home to an ungrateful nation. In the author's mind, the main character Rambo represented the disaffected youths of the Vietnam generation.[17] Rambo's nemesis, a small town sheriff named Teasle was "the establishment's representative," and the final confrontation between the two men showed that "in this microcosmic version of the Vietnam War and American attitudes about it, escalating force results in disaster. Nobody wins."[18] When Morrell's anti-war novel was translated to the screen, however, the message changed. According to screenwriter Michael Kozoll, producer Andrew Vajna wasn't interested in the political nuance of the novel: "Vajna told me, 'We have to clear out a lot of that crap and make it cleaner.'" Kozoll interpreted, "He meant, Make it a western."[19]

According to director Ted Kotcheff, the film's star Sylvester Stallone had a similar agenda: "Stallone said to me, 'This guy shoots like he's in a shooting gallery, and it's going to alienate the audience. What if he puts 'em out of action instead of killing 'em?' The second change was to transform Rambo from a foul-mouthed ranter into a stoical silent type. The last, and most important, was the ending."[20]

Stallone's modifications transformed Rambo from a disturbed killer into a sympathetic drifter—a character more like Kirk Douglas's alienated cowboy in *Lonely Are the Brave* than the troubled vet in Morrell's novel. Ironically, Kirk Douglas was originally hired to play the role of Trautman, the Army CO who arrives at the end of the novel to kill Rambo. After Stallone revised the ending, however, Douglas bowed out, explaining: "I thought that it would be better, dramatically, if my character realizes what a Frankenstein monster, amoral killer, and menace to society he has created, and KILLS STALLONE. If they'd listened to me, there would have been no [sequels]. They would have lost a billion dollars, but it would have been *right*."[21] Instead, Rambo became a hero and *First Blood* marked the beginning of a Hollywood campaign to mollify America's "Vietnam syndrome," and modify the popular perception of the war.

Sylvester Stallone as weary war hero John Rambo in *First Blood* (1982, Orion).

Soon after *First Blood* was released, James Cameron went to work on the screenplay for *Rambo: First Blood Part II* (1985), in which the weary war veteran returns to Vietnam to rescue American POWs. When he gets trapped behind enemy lines, he single-handedly re-fights the Vietnam War ... and wins. The story was intended as a morale-booster at a time when POW/MIA activist organizations were becoming especially vocal in America, but Rambo's creator was troubled by the mischaracterization of his haunted hero. Morrell dismissed the sequel, comparing it to World War II westerns and war films "that I hated and was terrified by as a kid," full of "violence without consequences."[22]

Of course, most people in Hollywood saw *Rambo* simply in terms of commercial appeal. While Cameron's script was still in development, the Cannon Group produced *Missing in Action* (1984) and *Missing in Action 2: The Beginning* (1985), starring Chuck Norris as an equally vengeful Vietnam vet. The martial arts champion-turned-action movie hero had, in a sense, been re-fighting the Vietnam War for years. In the 1978 film *Good Guys Wear Black*, he played a black ops leader who was left for dead in the jungles of Vietnam by a CIA bureaucrat. Five years after escaping from Southeast Asia, the discarded hero returns to war with the same corrupt politician who tried to bury him. Through the hero's actions, the film attempted to pay tribute to the unsung Vietnam vets who had willingly sacrificed their lives for their country. The actor later explained that the message was deeply personal for him—and why he was eager to repeat it:

> One of the secret dreams that I held close to my heart for many years was the desire to do something in honor of my brother Wieland's death in Vietnam. When film director Lance Hool showed me a screenplay about American prisoners of war in Vietnam [*Missing in Action*], I felt strongly that this was the vehicle

through which I could not only honor Wieland but also the more than two thousand other American soldiers who had not been accounted for in that horrific war.[23]

According to Norris, nobody in Hollywood wanted to make *Missing in Action* until after Reagan took office and "the country's mood improved."[24] Following Reagan's successful 1983 invasion of Grenada and a decisive victory over communist forces there, anti-communist films became a hot commodity. Norris, who had established a reputation as a modern-day cowboy hero in hidden westerns like *Silent Rage* (1982) and *Lone Wolf McQuade* (1983), replicated Rambo's war and became a cinematic tough guy on par with Clint Eastwood, Charles Bronson and Sylvester Stallone.

In the midst of this new heyday of the American action hero, it was inevitable that some filmmakers would attempt a return to the traditional western movie milieu. Writer/director Lawrence Kasdan obviously knew a thing or two about hidden westerns—having written two *Star Wars* sequels as well as *Raiders of the Lost Ark* (1981)—when he decided to make *Silverado* (1985), a film about a group of classic cowboys full of romantic agendas. Kasdan's leading man Scott Glenn described it as an ode to the studio-era western, explaining, "It's not an art western, it's not a send-up western, it's not a comedy western, and it's not a 'death-of-the-West' western with ancient airplanes, old telephones. If you were going to compare it to the westerns of the late '40s, and you had a western with Errol Flynn and Gary Cooper—Kevin Kline would be Flynn and I would be Cooper."[25] *Silverado* certainly unfolds with the same jauntiness of a Michael Curtiz or Cecil B. DeMille western. Unfortunately, it lacks the narrative stride of their classic films. Kasdan concedes: "Most westerns have been spare in story and character; it's a very austere form, and there's a real strength in that, as in any good, simple story. *Silverado*, though, is a terribly complicated story with too many characters in it."[26] The narrative excesses leave one yearning for what Kasdan called the "Hawksian spine" of *Raiders of the Lost Ark*, a straight-ahead story about a World War II–era American hero.[27] In contrast with that film, which added flesh to the bones of the lackluster 1969 Gregory Peck western *Mackenna's Gold* (1969), *Silverado* is a mishmash of old plots that never quite becomes a new whole. As a result, it failed to convince audiences that a western film in the 1980s could be anything more than an exercise in nostalgia.

Around the same time, Clint Eastwood rode into town with his own neo-classical western, laying out a plan for the resurrection of the form:

> In the sixties, American westerns were stale, probably because the great directors—Anthony Mann, Raoul Walsh, John Ford—were no longer working a lot. Then the Italian western came along, and we did very well with those; they died of natural causes. Now I think it's time to analyze the classic western. You can still talk about sweat and hard work, about the spirit, about love for the land and ecology. And I think you can say all these things in the western, in the classic mythological form.[28]

The filmmaker who conceived *High Plains Drifter* as a supernatural variation on *High Noon* likewise conceived *Pale Rider* (1985) as a supernatural variation on *Shane*. Like *Shane*, the film begins with the arrival of a mysterious drifter in a frontier community where hardworking settlers are being bullied by cutthroat corporate goons. In response to a young girl's prayer for a "miracle" to save her working-class family, Eastwood's rider rallies the settlers against their common enemy. Like the mystery man in *High Plains Drifter*, the Preacher in *Pale Rider* exists not as a human character, but as a symbol of change. When someone asks who he is, the Preacher answers, "Really doesn't matter, does it?" In essential terms, he is an ideological instigator—not necessarily a force for Good, but at least a force for political and economic fairness. Reflecting the filmmaker's observation that "the bureaucratic workings of nations and corporations have encouraged people to form counter-societies," *Pale Rider* illustrates hope that one man alone can inspire effective resistance to the malign influences of corporate America ... perhaps even in the era of Reaganomics.[29] The filmmaker summed up, "Basically I wanted to have contemporary concerns expressed within the classical tradition."[30]

Other filmmakers of the era adopted the same plan, employing the new generation of Hollywood cowboys to fight burgeoning political wars against communism, international terrorism and drugs. Chuck Norris fought Lebanese terrorists in *The Delta Force* (1986) and Colombian cocaine dealers in *Delta Force 2* (1990). Sylvester Stallone, having cured America's "Vietnam syndrome" in *Rambo*, went to war with the Soviets in *Rocky IV* (1985) and *Rambo III* (1988). Charles Bronson's vigilante Paul Kersey said no to drugs, cleaning up the streets of Los Angeles in *Death Wish IV: The Crackdown* (1987). Newcomer Mel Gibson also joined the war on drugs in *Lethal Weapon* (1987), playing a Vietnam veteran *and* rogue cop who refutes the notion that "there's no more heroes left in the world" by taking down an L.A. kingpin. South of the border, Nick Nolte squared off against a Mexican drug czar *and* a corrupt American paramilitary leader in Walter Hill's *Extreme Prejudice* (1987).

As Hill's film suggests, not all filmmakers embraced Ronald Reagan's policies, and offered a healthy dose of cultural criticism along with the decade's daydreams. When John Carpenter and Kurt Russell teamed up again, they made a playfully subversive commentary on the tradition of action movie heroes. One-upping his impersonation of Clint Eastwood in *Escape from New York*, Russell imitated another legendary westerner in the kung fu fantasy *Big Trouble in Little China* (1986). Carpenter remembered: "who better

East Meets Western: Kim Cattrall, Kurt Russell, Dennis Dun and Suzee Pai in *Big Trouble in Little China* (1986, 20th Century–Fox).

to stick into this kind of Asian underground than the man who won Vietnam for us in *The Green Berets*—namely John Wayne? Jack Burton is John Wayne, and Kurt Russell is playing it blow-hard John Wayne. And that's all he's doing. He's playing John Wayne, the man. It tickled me for a long time to do that because in all action movies—and it's still happening—the white American is always the cool guy."[31]

In *Big Trouble and Little China*, however, Jack Burton only *thinks* he's the cool guy. While Jack does all the talking, his silent partner Wang Chi does most of the fighting. Russell reflected on the Jack attack: "He's a lot of hot air, very self-assured, a screw up. He thinks he knows how to handle situations and then gets into situations he can't handle but somehow blunders his way through anyhow."[32] Although the film was a blatant criticism of America's gung-ho self-image during the Reagan era, it was ultimately not a mean-spirited one. Jack Burton, for all of his foibles, still wins the day and gets the girl. Why? Carpenter concludes, "I believe a great deal in America. I think it's the best there is. It's fucked beyond belief, but it's the best there is."[33]

Filmmaker Alex Cox's criticism was a more biting. Eager to make a western movie in an era when nobody wanted to finance western movies, the indie filmmaker pulled his friends together and shot *Straight to Hell* (1987), a spaghetti western spoof about a quartet of bumbling bank robbers who get trapped in a ghost town run by gang of caffeine-addicted cowboys. It's all fun and games until representatives of a ruthless oil company claim squatter's rights to the land, and start wiping out everyone around them. Cox, a revolutionary at heart, said he conceived the film as an expression of support for the Sandinista National Liberation Front, which was at the time fighting CIA-trained contras over control of the Nicaraguan government. Later, he even claimed he made the film instead of accepting a much more lucrative offer to direct HBO's comedy-western *Three Amigos* (1986). To him, the latter film was politically suspect, as he explained: "The script had these weird political overtones: it promoted the idea that Americans have the right to intervene in a violent way in foreign countries—for all that it was supposed to be a comedy, it was actually propaganda for the Monroe Doctrine."[34]

Not coincidentally, Cox's next film—another hidden western, written by Rudy Wurlitzer—presented an incendiary counterargument to the Monroe Doctrine. *Walker* tells the true story of Col. William Walker, an American lawyer in the mid–1800s who led several private military expeditions into Central America. His goal was to take over the local governments and install himself as leader. In the film, Walker sums up his personal philosophy as follows: "It is the God-given right of the American people to dominate the western hemisphere. It is our moral duty to protect our neighbors from

Ed Harris as the cold face of Manifest Destiny in *Walker* (1987, Universal).

oppression and exploitation. It is the fate of America to go ahead. That is Manifest Destiny." Although his fiancée argues that Manifest Destiny is "just a cover-up for slavery," Walker persists until he manages to wrest control of the government of Nicaragua. In reality, the American dictator's regime lasted from 1855 until 1857, leaving the country in a state of political unrest from which it has never fully recovered.

In the role of Walker, actor Ed Harris projected the same leadership qualities that defined John Glenn in *The Right Stuff*. His version of Walker was a clean-cut and humorless moral arbiter. Unlike Glenn, however, Walker is a stone-cold sociopath with no regard for human life. Although he claims to adhere to a "higher law," the self-professed "social democrat" exploits and enslaves an entire nation. Those he cannot rule, he kills. Cox's message—aimed directly at the Reagan administration—is that silver-tongued ideologues make natural tyrants. The filmmaker summed up, "Nothing has changed in the 130 years between Walker's genocidal campaign and that of Oliver North and the current crop of war criminals in the White House."[35] Walker's final speech, given as he literally watches "his" country burn, explicitly links the historic tragedy with American foreign policy in the mid–1980s:

> You all might think that there will be a day when America will leave Nicaragua alone, but I am here to tell you flat-out that that day will never happen, because it is our destiny to be here. It is our destiny to control you people. So no matter how much you fight and no matter what you think, we'll be back time and time again. By the bones of our American dead in grievous Grenada, I swear that we will never abandon the cause of Nicaragua. Let it occupy your every waking and sleeping thought.

Coming at a time of great political strength for Reagan—and of very little tolerance for preachy revisionist westerns—*Walker* failed to resonate with American audiences in 1987. For the time being, most of Hollywood's hidden westerns remained cautiously conservative and their heroes largely apolitical.

In 1988, rising star Bruce Willis paired up with old-timer James Garner for a completely innocuous romp through western territory. *Sunset* featured Willis as silent-era actor Tom Mix and transformed Mix into a cocky but affable sidekick to Garner's Wyatt Earp. Together, the two manufactured heroes pursue a murder mystery that culminates in a showdown at the first Academy Awards ceremony. The story is not entirely fictional—the real Wyatt Earp did come to Hollywood, where he met William S. Hart and Tom Mix (and possibly Allan Dwan and John Ford, who remembered him as "a man of few words, remarkable calm"[36]), but he died a few months before the first Academy Awards show. Nevertheless, Garner's Earp facetiously assures us that the story is basically true, "give or take a lie or two." Willis adopts his elder's wry sense of humor—a demeanor that served the actor well in his next hidden western, *Die Hard* (1988).

At one point in the latter film, terrorist Hans Grueber chides Willis's reluctant hero John McClane, calling him "just another American who thinks he's John Wayne, Rambo, Marshall Dillon." Perhaps remembering his ridiculous wardrobe from *Sunset*, McClane responds, "I was always kind of partial to Roy Rogers, actually. I really liked those sequined shirts." *Die Hard* managed to strike a perfect balance between larger-than-life heroics and down-to-earth humor, creating an everyman cowboy hero for the post–Reagan era. John McClane is Gary Cooper without the naiveté, John Wayne without the political bluster, Randolph Scott with a sense of humor. He's a more human Rambo, a less self-righteous Chuck Norris, a self-effacing Clint Eastwood. When McClane embraced his western movie roots, challenging terrorists with the words "Yippee ki-yay, motherfucker!" he signaled that America was ready for new generation of young guns.

CHAPTER XII

Young Guns
(1988–2001)

Today we do more than celebrate America. We rededicate ourselves to the very idea of America, an idea born in revolution and renewed through two centuries of challenge; an idea tempered by the knowledge that, but for fate, we the fortunate and the unfortunate might have been each other; an idea ennobled by the faith that our nation can summon from its myriad diversity the deepest measure of unity; an idea infused with the conviction that America's long, heroic journey must go forever upward.
—Bill Clinton, first Inaugural Address, January 20, 1993

In the final months of the 1980s, a historic breach of the Berlin Wall signaled the end of the Cold War. The subsequent dissolution of the Soviet Union established the United States as the world's only surviving superpower, and perpetuated a prosperous era during which most Americans could feel safe and confident for the first time since the end of World War II. The Gulf War of 1990–1991 projected a formidable illusion of U.S. military's mastery over all the nation's affairs, foreign and domestic. For the time being, America seemed to have regained control of its own destiny. As a result, it was possible for Hollywood to explore the western myth with renewed vitality and earnestness.

After years of non-traditional westerns, filmmakers were inclined to return to the classical form, but there was still some debate about what constituted the "authentic" western form. Reflecting on a series of made-for-TV westerns that revived the conservative myth of "rugged individualistic male protagonist with his own moral code," film historian David Pierson delineated six "authenticity markers" that distinguished the westerns of the 1980s and 1990s—from setting to familiar iconography like horses, cattle, six-guns, Winchester rifles, barrooms, cowboy boots and wide-brimmed hats.[1] At the top of the list was (1) established western writers and (2) a familiar western cast. Pierson noted the resounding popularity of writers Louis L'Amour, Zane Grey and Elmore Leonard, as well as actors Sam Elliott and Tom Selleck, and suggested that such figures represented the heart and soul of the genre. Theatrical westerns of the 1990s adopted the same reverential tone toward old-time westerners—including Jack Palance (in *Young Guns*), James Coburn (in *Young Guns 2*), Charlton Heston (in *Tombstone*), and Robert Mitchum (in *Dead Man*)—but these authenticity markers served mainly to pass the torch to a new generation of gunslingers, who proceeded to recapitulate the major trends of fifty years of Hollywood westerns and reboot the entire genre. In a sense, it was like 1939 all over again.

Emilio Estevez, Kiefer Sutherland, Charlie Sheen and Lou Diamond Phillips in "Hollywood's first heavy-metal western," *Young Guns* (1988, 20th Century–Fox).

One of the inaugural films of the new era was the surprise hit *Young Guns* (1988). Conceived by screenwriter John Fusco as a chronicle of the Lincoln County War, the film revolved around group of disparate outlaws led by Billy the Kid. Fusco remembers how the story idea came to him when he visited the Kid's grave in Fort Sumner, New Mexico:

> He's buried there with some of his regulators, and the epitaph on the tombstone is one word: "Pals." When I saw that years ago I knew I had my theme for *Young Guns*. And there's a point in that movie where the gang is in jeopardy of breaking up and Billy the Kid, trying to keep them together, says "you get yourself three or four good pals, then you've got yourself a tribe. And there ain't nothin' stronger than that." It's a key moment in that story and really defines this band of brothers.[2]

Actor Emilio Estevez, equally moved by the idea of an ensemble western, signed on to play the infamous outlaw. His tribe was a who's who of up-and-coming actors, including Charlie Sheen, Kiefer Sutherland and Lou Diamond Phillips. Although the young cast drew audiences to the theaters, critics generally dismissed the film as an inauthentic western. Estevez concurred, explaining, "John Fusco wrote a magnificent script, but then it was turned into what I call Hollywood's first heavy-metal western. It was just an excuse for a personality piece featuring all these young actors, and I was very disappointed."[3]

Aiming to correct the mistakes of the first film, Fusco wrote a sequel that would be bigger, better and more thematic. In *Young Guns 2* (1990), Billy is reunited with his "pals" courtesy of a corrupt governor who promises them a full pardon for their crimes. When the governor (unsurprisingly) betrays the gang, they set out to finish what they started:

eliminating corrupt bankers, politicians and lawmen, and dismantling the entire Lincoln County bureaucracy. This playfully irreverent western appealed to children of the 1980s just as similar populist fantasies like *Jesse James*, *When the Daltons Rode*, and countless "bad men" westerns appealed to young viewers in the early 1940s. Like those earlier films, it also inspired several like-minded westerns, including 1993's *Posse* (a black *Young Guns*) and 1994's *Bad Girls* (a pseudo-feminist *Young Guns*).

Just as the *Young Guns* films harkened back to the New Deal westerns, Kevin Costner's *Dances with Wolves* (1990) was reminiscent of early Civil Rights westerns like *Broken Arrow* and *Run of the Arrow*. Costner, who in the years since his breakout role in *Silverado* had become one of America's most bankable movie stars, conceived *Dances with Wolves* as a straightforward "love letter to the past"—the 1950s as well as the 1860s.[4] In the film, Costner plays a young, disillusioned Army scout named John Dunbar who befriends a tribe of Lakota Sioux Indians on the western frontier. Although taught to fear Indians, Dunbar comes to admire them for their friendliness, good humor and dedication to each other. When the soldiers of Manifest Destiny attack the Sioux, the hero chooses to fight alongside the Indians—not merely because they have become his friends but because he wants to preserve the "natural beauty" of the untamed West. *Dances with Wolves* presented a prelapsarian vision of America, nostalgically recapturing the early idealism of the baby boomer generation while avoiding the angry polemics of revisionist western films. Costner explained, "It wasn't made to manipulate your feelings, to reinvent the past, or to set the historical record straight. It's a romantic look at a terrible time in our history, when expansion in the name of progress brought us very little and, in fact, cost us deeply."[5]

The film resonated strongly with audiences, but it didn't convince Hollywood execs that audiences were ready for the return of the western genre. Clint Eastwood's *Unforgiven* (1992) did that by encapsulating the popular revenge westerns of the 1950s. American's reigning cinematic cowboy expressed admiration for *Dances with Wolves*,

Kevin Costner in his "love letter to the past," *Dances with Wolves* (1990, Orion).

but added that the film was not—from his own perspective—an authentic western: "It was kind of [about] a contemporary guy out West who was interested in ecology and women's rights and Indian rights. If you did it like it was [in the 1800s], people probably could've given a crap less about that in those days."⁶ The filmmaker responded with a film that focused on "the simplicity of the times" and "the idea of one person making a difference."⁷ Reflecting on the screenplay by David Peoples, he explained, "I just thought that this was a story I wanted to tell, my conclusion as to what the western mythology is. And if I was ever going to do a last western, it was the perfect one."⁸

Unforgiven's central character, played by Eastwood himself, is a reformed killer named William Munny. Although notoriously vicious at one time, Munny has become a peaceful farmer, a weary widower and father of two young children. Like Josey Wales, he seems to have escaped his violent past—until an aspiring bounty hunter hires him to avenge a brutalized prostitute. When his partner gets murdered, the hired killer's job becomes a matter of personal vengeance. From this point forward, *Unforgiven* is a traditional revenge western—but Eastwood, like Costner, has a progressive message. The filmmaker reflects on the brutally violent finale of his film: "You could see the triumph of vengeance there, but, deep down, no one wins anything at all in this story; everyone suffers some sort of loss, whether it's a part of themselves or ... their life. And that's what happens when people indulge in violence in order to obtain justice."⁹

According to Eastwood, the *Unforgiven* script was written in the late 1970s and had been floating around Hollywood for years before he decided that the time was right to tell the story. In the wake of the 1992 Los Angeles riots, the filmmaker felt that it "became more contemporary."¹⁰ Gene Hackman's character Little Bill Daggett, the lawman who

Clint Eastwood out for revenge in his "last western," *Unforgiven* (1992, Warner Bros.).

incurs Eastwood's wrath, was reputedly modeled on Los Angeles police chief Darryl Gates, a controversial hard-liner who resigned under heavy scrutiny after the riots.[11] Just as Munny does not think of himself as a hero, Daggett does not think of himself as a villain. When Eastwood comes gunning for him, he pleads, "I don't deserve this.... To die this way." Munny responds, "Deserve's got nothing to do with it." In the filmmaker's mind, violence begets violence. Eastwood muses, "An incident will trigger decisions, maybe the wrong decisions or the wrong reactions by people, and then there's really no way to stop things."[12] The line between Good and Bad gets lost in the gunsmoke.

Unforgiven, despite its contradiction of the traditional western movie idea that violence is a necessary evil, managed to please fans of the traditional western. While it demythologized the western hero, it reinvigorated the form. Perhaps most importantly, *Unforgiven* made the western film seem culturally relevant again, by offering commentary on a contemporary crisis that had been building since the early 1970s. As it turned out, the 1992 L.A. riots marked the peak of the decades-long escalation of crime rates in America. After President Bill Clinton's signed the Violent Crime Control and Law Enforcement Act in 1994, violent crime statistics began to fall dramatically. Viewed within that cultural context, Eastwood's final western does seem like an apt conclusion to his mythic journey that began in the deserts of Almeria.

Eastwood's subsequent films *In the Line of Fire* (1993) and *A Perfect World* (1993) serve as thematic postscripts to the journey. In the former, the actor plays a retired Secret Service agent who is haunted by the assassination of President John F. Kenned and terrorized by a similar threat to the current president. It's an unlikely story of redemption, but one that American audiences embraced in all its simplicity. In the latter—more complicated—film, Eastwood plays a grizzled Southern sheriff on the trail of an escaped convict. By casting Kevin Costner in the latter role, Eastwood crafted "a confrontation between two moralities, two purely American types of hero, two generations of actors."[13] Tellingly, *A Perfect World* is set in 1962, "just on the brink of a great turning toward the void that will take hold of America."[14] Eastwood's jaded lawman seems like a fallen hero, unable to connect emotionally with other people, while Costner's idealistic criminal seems never to have had an opportunity to be heroic. When they (almost) meet in the gulf between generations, the younger man asks, "Do I know you, friend?" The elder answers, "No, not really." Both characters present troubling images of stunted manhood to an innocent young boy caught between them. In *A Perfect World*, it remains unclear what lies in wait for the future of America's Generation X.

Writer/director Maggie Greenwald offered a counterpoint to such hyper-masculine mythology in *The Ballad of Little Jo* (1993), which the filmmaker based on the true story of "Little Joe" Monaghan, an Idaho rancher who lived most of her adult life masquerading as a man. Greenwald remembers:

> The only thing that's known is what was published in the newspaper article when she died, which gave me the information for the beginning and the end of the story. She was a society girl who had a child out of wedlock. It's believed her sister cared for the child, or someone else may have adopted him. Her family threw her out, and somewhere between the time she left the Northeast and arrived in the West she assumed the identity of a man and lived her whole life that way.[15]

When Greenwald started writing, her story was primarily a feminist western, bringing gender politics to the fore in a genre that habitually embraces gender stereotypes. Over time, however, she realized that she was actually writing "a classic western story about a rugged individualist."[16]

Just like the male western heroes of old, Little Jo lives by a personal moral code that defines her life and helps to define her community. She risks her life to save a Chinese man from being unjustly hanged and thereby makes an uncompromisingly loyal friend. Later, when a greedy cattle baron tries to scare her off of her land, Jo fights to hold onto the life she has created for herself—which earns her the respect and admiration of her neighbors, and makes her an authentic westerner. Greenwald reflects, "American history is full of women who did exactly that. Women came from all over the world to make lives for themselves, the same as men did."[17] Realizing how many of those stories remain untold, the filmmaker adds, "The people who say the western is dying are the ones who see it only as the domain of the white man, and who want to continue to repeat the same old stories. The stories of the minorities in the West—the Asians, blacks and Hispanics—and the women, can revitalize the whole genre."[18]

After the success of *Dances with Wolves*, some genre filmmakers focused for the first time on stories of Native Americans. *Young Guns* actor Lou Diamond Phillips played Navajo detective Joe Leaphorn in a 1991 adaptation of Tony Hillerman's murder-mystery novel *The Dark Wind*, while Val Kilmer played an FBI agent who rediscovers his Sioux heritage in *Thunderheart* (1992). *Dances with Wolves* also helped to launch the career of Cherokee actor Wes Studi, who went on to play the Indian warrior Magua in Michael Mann's remake of *The Last of the Mohicans* (1992) and the title character in Walter Hill's *Geronimo: An American Legend* (1993). Both of these films were classical pioneer narratives, dealing directly with the old myth of Manifest Destiny.

Mann regarded the literary source of his film, James Fenimore Cooper's 1826 novel, as a dubious political "justification for a massive land grab" implying "that the Euro-Americans will be a better steward of the riches that God bestowed upon American Indians."[19] Nevertheless, he was impressed with Philip Dunne's script for the 1936 screen adaptation, in which the hero Hawkeye (played by a young Randolph Scott) embodied politics of the day. Mann reflects: "Dunne did a very interesting thing. He was writing at a time of tremendous political struggle in the United States, a country caught in a depression and at the same time seeing events in Asia

Madeline Stowe and Daniel Day-Lewis in the "eastern western" *The Last of the Mohicans* (1992, 20th Century–Fox).

and Europe. The view here was isolationist, although some people with political agendas and attitudes saw the need to take part in international struggles against the rising tide of fascism. [...] Dunne essentially gave Hawkeye the political attitudes of the isolationists."[20] In the 1936 film, Hawkeye—a white man raised by Mohican Indians—is able to avoid involvement in the French and Indian War until the treacherous actions of a Huron Indian named Magua endanger his loved ones. The ensuing battle transforms the reluctant hero into an American soldier and frontiersman and dooms Magua and his fellow natives.

In Mann's film, Hawkeye (played by Daniel Day-Lewis) undergoes a similar transformation, but Magua becomes a more nuanced villain. Mann says he had a particular affinity for Magua because "he happens to be the only one who probably analyzes the politics." In his film, the villain recognizes that the white man's new frontier is the Indian's final fight and foresees "the loss that everybody shares at the end, looking into the frontier."[21] The historical context—focusing on the precise moment when multiculturalism gave way to cultural imperialism—was the filmmaker's reason for retelling the story. Mann says he aimed to show the "human politics" of the transition while remaining faithful to history: "I didn't want to take 1757, this story, and turn it into some kind of two dimensional metaphor for 1991. What I did want to do was go the other way and take our understanding of those cultures—and I think we understand them better today than Cooper did in 1826—and use our contemporary perspective as a tool to construct a more intense experience of realistically complex people in a complex time."[22]

Geronimo: An American Legend is a similarly complex study. Despite the title, Walter Hill's film is not a biopic of the famous Apache war chief but rather a story about the dynamic between the Apaches and the cavalrymen who lived and died with them. Hill explains: "It's as much about the Army as it is Geronimo. That came out of my reading of historical accounts and realizing that so much of what we think we know about the Indian campaigns is wrong. The Army is generally depicted as the enemy of the Apache, but in many cases, the people who were the most sympathetic to their plight were those soldiers [...] and tragically, it was these same soldiers who then had to go out and be the tip of the spear."[23]

The story revolves around a 22-year-old cavalryman named Britton Davis, who served in the U.S. Army under Brigadier General George Crook and Lt. Charles Gatewood when they were tasked with capturing the last remaining band of rogue Apaches. During the course of the Geronimo Campaign, Crook, Gatewood and Davis—as well as the prejudiced Army scout Al Sieber—learn to respect the men they are pursuing, making it harder to fulfill their mandate. Crook voices the hard reality of their position: "Settlers, prospectors, land speculators—they won't admit it, but the truth is they'd all like to see the Indian dead. They see the Army as their weapon." Somewhat hopefully, the general adds: "The Army that fights the Apache is the only real hope of keeping the Apache alive. Only the Army can protect them."

In the end, of course, nothing could protect Geronimo and his people from Manifest Destiny. They were rounded up and forced to live their lives in captivity, leaving Davis to mourn—like Kevin Costner in *Dances with Wolves*—the tragic extinction of a way of life that endured a thousand years. Hill concludes:

> As far as what I was trying to say in *Geronimo*, everyone agrees that what happened to the Apache and all the American Indians was a tragic thing, a sad thing, but nobody wants to talk about the fact that it was very nice people who did it. They like to think it was the terrible guy who worked for the government and

stole the Indian's beef shipment when it was due. One of the things I was trying to show in *Geronimo* is basically these were very good, decent people, very much the kind of people we see in the American heroic tradition.[24]

Geronimo is neither a classical nor a revisionist western, neither liberal nor conservative. It belongs to that rare breed of thoroughly humanistic westerns.

With a western revival well underway, Hollywood's biggest guns took aim at the law and order subgenre, and specifically at the symbolic centerpiece of the American heroic tradition. In the early 1990s, two films were being developed about the famous gunfight at the O.K. Corral, and the productions histories of *Tombstone* (1993) and *Wyatt Earp* (1994) are inextricably intertwined. According to screenwriter Dan Gordon, Kevin Costner expressed an interest in making a TV miniseries about Wyatt Earp around the time he completed *Dances with Wolves*. Costner hired Gordon to write a sprawling epic treatment of the famous lawman's life, from childhood to old age. His vision: "the western as *The Godfather*."[25] (Presumably Costner did not know that the epic disaster *Heaven's Gate* had been conceived in the same terms.) Around the same time, screenwriter Kevin Jarre, who was riding high on the success of his 1989 war film *Glory*, began writing a screenplay about the feud between the Earps and the Cowboys. According to producer James Jackson,

Kurt Russell and Val Kilmer as "flawed good guys" Wyatt Earp and Doc Holliday in *Tombstone* (1993, Buena Vista).

Jarre saw his project as a story of "flawed good guys" (the Earps and Doc Holliday) pitted against equally charismatic villains.[26]

While Jarre's *Tombstone* evolved into an ensemble piece that lured a stellar cast of old-time westerners (including Robert Mitchum, Charlton Heston, and Harry Carey, Jr.), *Wyatt Earp* suffered an identity crisis. Costner decided to make a feature film instead of a TV miniseries, and writer/director Lawrence Kasdan took over for Dan Gordon with the stated intention of crafting a "character study" that would capture "the spirit of *The Magnificent Seven*."[27] As Gordon points out, however, Kasdan and Costner's film ultimately went a different direction, focusing narrowly on the title character and allowing all the other characters to fall into the background. Kasdan later claimed that he wanted to focus on Earp because Earp's journey was essentially America's journey. He rationalized: "America started out with optimistic, innocent ideas. But in the settlement of America there was always a high level of violence and brutality. Americans have been good at it. We've been tough enough to face the challenges, but at some cost."[28] The director has suggested that his finished film reflects the failure of American interventions in Vietnam and, more recently, in Somalia: "Time and time again, you see that it doesn't work, because the situation cannot be cleaned up. Wyatt Earp found that out, too. He is like an exemplar of a certain aspect of American society. And was he compromised? Absolutely, as are most people. He was rigid and unforgiving, and loyal to his friends, and when you were an enemy he could not see you clearly. That's the American way."[29]

Unfortunately, Kasdan overemphasized his point by preventing moviegoers from seeing the enemy clearly. "He cut out the bad guys," Gordon complains. "You never knew what the hell was going on or why there was a rift between these guys or why there was this enmity between them. They were just a bunch of grubby guys going, 'Arrugh, kill the Earps!'"[30] Indeed, the biggest difference between Hollywood's dueling Earp movies is the presence of the villains. *Tombstone* boasts scene-stealers Powers Booth and Michael Biehn as Curly Bill Brocius and Johnny Ringo. Their strengths as villains enhance the strengths of Earp and Holliday. Eschewing politics in favor of characterization, *Tombstone* emerged as a testament to the basic vitality of the western myth and reduced Costner's film to an expensive afterthought.

The critical and commercial failure of *Wyatt Earp* may have hastened the end of the 1990s western revival, although there is evidence that Hollywood was already having trouble taking the genre seriously. In the summer of 1994, Costner's film was buffeted by *Maverick*, a tongue-in-cheek Mel Gibson vehicle (based on the popular TV series with James Garner), and *Wagon's East!*, a wheezy John Candy comedy. The former—essentially conceived as a *Lethal Weapon* sequel on horseback—was a financial success, but a very minor western. The latter, bogged down by the untimely death of its star, wasn't even good for a laugh. In 1995, only three westerns—Sam Raimi's *The Quick and the Dead*, Jim Jarmusch's *Dead Man*, and Walter Hill's *Wild Bill*—were produced for the big screen. Each took a different approach to the genre, attempting to capture the magic of some of the more esoteric westerns of years past.

Wild Bill was the most traditional of the three, although surprisingly theatrical for a western directed by actioneer Walter Hill. Like *I Shot Jesse James*, *The Gunfighter* and other existential westerns, the film examines our definition of a hero. The first half straightforwardly depicts the historical events which established Wild Bill Hickok's notoriety, culminating with the gunman's arrival in Deadwood in 1876. The second half unfolds more slowly and methodically, fictionalizing Hickok's relationships with Calamity

Jane, his most famous admirer, and Jack McCall, the young gambler who shot him in the back of the head. Hill uses details drawn from Thomas Babe's 1978 play *Fathers and Sons* and Pete Dexter's 1986 novel *Deadwood* to depict Hickok as a man worthy of his legend—though not in the way we might expect. Despite the filmmaker's laudable efforts to humanize and celebrate one of the genre's first icons, *Wild Bill*'s lack of action caused it to fizzle at the box office.

By contrast, Sam Raimi's *The Quick and the Dead* was conceived as a visually audacious spaghetti western. Screenwriter Simon Moore remembers: "I wanted to go back to the fundamental image of what I believed the western was, which is two people at either end of the street, and only one of them is going to make it. What I was trying to get across was really much more the Italian westerns of Sergio Leone and the Spanish-Italian spaghetti westerns rather than the more classical American westerns."[31] Moore built his story around a quick-draw contest in a town populated with colorful characters who are seeking thrills, money, fame, respect, redemption and revenge. At the center of the story is a "Woman with No Name," a descendant of *Hannie Caulder* who is out avenge her father's murder. When actress Sharon Stone expressed an interest in playing the lead role, splatschtick horror filmmaker Sam Raimi came on board as well, resolving to craft a western film with even more panache than the works of Sergio Leone. At times, the visuals in *The Quick and the Dead* are so outrageous that the film—despite being grounded by the performances of an exceptional cast—verges on parody. (In one scene, the winner of a quick-draw shootout is revealed through the gaping hole in a man's head.) Mainstream audiences apparently didn't know quite what to make of Raimi's strange blend of western clichés and comic book violence, and the filmmaker's emphasis on style over substance was blamed for the film's commercial failure.

Writer/director Jim Jarmusch's *Dead Man* was equally eccentric, but its innovations were more substantial. The film's cinematic ancestors seem to be the acid westerns of filmmakers like Monte Hellman, Dennis Hopper and Rudy Wurlitzer—films that were often overwhelmed by ideas. Jarmusch concedes that *Dead Man* is about many things: "history, language, America, indigenous culture, violence, industrialization."[32] The plot revolves around a timid eastern accountant named William Blake who kills a man out west, then spends the majority the film on the run from bounty hunters. The real story, however, is Blake's parallel spiritual journey into the land of the dead, guided by an enigmatic Indian character named Nobody. Jarmush reflects, "I wanted that simple story, and that relationship between these two guys from different cultures who are both loners and lost and for whatever reasons are completely disoriented from their cultures. That's the story for me, that's what it's about."[33] As the hero's metaphysical journey transcends the western plot, *Dead Man* demonstrates the true flexibility of the genre.

Filmmakers throughout the 1990s, like their predecessors in the 70s and 80s, continued to produce hidden westerns by importing familiar tropes and themes into action, science fiction and horror films. Action hero Jean-Claude Van Damme paid homage to *Shane* in *Nowhere to Run* (1993) and his rival Steven Seagal took up the mantle of *Billy Jack* in *On Deadly Ground* (1994). Filmmaker Michael Mann fused *Jesse James* and *The Wild Bunch* in the form of an urban crime drama (*Heat*, 1995) while Walter Hill translated *A Fistful of Dollars* into Prohibition-era Texas (*Last Man Standing*, 1996). Veteran indie filmmaker John Sayles made a contemporary revisionist western with shades of neo-noir (*Lone Star*, 1996) as Kevin Costner continued to celebrate western romanticism, even in a post-apocalyptic setting (*The Postman*, 1997). Newcomers Robert Rodriguez and

Quentin Tarantino crossed western mythology with local legends (*Desperado*, 1995) and vampire lore (*From Dusk Till Dawn*, 1996)—no doubt taking their cues from John Carpenter, who continued to populate his favorite genre with mutant creations. Carpenter's *Vampires* (1998)—a bloody pastiche of *Red River, The Searchers, El Dorado, Once Upon a Time in the West,* and *The Wild Bunch*—offered some encouragement for other weird westerns, including *Ravenous* (*The Shining* as a western, 1999), *Pitch Black* (*The Last Wagon* in space, 2000) and Carpenter's own *Ghosts of Mars* (2001), which transplanted *Rio Bravo* into a haunted mining colony on the Red Planet. Even Clint Eastwood made a hidden western, rallying fellow genre veterans James Garner and Tommy Lee Jones to make *Space Cowboys* (2000). Unfortunately, the escape to outer space was brief and the darkness at noon was not. A few weeks after the theatrical release of *Ghosts of Mars*, Islamic terrorists executed a coordinated attack on America, and the revitalized western became a quaint relic of a nostalgic era that had come to an abrupt end.

CHAPTER XIII

Fever Dream
(2002–2010)

> *Tonight we are a country awakened to danger and called to defend freedom. Our grief has turned to anger, and anger to resolution. Whether we bring our enemies to justice, or bring justice to our enemies, justice will be done.*
> —George W. Bush, address to the nation, September 20, 2001

In the weeks and months that followed the 1941 bombing of Pearl Harbor, Hollywood rallied behind the U.S. military as it prepared to wage war on two fronts. The film industry's dream machine became a propaganda machine, helping to unify public sentiment by producing a steady stream of patriotic war films and documentaries. The September 11, 2001, terrorist attacks likewise changed the tone of the films coming out of Hollywood, but in a very different way. Just a few days after the attacks, the Los Angeles Times reported that studio executives were cancelling disaster movies and action-espionage thrillers en masse, concerned that American audiences were too traumatized by recent events to embrace these subjects as entertainment.[1] War movies also became scarce, as Hollywood focused on generating escapist entertainment to soothe the nation's psyche. The same article mentioned a new TV series called *24* (2001–2010), and suggested that it would be something of a "test case" in the new entertainment climate. There was some concern that the series, about a counterterrorism specialist named Jack Bauer, would hit too close to home, and turn viewers off. Instead, *24* became an instant pop culture phenomenon, proving that Americans had an appetite—if not a need—for cathartic action. Even more than that, it showed that Americans had a need for new kind of hero for the new age.

Actor Kiefer Sutherland, who had risen to fame as a sensitive outlaw in the *Young Guns* films, spent much of the 1990s as a professional rodeo rider. Now he embodied a new type of cinematic cowboy—a rogue government agent willing to do whatever it took to safeguard his country. In *24*, Jack Bauer was a utilitarian hero who acknowledged the moral and political complexities of the 21st century and concluded (like U.S. president George W. Bush) that the physical safety of the many outweighed the individual rights of the few. In short, he was a westerner severed from libertarian moorings—a rugged individualist in the service of a higher power. To some, Bauer's personal integrity in combination with access to government secrets made him an ideal judge, jury and executioner. To others, he was a fascist cowboy whose escapades falsely suggested that torture can prevent terrorism. Series creator Joel Surnow, a self-proclaimed "right-wing nutjob,"

155

explained the popularity of the character and the series with one simple observation: "America wants the war on terror fought by Jack Bauer. He's a patriot."[2]

One of the few counterpoints offered during the time period was Joss Whedon's short-lived TV series *Firefly* (2002), a space western about a ragtag group of rebels struggling to fly below the radar of an authoritarian government. The hero at the center of the show is Captain Mal Reynolds, a lovable curmudgeon who previously fought against the Alliance in an intergalactic Civil War, and lost. As a result, he is decidedly anti-authoritarian, a patriot of lost causes and a man with no country—a very different type of hero than Jack Bauer. Whedon explains: "Mal's politics are very reactionary and 'Big government is bad' and 'Don't interfere with my life.' And sometimes he's wrong—because sometimes the Alliance is America, this beautiful shining light of democracy. But sometimes the Alliance is America in Vietnam: we have a lot of petty politics, we are way out of our league and we have no right to control these people."[3] *Firefly* was an essentially liberal-minded western at a time when liberal sentiments were not especially popular. Perhaps for that reason, the show was eclipsed by *24*—for the time being.

By 2004, the United States had become engaged in a long-term war in the Middle East, and public opinions began to shift. Amidst controversies about the failure to find weapons of mass destruction in Iraq and demoralizing evidence of illegal torture practices by American soldiers at Abu Ghraib, many people began to question the U.S. government's motives and methods. As it turned out, this was a fortuitous time for a reconsideration of America's western mythology. A groundswell of interest in Joss Whedon's cancelled series *Firefly* led to a feature film spinoff, *Serenity* (2005), while another TV series popularized the genre for a new generation.

Writer/producer David Milch, creator of the HBO series *Deadwood* (2004–2006), made the western genre relevant again by depicting the Old West as a community governed by ruthless opportunists—pioneers in search of money, power and personal freedom. This was, in the creator's mind, a more honest depiction of American history than white hat/black hat ideology. In a 2005 interview, Milch reflected, "The idea of the western, I believe, as people conceive of it, is really an artifact of the Hays Production Code of the Twenties and Thirties and it has really nothing to do with the West, and much to do with the influence of middle-European Jews who had come out to Hollywood to present to America a sanitized heroic idea of what America was."[4] By contrast, *Deadwood* followed the lead of recent mud-and-rags westerns like *Unforgiven* and *Wild Bill*, abandoning simple ideas in favor of complex (often morally ambiguous) characterizations. Making a significant impact on pop culture, *Deadwood* was no doubt partly responsible for the subsequent arrival of other western miniseries like Steven Spielberg's *Into the West* (2005) and Walter Hill's *Broken Trail* (2006).

On the big screen the resurgence of western formulas was more tenuous, but some filmmakers began rallying as early as 2003. Robert Rodriguez made *Once Upon a Time in Mexico* (2003), a belated sequel to *Desperado* that paid homage to the spaghetti westerns of Sergio Leone, and Quentin Tarantino drew inspiration from Leone, Sergio Corbucci, and Giulio Petroni's *Death Rides a Horse* for his epic samurai revenge western *Kill Bill* (2003–2004). Edward Zwick partly conceived *The Last Samurai* (2003), a film revolving around a disillusioned Civil War veteran who finds redemption in the Far East, as an elegiac western about "heroes who stand tall against the tide of time."[5] Kevin Costner, meanwhile, mounted a full-scale return to the classic tradition with *Open Range* (2003), the first major Hollywood western of the 21st century.

XIII. Fever Dream

Sturm und Drang: Kevin Costner and Robert Duvall in *Open Range* (2003, Buena Vista).

In a 2003 interview, Costner claimed that his goal for *Open Range* was to revitalize the genre by evading the clichés that had been dogging it for years. Reflecting on recent westerns, especially made-for-television westerns, he said: "They've been kind of lazy, they've been stupid, they've been predictable, they've been simple, and they've been essentially costume parties. If you put on a hat and you wear a gun, that's a western, right? Well, it is to a lot of people."[6] For Costner, as for filmmakers like John Ford and Anthony Mann, real westerns are profoundly *naturalistic*: characters echo the austerity of the harsh landscape, and stories follow the fluent rhythms of nature, with sudden bursts of elemental violence. *Open Range* tells the uncomplicated story of two cowboys who find themselves at odds with a greedy rancher. After the rancher kills one of their friends, the two free-rangers fight back. The *Sturm und Drang* is punctuated by picaresque glimpses of tenderness and humor: a rugged cowboy struggling to hold a dainty teacup in front of the woman he loves. The story builds slowly toward a climactic shootout that asserts the core belief of the classic American westerns: Violence is always ugly, but sometimes still necessary. This message was particularly well-suited to the early years of the War on Terror, when U.S. morale was high.

The success of *Open Range* suggested that it was a prime time for westerns. Walt Disney Pictures responded by releasing three western-themed films in the spring of 2004. First out of the gate was *Hidalgo*, John Fusco's Middle East-meets-West story about a man and his horse. Like *The Last Samurai*, it told the story of a disillusioned U.S. cavalryman who finds new meaning in a foreign land, but *Hidalgo*'s cultural exchange was more one-sided, celebrating the superiority of the American "cowboy way." The animated western-comedy *Home on the Range* and a lavish remake of *The Alamo* followed soon after. The former was playfully diverting; the latter painfully solemn. In contrast to John

Wayne's shamelessly jingoistic *The Alamo*, which played fast and loose with historical facts, the new version was slavishly faithful to new scholarship about the people who fought and died in the 1836 Battle of the Alamo. Director John Lee Hancock, who inherited the film from producer Ron Howard, tried to balance factual truth with the "emotional truth" of the legend, but the film ultimately failed to inspire moviegoers the way its namesake inspired American pioneers.[7]

After escaping *The Alamo*, producer Ron Howard decided to tackle a western with less baggage. For him, the appeal of *The Missing* (2003) was not its mythic resonance, but its character drama. The story revolves around a pioneer woman who enlists the help of her estranged father to find her abducted daughter. Howard said, "I thought that the characters were very surprising to be in a 'western,' and I felt the father-daughter estrangement story was something that, dramatically, would be a great opportunity. I was also fascinated by the fact that these two characters were struggling with their feelings, because they didn't have the Freudian vocabulary which hadn't been invented yet, so they had no Dr. Phil to explain the abandonment issues."[8] *The Missing* unfolds as a primitive psychological drama that just happens to be set in the Old West, and thus it sidestepped some of the scrutiny that modern-day westerns face in terms of "authenticity." Neither Cate Blanchett's searcher nor Tommy Lee Jones's wanderer emerges as a conventional western hero—although, to be fair, Jones still delivers a certain amount of western authenticity.

Filmmaker Oliver Stone once said of Tommy Lee Jones, "He is definitely the kind of man who would have ridden with Sam Houston to the Alamo. He is very strong in his beliefs and close to the land."[9] An eighth-generation Texan and cattle rancher, Jones made his western genre debut in the popular TV miniseries *Lonesome Dove* (1989), and went on to direct and star in the TV film *The Good Old Boys* (1995). After *The Missing*, he returned to the director's chair to make *The Three Burials of Melquiades Estrada* (2005), a contemporary western that defies the usual expectations for the genre. In the film, Jones plays a modern-day Texas cowhand seeking justice for a fallen friend who was accidentally killed by a border patrol agent. When local authorities cover up the incident, demonstrating their contempt for the life of Mexican immigrants, Jones's cowboy Pete Perkins abducts the killer and forces him to return the body to Mexico for a proper burial. At that point, the Peckinpah-esque revenge western veers into new territory. At the end of his journey, Perkins learns that his friend's identity was mostly a construct of imagination. He never really knew the man that he has been fighting for.

The actor/director recalled that his initial inspiration for the story was a personal one:

> I guess the spark that started everything was an incident that occurred about three or four years ago in the town of Redford, right on the Rio Grande Valley. A high school kid, a pitcher on the baseball team, a kid of Mexican descent, was out tending to his father's goats. He had a 22 rifle with him to protect the goats against coyotes. He saw a coyote, shot at it and there happened to be three marines, United States marines, in the area, in camouflage, on a stakeout, looking for drug smugglers, and I suppose out of boredom or fear or stupidity, or all three, decided they were taking fire and they gunned the kid down and they shot him dead. They were whisked away and no one was ever brought to trial or held responsible for this murder. Many of us who lived out there were insulted by that and it led to all kinds of thoughts about the Federal Government's attempted imposition of what is actually an arbitrary international border created by wars of the 19th century. That was, sort of, the beginning of the idea.[10]

From there, the story evolved into an existential drama comparable to John Sayles' *Lone Star*, about one man's journey through the illusions and delusions that define life on the border between the United States and Mexico. More than a western, Jones insists, *Melquiades Estrada* is "a journey picture," following a much older mythic tradition that includes works like *The Odyssey* and *Don Quixote*.[11]

Jones's character in the subsequent wartime drama *In the Valley of Elah* (2007) follows a similar path from loss and anger to disillusionment and surrender. Based on a true story, *Elah* begins when Army veteran Hank Deerfield receives a message that his enlisted son has gone AWOL after returning from Iraq. The suspicious father immediately starts searching for his boy, only to learn that he has been murdered by one of his fellow soldiers. When Deerfield realizes that the Army is concealing that shameful secret, the murder mystery becomes a hard-hitting drama about disillusionment and PTSD—or what some pop psychologists have termed "the John Wayne syndrome."

Real-life cowboy Tommy Lee Jones tackles "John Wayne syndrome" in *In the Valley of Elah* (2007, Warner Bros.).

In much the way that Ang Lee's *Brokeback Mountain* (2005) is "a tragedy of emotional deprivation, as not a few western stories are," *In the Valley of Elah* is a film about the masculine mystique embodied in classic American westerns.[12] Not coincidentally, writer/director Paul Haggis notes that Clint Eastwood played a crucial role in getting the film made, and that it is "very similar in tone and feel" to John Ford's *The Searchers*.[13] In the film, Tommy Lee Jones's character represents the John Wayne stereotype of laconic, patriotic cowboy-soldier—a breed of man that seems to be defined by some secret vow of silence about the dehumanizing effects of violence. His son Mike takes that projected image of manhood to heart and stoically follows his father's footsteps to war. The boy's mother explains, "Livin' in this house, he never could have felt like a man if he hadn't gone."

When the reality of the war turns out to be far different from the romantic projections of an old John Wayne movie, Mike calls home and asks his father to save him. Instead, Hank reinforces the macho code, saying, "That's just nerves talking." Desperate to make the old man proud, the young soldier represses his fear and disgust and takes his vow of silence—but, after that, he never again feels like a hero. When Hank Deerfield finally finds himself sitting in front of his son's murderer, he realizes that his son and the killer have both been destroyed by the same set of circumstances. At that point, Hank Deerfield finally breaks his vow of silence. Although he remains proud of his son's bravery and service, the old patriot cannot continue to support the war or the way of thinking and behaving that destroyed his boy.

In the Valley of Elah was one of five major Hollywood films released in the fall of

2007 that conveyed growing disgust with the Iraq war and the George W. Bush administration. These five films—beginning with *Redacted* and *The Kingdom*, and culminating with *Rendition* and *Lions for Lambs*—signaled a tonal shift like the one that occurred after the end of World War II with the rise of film noir and again in the midst of the Vietnam War with the rise of New Hollywood. The former set the stage for the golden era of Hollywood westerns, while the revisionist tendencies of the latter delivered a crippling blow to the declining genre. Interestingly, the fall of 2007 was another pivotal time for Hollywood westerns, owing to the release of Christopher Cain's *September Dawn*, James Mangold's remake of *3:10 to Yuma*, Andrew Dominik's *The Assassination of Jesse James by the Coward Robert Ford*, the Coen Brothers' *No Country for Old Men*, and Paul Thomas Anderson's *There Will Be Blood*. This incredibly diverse collection of films spoke directly to the time in which they were made and showed the 21st century western continuing to grow beyond easy definitions of the genre.

September Dawn was a consciously post–9/11 narrative, a polemical western on par with *Soldier Blue*. In much the way that *Soldier Blue* used the 1864 San Creek Massacre as an allegory for America's crisis in Vietnam, *September Dawn* uses the Mountain Meadows Massacre (which took place on September 11, 1857, in Utah territory) to reflect on contemporary wars in the Middle East. According to the film, the tragedy in Mountain Meadows occurred when "two different worlds met on this spot: one of love, one of hate." The world of love belonged to a band of Christian pioneers from Missouri and Arkansas: good country folk who believed in women's rights, monogamy, and the divinity of Jesus Christ. The world of hate belonged to Mormon settlers, led by a zealous bigot named Jacob Samuelson who insisted that you "can't trust anyone from Missouri" and ordered his people to kill the immigrants in the name of God. Within the Mormon community, Samuelson's claim to divine inspiration was so strong that his "chosen ones" massacred the pioneers in cold blood.

For the actor who played Samuelson, Jon Voight, the film's message was simple. Voight explained: "The movie is a true documented event of a group of fanatic religious believers who received one man's evil permission to massacre another religion—that's the way I summed it up for myself. And it's interesting that we have the same problem facing us now with the Islamic fanatics calling for the destruction of America and all of democracy. It seems there's always a face of evil putting on a mask of God-like beliefs to destroy true believers of innocence and good."[14]

Voight wisely makes a distinction between the corrupting influence of one man and the simpler notion of a uniform group of "bad guys." Because the film makes the same distinction, it can be viewed as a complement to *In the Valley of Elah*'s anti-war rhetoric—especially scenes revolving around Samuelson's younger son, whose role in the massacre leads him to self-loathing and suicide. As writer/director Christopher Cain suggests, *September Dawn* is best viewed as a thinly-veiled warning for *any* culture that promotes religious fanaticism. Cain reflects: "What makes a young kid—of any faith, in any part of the world—strap a bomb on his back and walk into a school, or a mosque, or get on a bus full of innocent people, and blow himself and them all up? You ask yourself that question, and as you do, you start looking around and all of a sudden, it's what religious fanaticism can turn into."[15] Unfortunately for Cain, the film's message didn't rouse audiences in 2007 the way that *Soldier Blue* had in 1970, possibly because it offered no heroic counterpoint to tragedy.

A more conventional western story was *3:10 to Yuma*, with even greater nuance about the notions of good and evil. Director James Mangold said that the original *3:10 to Yuma*, about a hero who risks his life to do what's right, had always inspired him. In fact, he claimed that his earlier film *Cop Land* (1997), about a beleaguered small-town sheriff who stands along against powerful peers, was "in a way based on it."[16] That film's moral dilemma was summed up in a single line of dialogue: "Being right is not a bulletproof vest." The main character in Mangold's *3:10 to Yuma* faces a similar dilemma. When crippled war veteran Dan Evans agrees to help the authorities bring outlaw Ben Wade to justice, he is simultaneously supporting his family and potentially abandoning them. On the verge of losing his home due to late mortgage payments, Evans explains to his wife that their entire existence hinges on one decision: "If I don't go, we gotta pack up and leave. And God knows where. I'm tired of watching my boys go hungry. I'm tired of the way that they look at me. I'm tired of the way you don't. I've been standin' on one leg for three damn years, waiting for God to do me a favor. And He ain't listening." Evans risks his life, not because he has an overwhelming sense of civic or moral responsibility, but because he is living at the mercy of institutional forces beyond his control. Mangold felt that 21st century Americans could easily identify with "with the hesitancy and thwarting of what modern life, and family life, can be, and earning and holding the respect of your wife and children, and how hard that can be in a world filled with compromise and power greater than your own."[17] Dan is doing the job because it is the only way he can support his family—at least, the only "honest" way.

The outlaw Ben Wade represents the alternative: survival of the fittest. "It's man's nature to take what he wants," Wade chides Evans. Over the course of the film, the charming villain offers the reluctant hero many opportunities to walk away from the job and still make the money he needs. Evans refuses, silently confessing that there is more at stake than financial or even physical survival. He is fighting for his own self-respect, and for one thing more. In the end, Evans risks his life so that his boy will know what it means to be a hero. His actions convey the message that being right is not a bulletproof vest, but being alive is not enough to live for. Even Ben Wade understands that message, and Dan's sacrifice ultimately transforms him as well.

By the time the credits roll, Mangold's *3:10 to Yuma* has thoroughly dismissed simple-minded ideas about heroes and villains. The filmmaker insists that it is exactly this type of real-world ambiguity that has always defined the great westerns. "I think part of the reason people have tuned out of the western is this assumption that it actually isn't borne out by reality," he says, arguing that the most famous westerns were never "simplistic stories":

> The traditional westerns are really mistyped as bad guy/good guy movies. Most of them, you go back, who's the bad guy and good guy in *Shane*? Shane's a killer but he saves the family. Jack Palance wants some office property. Is he bad? Is he good? Everything is gray in the great westerns. *The Searchers*, is John Wayne a good guy or a bad guy? [...] *3:10 to Yuma*, 1957, that's not a movie about clear-cut good guys and bad guys. *Rio Grande*, *Rio Lobo*, on and on I could go. These are all movies about the gray between good and bad.[18]

Mangold's argument suggests that the popularity of the western depends less on a ready-made formula than on the way that thoughtful storytellers interpret those formulas. As film critic Robin Wood once pointed out, genre films offer "a collection of convenient conventions which allow the director to escape from the trammels of contemporary surface reality and the demand for verisimilitude, and express certain fundamental human urges or explore themes personal to him."[19] A serious filmmaker embraces the conventions and transforms them, making them his own. Or, to quote filmmaker Jean Renoir: "The

Black hat Russell Crowe and white hat Christian Bale explore shades of gray in *3:10 to Yuma* (2007, Lionsgate).

marvelous thing about westerns is they are all the same movie. That gives a director unlimited freedom."[20]

Mangold concludes that too many modern-day western filmmakers lazily pander to audience expectations or outright reject the formulas and conventions that are the basic strength of the genre. The former tendency produces a mélange of western movie clichés: "a movie about movies" instead of "a movie about the characters on the screen." The latter produces historical epics with all the trappings of a western but none of the spirit. The director sums up his western movie ideal: "My feeling is that they are a kind of fever dream of America. [...] They are American yearnings and fears, angst and quests laid out in a kind of really beautifully barren and pure landscape that allows these themes to resonate in ways that they can't in other settings."[21]

"Fever dream" is an apt description for writer/director Andrew Dominik's *The Assassination of Jesse James by the Coward Robert Ford*, a psychological western in the tradition of Samuel Fuller (*I Shot Jesse James*) and a meditative western in the tradition of Terrence Malick (*Badlands, Days of Heaven*). Dominik's film, based on the novel by Ron Hansen, ruminates on violence at the heart of American celebrity culture by unraveling the relationship between legendary outlaw Jesse James and his murderer Robert Ford. Throughout the film, the outlaw (played by A-list celebrity Brad Pitt) remains reliably mercurial: alternately playful and murderous, nonchalant and suicidal. He is a man haunted by self-contradictions as well as glaring discrepancies between his personal life and public legend. Because Jesse James seems like a walking enigma, young gun Robert Ford is drawn to him like a star-struck fanboy mooning over an untouchable tabloid celebrity. When Jesse rejects his affections, Ford responds with the hellish fury of a fan scorned. The subsequent coda about an outlaw trapped within his own notoriety is as old as the 1950 western *The Gunfighter*, while the story of a culture that obsessively creates and destroys its legends is as current as the morning news.

No Country for Old Men is an equally sobering meditation on violence in 21st century America. Based on a novel by Cormac McCarthy, the film juxtaposes three characters—in western terms: the Good, the Bad and the Ugly. The Good is sheriff Ed Tom Bell, a world-weary Texas lawman struggling to understand cultural changes taking place on the U.S./Mexico border during the drug wars of the early 1980s. The Bad is sociopathic criminal Anton Chigurh, a killer who lives by a personal code that leaves no room for sympathy or morality. Void of human feeling, he stalks the borderlands like an agent of cruel or indifferent Fate. The Ugly is Llewelyn Moss, a decent and capable everyman with a tragic flaw: greed. The story is mostly about what might happen if these three men collide.

No Country for Old Men is also a film about colliding genres. Ed Tom Bell embodies the sadness of traditional western hero in an amoral world. He is baffled when he encounters Anton Chigurh, an apocalyptic horror movie villain like Leatherface in *The Texas Chainsaw Massacre* (1974) or "The Shape" in John Carpenter's *Halloween* (1978). Bell realizes that he can no more reason with Chigurh than one could reason with a flood or a hurricane. Afraid that a confrontation with the man will shatter his already-tenuous faith in God, Bell abandons the chase, leaving Chigurh at large—an enduring symbol of a country that (according to the would-be hero in the film's feverish final scene) has become too randomly violent to support the only kind of idealism he understands. Director Joel Coen reflects: "The stuff about things getting worse is very interesting. How much of that perspective on things is old age talking, and how much is true? Cormac put in Bell's conversation with his uncle, which we always felt was the center of the story;

Javier Bardem is apocalyptic horror movie villain Anton Chigurh in *No Country for Old Men* (2007, Paramount).

it suggests 'This is just the world, it's not anything new.' But if you were living in Germany in 1939 and said things were getting worse, you'd be right. So it's not just old age."²² Coen is not suggesting that America in 1980 or 2007 is comparable to Germany in 1939, but rather that conscionable citizens—in any place and time—have to pay close attention to the moral and ethical struggles that define their culture.

No Country for Old Men resonated strongly with film critics and audiences in 2007, perhaps because it captured the moral fatigue of the final years of the George W. Bush presidency. By that point, it was clear to most Americans that gung-ho patriotism could not win the War on Terror. In place of the classic western myth, *No Country* offered a nihilistic vision of a future determined by random, uncontrollable forces, instead of a future crafted by a singular sense of destiny. McCarthy's story is a eulogy, delivered by the world-weary hero, and it reads like this:

> I think I know where we're headed. We're bein bought with our own money. And it aint just the drugs. There is fortunes bein accumulated out there that they don't nobody even know about. What do we think is going to come of that money? Money that can buy whole countries. It done has. Can it buy this one? I don't think so. But it will put you in bed with people you ought not to be there with. It's not even a law enforcement problem. I doubt that it ever was. There's always been narcotic. But people don't just up and decide to dope theirselves for no reason. By the millions. I don't have no answer about that. In particular I don't have no answer to take heart from.²³

There Will Be Blood, released in the final days of 2007, played out this set of ideas like a ready-made sequel. Loosely based on Upton Sinclair's 1927 novel *Oil!*, the film presents petroleum as America's drug of choice—another timely observation, with several wars raging in the Middle East. Just as *No Country for Old Men* partly told the story of a man undone by greed, so *There Will Be Blood* revolves around a prospector who sells his soul for black gold. Daniel Day-Lewis's oil prospector Daniel Plainview eagerly presents himself as a community leader, but the truth is that he's a misanthrope who only wants to build a personal empire of money and power. "I have a *competition* in me," he confesses, and adds, "I want no one else to succeed. I hate most people [...] I want to earn enough money [so] I can get away from everyone." In time he becomes the traditional western villain: a ruthless capitalist. In *There Will Be Blood*, however, there is no hero to counterbalance this villain's destructive appetite. We, the audience, are at his mercy.

Plainview's only nemesis, or sparring partner, is an opportunistic young preacher named Eli Sunday, who also knowingly exploits the people around him in order to build his own empire. So long as an alliance can be mutually beneficial, Plainview and Sunday tolerate each other, but (as the film's title promises) this matchup between capitalism and Christianity can only end in violence. The final scene is a haunting parallel to the ending of the classic western *My Darling Clementine*: The tough, single-minded outsider, having exploited and abandoned the community he claimed to serve, withdraws again into solitude. *There Will Be Blood* is, like the urban westerns and horror-westerns of the 1970s, a post-frontier parable of the bleakest kind. When Daniel Plainview says "I'm finished," what he means is that there are no more worlds left to conquer. His empire is complete. He has fulfilled his dark destiny.

There Will Be Blood might have seemed like another tombstone for the American western film—except that, for many viewers, it wasn't a western. More than three decades of revisionist westerns, anti-westerns, alternative westerns and post-westerns have not been able to definitively squelch the myth of the heroic gunslinger. In 2008, the year that president Barack Obama was elected on a wave of hope for the future, actor/director Ed

Harris made *Appaloosa*, a thoroughly traditional western. Harris's character, Virgil Cole, is the quintessential American cowboy hero: simple, honest, righteous, duty-bound, and deadly. He is Wyatt Earp in *My Darling Clementine*, and his sidekick Everett Hitch is as cool and as loyal as Doc Holliday. Together, these two town-tamers confront the usual problems: greed, corruption, and lawlessness. Things don't go exactly as planned, but each man remains true to his ideals. Virgil serves the law, and Everett breaks the law in order to serve his friend. The film ends on this note of self-sacrifice, and thus on the traditional suggestion that self-sacrifice is the defining act of a western hero.

Clint Eastwood came to the same conclusion in his 2008 film *Gran Torino*. Although not a western, the film is (so far) the final film that Eastwood both directed and starred in, making it a significant addendum to the filmmaker's personal mythology. *Gran Torino*'s main character, Walt Kowalski, is a semi-parodic extension of Eastwood's gruffest characters. On the surface, he's a bitter, racist curmudgeon, psychologically scarred by his long-ago service in the Korean War. Beneath that icy exterior, however, he's got a soft heart. Like the Man with No Name (in *A Fistful of Dollars*) and Dirty Harry, he fights for innocents who can't protect themselves. At the same time, like the outlaw Josey Wales, he genuinely wants to overcome his overwhelming impulses toward violence. Unlike Will Munny (in *Forgiven*), he eventually finds another way. Walt Kowalski walks into in a western-style shootout with no gun—and that is precisely how he saves himself and his surrogate son.

If *Gran Torino* is the latest in a long line of final acts for the cinematic westerner, the Coen Brothers' 2010 remake of *True Grit* is something of a postmortem. The filmmakers knew from the beginning that they were treading on sacred ground, that their project (or at least, the critical responses to their project) would be haunted by the ghost of Hollywood's ultimate cowboy. Rather than address that fact, they consciously avoided rewatching the 1969 film that earned John Wayne his Oscar, and based their film solely on Charles Portis's source novel.[24] Compared to its predecessor, the new *True Grit* is less a film about a western hero than a coming-of-age narrative. The film presents the Old West through the eyes of Mattie Ross, just as *Shane* presented an idealized West through the eyes of young Joey Starrett. Unlike Joey, however, Mattie sees her western hero as a flesh-and-blood human being. Jeff Bridges's Rooster Cogburn is vulgar, boorish and

Jeff Bridges as Rooster Cogburn in the remake of *True Grit* (2010, Paramount).

patronizing—a flawed hero, to be sure—but he nevertheless restores her faith in people by risking his life to save her. In its biggest departure from the 1969 adaptation, the film ends on a solemn note, emphasizing the hero's mortality rather than his mystique. But what resonates for Mattie Ross, after she awakens from her fever dream, is the *vitality* of her memories. The same was true for audiences. *True Grit* became the most commercially and critically successful western of the 21st century.

So far.

Afterword
Destiny or Dust?

> *Throughout the history of the motion picture industry, western films have served as the staple entertainment commodity despite the multitude of vogues and changes. And westerns will become more and more popular as time goes on. Time itself enhances the color and adventure of a form of life in the United States that will never be lived again. Already the western has become a form of folklore, based primarily on the American pioneer spirit. As technological achievements bring us closer and closer to push-button automation, the need for the western film for complete escape will become more apparent.*
> —Budd Boetticher

Since the 1920s, people have been declaring the western dead. Most of these pronouncements have been about the commercial viability of films set in a specific historical milieu and dealing with specific types of conflicts between cowboys and Indians, lawmen and badmen, heroic gunslingers and dangerous outsiders. More thoughtful examinations suggest a broader definition of the genre, exploring a wide assortment of variations on familiar formulas and themes. These variations are prolific enough that, a decade and a half into the 21st century, it is difficult to determine precisely where the western genre begins and ends. Like most film genres, the western thrives by mutation. As a result, for many filmmakers and viewers, the western is no longer an embodiment of a distinct American mythology so much as a platform for deconstruction and reconstruction—no longer a collective vision, but a heap of potentially revelatory fragments.

The most popular Hollywood western in recent years, Quentin Tarantino's *Django Unchained* (2012), is a sophisticated mash-up of spaghetti westerns and blaxploitation movies. It offers, rather than a celebratory western narrative (Tarantino has made it clear that he has no love for John Ford's vision of America), an incendiary slave narrative that explodes in righteous anger. Other recent western hybrids like *Jonah Hex* (2010), *Cowboys and Aliens* (2011), *Rango* (2011), *John Carter* (2012) and *The Lone Ranger* (2013) have tried to capture the same anarchic energy without much success, while hidden westerns like Nicolas Winding Refn's *Drive* (2011) and contemporary western TV series like FX's *Justified* (2010–2015) and A&E's *Longmire* (2012–2015) testify to the vitality of the form.

In spite of its persistent identity crisis, the Hollywood western is still alive and kicking, as evidenced by the largest crop of big-budget oaters in decades: Tommy Lee Jones's *The Homesman* (2014), *Slow West* (2015) starring Michael Fassbender; Tarantino's *The Hateful Eight* (2015); *24* producer/director Jon Cassar's *Forsaken* (2015) starring Kiefer

Sutherland; *The Revenant* (2016) starring Leonardo DiCaprio; *Bone Tomahawk* (2016) starring Kurt Russell; *Jane Got a Gun* (2016) starring Natalie Portman; Ti West's *In a Valley of Violence* (2016); Antoine Fuqua's remake of *The Magnificent Seven* (2016) and HBO's serialization of *Westworld* (2016). If the genre has lost its original sense of destiny, it is nevertheless a genre returned from the dust. As to what the future holds for this new wave of range riders, only time will tell.

Appendix: Filming Locations

Hollywood, California

There are not many remnants of the Old West in Hollywood. Even in the early days, filmmakers found it difficult to pass off Tinseltown as a wild western frontier.

History enthusiasts will want to visit the **Hollywood Heritage Museum**, the symbolic birthplace of Hollywood. The museum features a wealth of silent-era memorabilia and is housed in the old Lasky-DeMille Barn, first featured in Cecil B. DeMille's 1914 western film *The Squaw Man*. At the time the film was made, the barn sat on the corner of Selma and Vine Streets in Hollywood. It was later moved to the Paramount Pictures studio backlot (where according to one filmmaker, it served as a gym), and then to its present site on Highland Avenue, across from the Hollywood Bowl. The non-profit Hollywood Heritage organization runs the museum, and also hosts special events, silent movie screenings and historic walking tours of nearby Hollywood Boulevard.

The best resource for information on the history of the Old West is the **Gene Autry National Center of the American West**, adjacent to Griffith Park. Permanent installations include the "Imagination Gallery," which presents classic western films within 20th century historical context.

Also in Griffith Park is the famous **Bronson Canyon** cave. This is where John Wayne rescued Natalie Wood at the end of *The Searchers* (1956). It is also where Gene Autry descended into an underground civilization in the sci-fi/western serial *The Phantom Empire* (1935). Harry Medved says that the canyon has "suited hundreds of TV and movie westerns including *Carson City* (1952), *Massacre Canyon* (1954) and *Thunder Pass* (1954)," but the location is best known from appearances in countless science-fiction films, including *Invasion of the Body Snatchers* (1956), as well as the *Batman* TV series (1966–1968).

Western fans may also want to visit the nearby **Gower Gulch Sunset Shopping Center**. The western décor memorializes this intersection's historic reputation as a meeting place for authentic cowboys who aspired to be in the film business. John Wayne, Gary Cooper and many others got their start here in the 1930s, when "Gower Gulch" was conveniently located between the headquarters for Columbia Pictures (now Sunset Gower Studios) and Monogram Pictures (now KCET). Many of Columbia's westerns—including *High Noon* (1952)—were shot on a backlot off Hollywood Way in Burbank, which is now part of Warner Bros. Many of Monogram's westerns were shot at Republic Studios in Studio City, now the CBS Studio Center. Neither Warner Bros. nor Columbia currently has a western street set. (David Rothel was apparently one of the last people to visit the Republic western street before it was demolished in 1988. He claims that the street's last onscreen appearance was in *Michael Jackson's Moonwalker*.)

Universal Studios does still have a functioning western street set. "Six Points, Texas" is featured in several studio films starring James Stewart, including *Destry Rides Again* (1939) and *Winchester '73* (1950), and several of Audie Murphy's best westerns, including *No Name on the Bullet* (1959). Tourists on the studio tram tour can catch a glimpse of the street, along with the nearby Mexican village set, prominently featured in *Invitation to a Gunfighter* (1964) and more recently in the Brad Pitt vehicle *The Mexican* (2001).

Santa Monica Mountains, Conejo Valley and Simi Valley, California

Paramount Ranch in the Santa Monica Mountains is home one of the most impressive western movie sets in Los Angeles. And, thanks to the National Park Service, it's open to the public! Well preserved from a lengthy stint as the setting of the TV series *Dr. Quinn, Medicine Woman* (1993–1998), Paramount's western town is a reconstruction of an earlier set that was located closer to the present-day Ventura Freeway. The earlier set was featured in the first screen adaptation of the classic tale *The Virginian* (1929), and John A. Murray claims that it also appeared in *The Plainsman* (1936), *Wells Fargo* (1937) and *Gunfight at the O.K. Corral* (1957). Most recently, the ranch was featured in *Bone Tomahawk* (2015).

Just down the road is **Malibu Creek State Park**, which was once the 20th Century–Fox Ranch. The studio built a Welsh mining village near the present-day parking lot for John Ford's *How Green Was My Valley* (1940) and an Ape Village near Century Lake for *Planet of the Apes* (1968). In the years between, several notable westerns were shot on site, including *Viva Zapata!* (1952), *Broken Lance* (1954), *The Proud Ones* (1956), *Love Me Tender* (1956), *The True Story of Jesse James* (1957), *Flaming Star* (1960) and *Ride the High Country* (1962), as well as the western TV series *Broken Arrow* (1956–1958) and *Daniel Boone* (1964–1970). According to Harry Medved, Marlon Brando's Zapata was marched to prison on Crag's Road, and rescued by peasants who swarmed the adjacent hillside. The famous river-jump scene in *Butch Cassidy and the Sundance Kid* (1969) was staged on the opposite side of Crag's Road, at Century Lake.

Warner Bros. had its own movie ranch in nearby Calabasas, near the present-day **Calabasas Country Club**. Jerry L. Schneider says that the ranch included two western streets, one built for *Dodge City* (1939) and another built for *San Antonio* (1945), as well as a Mexican town built for *Juarez* (1939). Other westerns shot on this property include *The Oklahoma Kid* (1939) with James Cagney, *Colorado Territory* (1949) with Joel McCrea, all of Errol Flynn's subsequent westerns and nearly all of Randolph Scott's early 1950s westerns. Among the last films shot there were *The Left-Handed Gun* (1958) with Paul Newman and *One-Eyed Jacks* (1961) with Marlon Brando.

During the 1930s and 1940s, Warner Bros. filmed scenes for some of its biggest westerns at nearby Lasky Mesa/Barrett Ranch, on land that was later incorporated into the **Upper Las Virgenes Canyon Open Space Preserve**. Lasky Mesa was named for its onscreen appearance in producer Jesse Lasky's *The Thundering Herd* (1925). The location later provided epic vistas for *The Charge of the Light Brigade* (1936), Custer's Last Stand in *They Died with Their Boots On* (1941) and the horsemen's revolt in *Duel in the Sun* (1948). (For a more comprehensive list, see Carlo Gaberscek and Kenny Stier's *In Search of Western Movie Sites*.)

Adjacent to the Upper Las Virgenes Preserve is **Cheseboro/Palo Comado Canyon**, which includes land that used to be part of the Agoura/Albertson Ranch. Tinsley Yarbrough identifies this as a filming location used in *Brigham Young* (1940) as well as the site of Gene Autry's "Radio Ranch" in *The Phantom Empire* serial (1935). Further north and east inside the Cheseboro/Palo Comado park is an area called China Flat. Accessible via a hiking trail off of Lindero Canyon Road, China Flat served as the location for the McFly farm in *Back to the Future Part III* (1990).

Further north in Simi Valley, **Big Sky Movie Ranch** is a private ranch featured in several western TV series, including *Gunsmoke* (1955–1975) and *Rawhide* (1959–1965). More recently, it provided settings for *Django Unchained* (2013).

Further west, near the town of Thousand Oaks, is **Wildwood Regional Park**. Formerly part of the Janss Conejo Ranch, this site was (according to Harry Medved) a filming location for *The Left-Handed Gun* (1958), *Flaming Star* (1960), *The Man Who Shot Liberty Valance* (1962) and *Cheyenne Autumn* (1964), along with countless hours of TV westerns. According to Jerry Schneider, a western town was built nearby on the future site of California Lutheran University for the film *Welcome to Hard Times* (1967). Boyd Magers has suggested that the town set existed as early as 1947, and on the southwest edge (rather than northeast) of Wildwood park. Tinsley Yarbrough mediates, identifying this secondary location as "North Ranch" and stating that it was also used for *Texas Across the River* (1966) and *Firecreek* (1968).

Also in Thousand Oaks is the **Joel and Frances McCrea Ranch**—not a filming location, but a real working ranch where the iconic western actor and his favorite actress lived from 1933 until their deaths. In 2004, the McCrea family donated 225 acres of the ranch, including the family home, to the Conejo Recreation and Park District. The ranch opened to the public in 2011.

West of the Santa Monica Mountains, there is one more important western movie location. **Santa Catalina Island** is visible from the coast of Malibu, which has made it an attractive getaway for Hollywood players since the early 1900s. D.W. Griffith shot a film here in 1911, and the first Catalina western (a Tom Mix movie) was made in 1920. According to Lee Rosenthal, filmmakers imported twenty-four bison to the island for the filming of the Zane Grey western *The Vanishing American* (1925). When filming was completed, the filmmakers released the bison into the wild. In the following years Catalina was used mostly as a South Seas locale, but the island interior now has a healthy bison population to match its rugged western-ready terrain.

Chatsworth, Santa Clarita and Antelope Valley, California

Iverson Ranch was once the most famous western movie ranch in Los Angeles. Located in the far northwest corner of the San Fernando Valley, far from the action of Hollywood, its distinctive rock formations—particularly the Lone Ranger Rock (which appears at the end of every episode of the long-running TV series) and the Garden of the Gods (which appears in countless western movies, including John Ford's *Stagecoach*,

The Oklahoma Kid with James Cagney, *The Man from Colorado* with Glenn Ford, *Tall Man Riding* with Randolph Scott, and Roger Corman's directorial debut *Five Guns West*)—are instantly recognizable. Today the ranch has been developed completely into residential communities. The famous rock formations of Lower Iverson remain accessible via Red Mesa Drive, thanks to the efforts of the Santa Susanna Conservancy, but Middle and Upper Iverson (as well as the neighboring Brandeis Ranch) belong to a gated community on the north side of the Ronald Reagan Freeway. Much has been written about the ranch over the years, with Robert G. Sherman producing the most comprehensive history so far.

Corriganville Regional Park earned its name in 1937, when B western actor Ray "Crash" Corrigan bought property on the edge of Simi Valley and promoted it as a movie ranch. Dozens of B westerns were filmed there in the late 1930s and 1940s, including several films starring John Wayne, who later returned to shoot the elaborate *Fort Apache* (1948). Buoyed by the success of that film, Corrigan converted the ranch into one of the most popular amusement parks in the United States. Corriganville Movie Ranch remained active as a filming location—hosting films like *The Man from Colorado* (1948), *The Baron of Arizona* (1949), *Escape from Fort Bravo* (1953), and *The Naked Dawn* (1955)—until it closed in 1966, the year that *Billy the Kid Meets Dracula* and *Jesse James Meets Frankenstein's Daughter* were shot on the property. Most of the remaining sets were destroyed by wildfire in 1970. Today the park is preserved and maintained by the Rancho Simi and Park Recreation District, which has posted historical markers at the most iconic sites—Silvertown (the main western street), Vendetta Village (built for the Howard Hughes film *Vendetta* in 1946), Fort Apache (constructed on a plateau called Table Mountain, above Silvertown), Canyon Rock, Hideout Rock and Robin Hood Lake. Jerry Schneider has chronicled the rise and fall of Corriganville, and the man who created it, in a series of publications under the banner of his Corriganville Press.

On the northern edge of the San Fernando Valley, the Newhall Pass provides a thoroughfare to the Santa Clarita Valley, where silent western stars William S. Hart and Harry Carey made their homes (accessible to the public as the **William S. Hart Ranch and Museum,** and **Tesoro Adobe Historic Park**) and where many movie ranches have sprung up over the years.

Western fans may be interested in a particular feature of the pass, just off of the Old Sierra Highway, called **Beale's Cut**. This distinctive location was a favorite of director John Ford, who used it in *Straight Shooting* (1917), *The Iron Horse* (1924), and *Stagecoach* (1939).

Also nearby is the unlikely ghost town of **Mentryville**, home to the first commercially successful oil well in the United States as well as a 13-room Victorian mansion featured in the John Wayne film *The Lonely Trail* (1937), the Roy Rogers vehicle *Days of Jesse James* (1939), and more recently in the TV series *Big Love* (2006–2011).

The most famous movie ranch in Santa Clarita is **Melody Ranch**. Primarily used by the so-called poverty row studios in the 1930s and 1940s, it was known as Monogram Ranch and Placeritos Ranch, it was purchased and renamed by singing cowboy Gene Autry in 1952. Over the course of the following decade, the property became the primary shooting location for several western TV series. It was also featured in several films, including *Stranger on Horseback* (1955) and *Wichita* (1955) with Joel McCrea, *Man of the West* (1958) with Gary Cooper, and *Last Train from Gun Hill* (1959) with Kirk Douglas and Anthony Quinn. In 1962, many of the old movie sets were destroyed by wildfire and filming was less frequent in the following years. In 1991, Renaud and Andre Veluzat purchased and restored the ranch. The reconstructed western street was featured in *Maverick* (1994), *Wild Bill* (1995), *Last Man Standing* (1996), *Django Unchained* (2013) and the TV series *Deadwood* (2004–2006). Today Melody Ranch is closed to the public, except for one Saturday every spring, when the Veluzats invite the public to their annual Santa Clarita Cowboy Festival on the property.

Renaud and Andre Veluzat also own and operate two other private movie ranches in the Santa Clarita Valley, **Blue Cloud Ranch** and **Veluzat Movie Ranch**. The latter has a Mexican village set that was featured in *El Diablo* (1990), *Wild Bill* (1995) and *Last Man Standing* (1996), among other films.

Some additional scenes for *Wild Bill* (1995) were filmed north of the Santa Clarita Valley, at privately-owned **Tejon Ranch,** the largest working ranch in California.

Just south of Santa Clarita, in Placerita Canyon, are several small ranches that were used for filming in the heyday of the Hollywood western. The only one accessible to the public is Walker Ranch, now the **Placerita Canyon Natural Area**. Visitors can see the Oak of the Golden Dream, the site of the first California gold discovery in 1842, and the historic Walker Cabin, featured in a plethora of B westerns in the 1930s and 1940s.

Adjacent to the old Walker Ranch is **Disney's Golden Oak Ranch**, which had its own western street from 1978 (when it was created for *Roots II*) until 2008, when the street made its final appearance in *Prairie Fever* (2008). In the late 1990s, Disney bought the adjacent Andy Jauregui Ranch and incorporated it into Golden Oak.

Also nearby are **Sable Ranch** and **Rancho Maria**, both owned by the same family. The latter has a small western street, originally built (according to Tinsley Yarbrough) for the TV movie *Gambler III: The Legend Continues* (1987).

East of Placerita Canyon, along highway 14 in the town of Agua Dulce, is one of the most famous movie locations in Hollywood history. **Vasquez Rocks Natural Area Park**, named for the notorious bandit Tiburcio Vasquez (who reputedly roamed these hills in the 1870s), made one of its earliest onscreen appearances in the Bob Steele western *The Land of Missing Men* (1930). Over the years the distinctive rock formations have been featured in a variety of films, including *Law and Order* (1932), *The Arizonian* (1935), *The Outlaw* (1943), *Along Came Jones* (1945), *Whispering Smith* (1948), *The Duel at Silver Creek* (1952), *Apache* (1954), *The Lonely Man* (1957), *Gunfight at Dodge City* (1959), *Skin Game* (1971), *The Magnificent Seven Ride!* (1972), *Blazing Saddles* (1974), *Hearts of the West* (1975), *Spacehunter: Adventures in the Forbidden Zone* (1983), *Hell Comes to Frogtown* (1987), *Star Trek* (2009) and *John Carter* (2012). Vasquez has also appeared in dozens of TV series. The park is open to the public, and an inviting visitor's center was completed in 2013.

Antelope Valley is a prime location for films about desolation. According to Tinsley Yarbrough, sparsely-populated Lake Los Angeles was used as a filming location for numerous westerns, including *MacKenna's Gold* (1964), in which Gregory Peck and Omar Shariff are attacked by the cavalry amid the Lovejoy Buttes. **Saddleback Butte State Park** offers easy hiking access.

While you're in the neighborhood, check out the **Antelope Valley Indian Museum State Historic Park**, featured in *The Magnificent Seven Ride!* (1972) and *The Stone Killer* (1973) with Charles Bronson.

Mojave Desert, Eastern Sierras and Beyond, California

Along state highway 14, south of the Eastern Sierras, is **Red Rock Canyon State Park**. Hollywood filmmakers began making the long trek to the picturesque site as early as 1925, when *Wild Horse Canyon* was shot there. Owner Rudolf Bart Hagen quickly recognized a business opportunity and, over the following decades, more than a hundred films (including many westerns) were shot on his family property before it became a state park in 1968. Richard J. Schmidt provides a comprehensive list of the films, and detailed maps to the areas in which they were shot. The films include *Stagecoach* (1939), *Four Faces West* (1948) with Joel McCrea, Val Lewton's *Apache Drums* (1951), *Along the Great Divide* (1951) with Kirk Douglas, *Law and Order* (1953) with Ronald Reagan, *Tumbleweed* (1953) with Audie Murphy, *The Bounty Hunter* (1954) with Randolph Scott, *Man of the West* (1958) with Gary Cooper, *The Big Country* (1958) with Gregory Peck, and *Westworld* (1973) with Yul Brynner.

Further north, along state highway 395, is the town of Lone Pine, home of the **Alabama Hills**. Perhaps no landscape is more familiar to western movie fans than these bold and beautiful foothills between the High Sierra mountains and the lowlands of Death Valley. Hollywood first discovered the location in 1920 (when the Fatty Arbuckle short *The Roundup* was filmed there), and it wasn't long before the distinctive hills became part of the iconography of the screen western, through the B movies of stars like William Boyd, Roy Rogers, Gene Autry, and Tim Holt, and films like *Frontier Marshal* (1939), *Tombstone: The Town Too Tough to Die* (1942), *West of the Pecos* (1945), *Yellow Sky* (1948), *Bad Day at Black Rock* (1955), *Seven Men from Now* (1956), *The Tall T* (1957), *3:10 to Yuma* (1957), *From Hell to Texas* (1958), *Hell Bent for Leather* (1960), *How the West Was Won* (1962), *Showdown* (1963), and *Joe Kidd* (1972). Many of these films were shot on "movie road," and Dave Holland has written an incomparable pictorial guide to that area. If you prefer an in-person tour of the Alabama Hills, you can attend the annual Lone Pine Film Festival, which takes place every October. Be sure to stay at the Dow Villa Hotel (where the stars stayed) and plan to spend your nights watching movies at the Lone Pine History Museum.

Southeast of Lone Pine is **Owens Dry Lake** (bled dry by the Los Angeles Aqueduct in 1924) and the **Olancha Sand Dunes**. According to Carlo Gaberscek and Kenny Stier, the former was featured in *Westward Ho!* (1935) with John Wayne, as well as Henry Hathaway's *From Hell to Texas* (1958) and *Nevada Smith* (1966). The latter appeared in Raoul Walsh's *Along the Great Divide* (1951) as well as Budd Boetticher's *Seven Men from Now* (1956) and *Ride Lonesome* (1959). The nearby ghost towns of Cerro Gordo and Dolemite can be glimpsed in the opening of *Nevada Smith*.

Death Valley National Park needs no introduction. Its forbidding name conveys the place's reputation as a no-man's land, named by a band of unlucky pioneers who got stranded there in the summer of 1849. Death Valley has always been full of haunting mystery and mythic beauty, which is why Hollywood filmmakers have been going there since 1923, when Erich von Stroheim made *Greed* on site at Badwater, the lowest elevation in the continental United States. Many years later, a couple of "space cowboys" looked down on the same area from Dante's View in *Star Wars* (1977). Equally popular among filmmakers are the rolling dunes of Stovepipe Wells, featured in *Yellow Sky* (1948), *The*

Walking Hills (1949), *Along the Great Divide* (1951) and *Ride Lonesome* (1959). Zabriskie Point, made famous by a Michelangelo Antonioni film of the same name, appears in *The Law and Jake Wade* (1958) and at the beginning of *One-Eyed Jacks* (1961). Golden Canyon appears in John Sturges's *Escape from Fort Bravo* (1953), and The Devil's Golf Course appears in *The Professionals* (1966). For the most comprehensive overview of Death Valley, see John Ford's *Three Godfathers* (1948), which features locations throughout the park.

A bit further north on 395, and at a much higher elevation, the **Mammoth Lakes** region hosted Hollywood filmmakers as early as the 1920s. Carlo Gaberscek and Kenny Stier note that Convict Lake was featured in *The Return of Frank James* (1940) as well as several Henry Hathaway films: *Nevada Smith* (1966), *How the West Was Won* (1962), and *Shoot Out* (1971). Harry Medved adds *Will Penny* (1967) to the list, but Gaberscek and Stier suggest that most of the scenes for that film were shot further north, in the Bishop area. Mammoth's Twin Falls Picnic Area and Horseshoe Lake were featured briefly in Sam Peckinpah's *Ride the High Country* (1962).

Scenes for *Nevada Smith* (where Steve McQueen meets his mentor and later has a showdown with his nemesis) and *True Grit* (where John Wayne and company first encounter the outlaws they're tracking at a rustic cabin) were filmed at nearby **Hot Creek Geological Site**, a favorite filming location of director Henry Hathaway. The natural spring was also featured in Hathaway's *From Hell to Texas* (1958), *North to Alaska* (1960), and *Shoot Out* (1971).

On the opposite side of 395, **Convict Lake** hosted an additional scene in *Nevada Smith* (where McQueen learns how to play cards) as well as the opening scene in *How the West Was Won* (1964). Convict Lake, named for events recounted in the 1951 film *The Secret of Convict Lake*, is a particularly popular destination in October, when photographers swarm the Eastern Sierras to capture fall colors.

Further north along 395 is the vast and otherworldly **Mono Lake**. Western fans will want to visit the south shores of the lake, off of Mono Lake Basin Road, to see the salty shores where Clint Eastwood built a ghost town (and painted it red) for *High Plains Drifter* (1973). The set is long gone, but there is a real ghost town just north of the lake.

Bodie State Historic Park was founded as a gold mining town in 1859. By 1915, it was being labeled as a ghost town, and by the 1940s it was all but abandoned. Despite its authentic beauty, Hollywood has shown only a passing interest in it. A few scenes for *Hell's Heroes* (1930), an early adaptation of Peter B. Kyne's novel *The Three Godfathers* (later adapted by John Ford), were filmed here. In 1962, Bodie became a state park. Since then it has been preserved in a state of "arrested decay," and it remains one of the most impressive remnants of the Old West in California. There are several books on the history of Bodie, including *Big Bad Bodie: High Sierra Ghost Town* by Doug Brodie and James Watson, and *Bodie's Gold: Tall Tales and True History from a California Mining Town*, by Marguerite Sprague.

Relatively few films have been shot at California's best-known park, **Yosemite National Park**, but there are some noteworthy examples, from the 1920 adaptation of *The Last of the Mohicans* to the 1994 remake of *Maverick* (which features Mel Gibson swindling a tourist at Washburn Point). Harry Medved notes that the opening sequence of *Star Trek 5: The Final Frontier* (1989) was filmed near the wide side opening of the Wawona Tunnel.

On the other side of Yosemite, west of the Sierras, location seekers will find three filming locations from the classic western *High Noon* (1952). The opening scenes of the film were shot at Iverson Ranch and most of the western street scenes were filmed at the Columbia Ranch, but some scenes were also shot on location at **Columbia State Historic Park**, a well-preserved mining town. **St. Joseph's Catholic Church** in nearby Tuolumne City is where Gary Cooper's weary sheriff appealed to his fellow citizens for help.

A little further south, at **Railtown 1897 State Historic Park** in Jamestown, visitors can ride the railroad from *High Noon*. The "Sierra Dinner Train," which runs from Railtown to Oakdale, California, has also been featured in *Dodge City* (1939), *Duel in the Sun* (1947), *Man of the West* (1958), *The Great Northfield Minnesota Raid* (1972), *The Long Riders* (1980), *Pale Rider* (1985), *Unforgiven* (1992) and *Bad Girls* (1994), among many others.

According to Tinsley Yarbrough, the historic Hill Valley set was built a few miles southwest of Jamestown for *Back to the Future Part III* (1989). Unfortunately, the set burned down in 1996.

Dedicated location hunters can continue traveling southeast to see one of the few western filming locations with a view of the Pacific Ocean. Marlon Brando set his existential western *One-Eyed Jacks* (1961) along the coastline of the **Monterey Peninsula** ... not far from Clint Eastwood's hotel/restaurant, Mission Ranch, in the mythic-sounding city of Carmel-by-the-Sea.

Inland Empire, California

One of the oft-told clichés about the greater Los Angeles area is that residents are always within easy driving distance of all terrains: coastline to the west, mountains to the north and east, and desert beyond that. Just east of San Bernardino is one of the region's most distinctive getaways. The dense forest and cool temperatures of the San Bernardino National Forest offer the illusion that one is not in Southern California at all. Accordingly, Hollywood filmmakers have gone there to film "northern westerns" and "eastern westerns" such as *The Call of the North* (1914), *The Trail of the Lonesome Pine* (1936), *Brigham Young* (1940), *Northwest Mounted Police* (1940), *The Shepherd of the Hills* (1941), *The Spoilers* (1942), *North to Alaska* (1960), *Paint Your Wagon* (1969), and *Almost Heroes* (1998). Scenes for all of those films were shot in the mountains near **Lake Arrowhead**, **Big Bear Lake** and nearby **Cedar Lake**. David Rothel visited the Cedar Lake mill set, originally constructed for *Lonesome Pine*, in the fall of 1988. His photos were among the last taken of the set before it was torn down. Shay Ranch cabin, featured most prominently in *Brigham Young* and the TV series *Gunsmoke* (1955–1975), still stands on private property owned by the Inn Der Bach.

North and east of the San Bernardino National Forest is the forbidding Mojave Desert. Western fans may be interested in visiting **Lucerne Valley**, as it is one of the many locations featured in John Ford's *Stagecoach* (1939). Yakima Canutt's death-defying stunt sequence, in which he jumps from horse to horse while the team is pulling a stagecoach at top speed, was filmed on the Lucerne Dry Lake bed. This is also the area where Wes Craven filmed his horror-western, *The Hills Have Eyes* (1977).

A bit further north, just east of Barstow, are two locations used by Quentin Tarantino in his horror-western, *From Dusk Till Dawn* (1996). **Peggy Sue's 50s Diner** in Yermo, a Route 66 staple, is where Harvey Keitel's family has lunch at the beginning of the film.

The nearby **Calico Dry Lake Bed** was the location of the film's vampire-friendly strip club, the Titty Twister. For better or worse, the set is no longer there ... but curiosity seekers shouldn't pass up an opportunity to visit the Calico Ghost Town.

Southeast of Lucerne Valley, in Yucca Valley, is a surprisingly little-known filming location known as **Pioneertown**. This is a working town ... but just barely. Built in the 1946 as a filming location, Pioneertown never quite achieved its potential. Several B westerns, often featuring Gene Autry, were shot there over the following years, but today the western street belongs entirely to the residents.

There has been plenty of filming in nearby **Joshua Tree National Park** over the years, but not many westerns (unless you're willing to count Craven's 1985 sequel *The Hills Have Eyes Part II*, which featured the Desert Queen Mine).

The same is true of the **Coachella Valley**. Scenes for Robert Redford's *Tell Them Willie Boy Is Here* (1969) were filmed in the Coachella Valley Preserve, and *The Professionals* (1966) and *The Rare Breed* (1966) featured the Mecca Hills Wilderness/Painted Canyon, but this area remains largely unexplored by Hollywood's mythmakers.

Nevada

Surprisingly, Nevada has not been used frequently as a filming location for A-westerns. One of the first and best-known productions, *The Covered Wagon* (1922), was shot in **Snake Valley**, near the Utah border. In the decades to come, Hollywood filmmakers migrated to the southwest corner of Utah, but mostly stayed away from the rural parts of Nevada.

Much of the filming in the state has been done in and near the urban centers of Reno and Las Vegas. John Huston's *The Misfits* (1961) was firmly rooted in the culture of mid–20th century Nevada, and filmed in **Reno** and nearby Dayton. Prominent locations include the Washoe County Courthouse on Virginia Street, Dayton State Park, and Quail Canyon near Pyramid Lake. The most memorable part of the film is the final sequence, shot in an area off of Route 50, between Dayton and Silver Springs, which has come to be known as Misfits Flat. According to John A. Murray, director John Ford also shot some sequences for his early epic *The Iron Horse* (1924) in this area.

South of Reno, principal filming for John Wayne's final film *The Shootist* (1976) was completed in **Carson City**. The boarding house where Wayne stayed with Lauren Bacall is the Krebs-Peterson House at 500 Mountain Street in the town's historic district. The buggy ride scene was shot at nearby Washoe Lake State Park.

Countless films have been made in **Las Vegas**, but perhaps the most notable western film is *The Electric Horseman* (1980), which stars Robert Redford as a rodeo cowboy at odds with the glitz and glamour of modern-day America.

More awe-inspiring than all the lights of Las Vegas are the natural colors of nearby **Valley of Fire State Park**. Fire Canyon is memorably featured in *The Professionals* (1966), where it stands in for rural Mexico. Other films shot inside the park include *The Stalking Moon* (1968), *The Ballad of Cable Hogue* (1970), *Ulzana's Raid* (1972) and *Bite the Bullet* (1975).

Utah

In contrast to Nevada, Utah has an extensive history as a filming location, especially for westerns. James V. D'Arc has written the definitive book on moviemaking in Utah. His history begins with the filming of the Tom Mix western *The Deadwood Coach* (1924) at **Zion National Park** and **Bryce Canyon National Park**. Subsequent films made in these areas included *Arizona Bound* (1927) and *Nevada* (1927) starring Gary Cooper.

In the following years, several B westerns—including *Ramrod* (1947) with Joel McCrea—were shot in the ghost town of **Grafton**, just outside of Zion National Park. The town's most famous onscreen appearance, however, was in the 1969 megahit *Butch Cassidy and the Sundance Kid*. This is where Paul Newman and Katharine Ross ride a bike to the tune of Burt Bacharach and Hal David's "Raindrops Keep Falling on My Head." Today, the town is owned and maintained by the Grafton Heritage Partnership.

At the end of the 1930s, the hub of activity was **Cedar City**. Second-unit filming for Cecil B. DeMille's *Union Pacific* (1939) was accomplished in nearby Iron Springs, a plain west of town, around the same time that John Ford chose nearby Dixie National Forest (east of town) as a primary filming location for *Drums Along the Mohawk* (1939). Second unit filming for *Brigham Young* (1940) was also accomplished on the plains west of Parowan Gap, north of town.

With the increasing popularity of westerns, Hollywood filmmakers moved south to the city of **Kanab**, which became known in some circles as "Little Hollywood." Films shot in or near Kanab include *Western Union* (1941) and *The Desperadoes* (1943) starring Randolph Scott, *In Old Oklahoma* (1943) starring John Wayne, *Buffalo Bill* (1944) starring Joel McCrea, and dozens of others. The most popular filming locations were Johnson Canyon, Kanab Canyon (now known as Angel Canyon) and Old Pariah. Particularly noteworthy is an old town set about 8 miles up Johnson Canyon. Some locals refer to it as the "*Gunsmoke* set," but Tinsley Yarbrough notes that it was originally constructed for *Westward the Women* (1952). The town set is on private property, but visible from the road. Old Pariah also had a western town set—which was featured in *Sergeants Three* (1962), *Duel at Diablo* (1966), *Ride the Whirlwind* (1965), *The Shooting* (1966), and *The Outlaw Josey Wales* (1976)—but it was dismantled years ago. Only one of the buildings was saved, and transplanted to the Little Hollywood Movie Museum in Kanab. The museum, along with the nearby Parry Lodge and the Crescent Moon Theater, is the center of activity for the town's annual Western Legends Roundup festival, which takes place in August.

West of Kanab, near the city of St. George, is another recognizable western setting: **Snow Canyon State Park**. The park is best known as the filming location for *The Conqueror* (1956), a Genghis Khan biopic starring John Wayne, but it was also featured in Sam Fuller's *Run of the Arrow* (1957), Gary Cooper's final film *They Came to Cordura* (1959), *The Appaloosa* (1966) with Marlon Brando, and three late-era Audie Murphy westerns: *Six Black Horses* (1962), *Bullet for a Badman* (1964) and *Gunpoint* (1966). Snow Canyon has also been a popular spot for Robert Redford, who went there to make *Butch Cassidy and the Sundance Kid* (1969), *Jeremiah Johnson* (1972), and *The Electric Horseman* (1979).

Unquestionably the most famous filming location in Utah (and arguably the entire American West) is **Monument Valley** and the nearby town of **Mexican Hat**. The valley made its first appearance in the silent western *The Vanishing American* (1925), but Hollywood's long-term infatuation with the place began in 1938, when local sheepherder and trading post operator Harry Goulding traveled to L.A. and convinced John Ford to film his classic western *Stagecoach* (1939) in the Navajo-owned valley. In the years to come, Hollywood and Ford returned to Monument Valley many times for many films, including *Kit Carson* (1940), *Billy the Kid* (1941), *My Darling Clementine* (1946), *Fort Apache* (1948), *She Wore a Yellow Ribbon* (1949), *The Searchers* (1956), *Sergeant Rutledge* (1960), *How the West Was Won* (1963) and *Cheyenne Autumn* (1964). By the time Sergio Leone filmed his masterpiece *Once Upon a Time in the West* (1968), he had to contend with the idea of infringing on "Ford's West" by shooting in Monument Valley. Later films like *Easy Rider* (1969), *Back to the Future Part III* (1990) and *The Wild, Wild West* (1999) have featured the location as a pointed invocation of Ford's "reel West." The valley's famous rock formations remain a popular tourist attraction, as do Goulding's original house (featured in *She Wore a Yellow Ribbon*) and trading post (now a museum).

Although Monument Valley is better known, nearby **Moab** is the more popular filming location. Its history begins with director John Ford, who went looking for a new filming location after he completed *She Wore a Yellow Ribbon* in Monument Valley. The filmmaker shot his next two films, *Wagon Master* (1950) and *Rio Grande* (1950), in Moab's Professor Valley on the Colorado River. Over the following years, filmmakers explored the greater Moab area, shooting in nearby Castle Valley (beginning with *Taza, Son of Cochise* in 1953), Arches National Park (beginning with *The Battle of Apache Pass* in 1952) and Dead Horse Point State Park (beginning with *Warlock* in 1959). For a comprehensive account of films shot in the region, see Bette L. Stanton's book, James V. D'Arc's book, or visit the Moab Museum of Film & Western Heritage at Red Cliffs Lodge. You can also request an official auto tour guide from the Moab Area Travel Council.

Capitol Reef National Park, east of Moab, may also be of some interest for hardcore movie geeks that will recognize it from Al Adamson's Z-grade westerns *Halfway to Hell* (1963), *The Female Bunch* (1969), *Five Bloody Graves* (1970) and *Jessi's Girls* (1975).

Due east of Monument Valley, along the Utah/Arizona state line, is another well-known area for filming. **Glen Canyon National Recreation Area** provided the setting for *Mackenna's Gold* (1969), as well as non-westerns *The Ten Commandments* (1956), *Planet of the Apes* (1968) and John Woo's *Broken Arrow* (1995). According to John A. Murray, Warner Bros. built an entire western town below the high water line at the mouth of Crosby Canyon on Lake Powell for their 1994 film *Maverick*. The set was removed after production wrapped.

Arizona

According to author Joe McNeill, Arizona also has its own "Little Hollywood." That's what the locals called **Sedona** in the 1940s and 1950s, when the city was a hotbed of filming activity. McNeill has written an amazingly comprehensive book about Sedona's filming history, with detailed information about the making of dozens of classic westerns, beginning with *Call of the Canyon* (1923) and including *Stagecoach* (1939), *Virginia City* (1940), *Billy the Kid* (1941), *Tall in the Saddle* (1944), *Angel and the Badman* (1947), *Blood on the Moon* (1948), *Rancho Notorious* (1952), *Johnny Guitar* (1954), *Apache* (1954) and the films of director Delmar Daves. Though not as well known as John Ford, Daves had an equally strong commitment to the genre and to his favorite filming location. Among the films he made in Sedona were *Broken Arrow* (1950), *Drum Beat* (1954), *The Last*

Wagon (1956) and *3:10 to Yuma* (1957). Although Sedona hasn't been used much as a filming location since the early 1970s, visitors can still marvel at the natural beauty of the famous rock formations between Slide Rock State Park (northeast of town) and Red Rock State Park (southwest of town). The most famous filming locations are Oak Creek Canyon, Schnebly Hill, Little Horse Park, Courthouse Butte, Bell Rock, Coffee Pot Rock, Cathedral Rock and Red Rock Crossing. If you take a Jeep tour, you can even find the Van Deren Cabin from *Blood on the Moon*, deep within Boynton Canyon. A word of advice: Avoid the movie "museums" in town, which are thin covers for timeshare operations; use the Bradshaw tour company ("A Day in the West") or McNeill's book as your guide.

To the west of Sedona, the city of **Prescott** has been used occasionally for filming since the early days of Tom Mix westerns. Modern films shot there include *Billy Jack* (1971), Sam Peckinpah's *Junior Bonner* (1972) and Peter Fonda's *Wanda Nevada* (1979). The latter two films both included scenes at The Palace Restaurant and Saloon.

Apacheland Historical Museum, located east of Phoenix at the edge of the Superstition Mountains, claims to be "the western movie capital of the world." Built as an amusement park in 1956, the Apacheland studio was first featured in *Gunfight at the O.K. Corral* (1957) and later appeared in several TV series and minor western films. It was last featured in *A Time for Dying* (1969), Audie Murphy's final film, which was shot just before a devastating fire destroyed the entire western town except for the barn and the chapel. The town was rebuilt, only to be devastated again by fire in 2004. Today the two original buildings are part of the Superstition Mountain Museum complex in Apache Junction. The history of the studio is celebrated every January at the "Apacheland Days" festival.

An even more compelling destination for tourists is **Old Tucson Studios**. Originally built for the film *Arizona* (1940) starring Jean Arthur and William Holden, the elaborate western town sets were allowed to deteriorate for several years before Hollywood returned. Old Tucson was a particularly popular shooting location in the 1950s, when it provided settings for *Winchester '73* (1951), *Ten Wanted Men* (1955), *Gunfight at the O.K. Corral* (1957), *Walk the Proud Land* (1957), *Buchanan Rides Alone* (1958) and *Rio Bravo* (1958). In 1960, the studio was transformed into an amusement park, but it has continued to appear onscreen in many films: *The Deadly Companions* (1961), *McLintock!* (1964), *Hombre* (1967), *Joe Kidd* (1972), *Death Wish* (1973), *The Last Hard Men* (1976), *Three Amigos!* (1986), *Young Guns 2* (1991) and *Tombstone* (1993). Fire destroyed many of the original buildings in 1995, but Old Tucson has since returned to life as a movie studio and an amusement park. Paul J. Lawton has compiled a photo essay on the place, as well as an extensive list of the films shot there (available in the studio's gift shop).

East of Tucson, on the edge of the Rincon Mountains, the makers of the film *Monte Walsh* (1969) built a western set that later fell under the ownership and management of Old Tucson Studios. The site, eventually named **Mescal**, has been used extensively in several modern westerns, including *The Life and Times of Judge Roy Bean* (1972), *The Outlaw Josey Wales* (1976), *The Frisco Kid* (1979), *Tom Horn* (1980), *Tombstone* (1993) and *The Quick and the Dead* (1995). Mescal is not open to the public.

Hardcore western fans will want to visit the wide-open ranchlands south of Mescal, where Howard Hawks filmed much of his classic *Red River* (1948) on the privately-owned **Empire Ranch** in Elgin, near Rain Valley and the Whetstone Mountains. The San Pedro River stood in for the Red River of the title. According to Carlo Gaberscek and Kenny Stier, other films shot on Empire Ranch, as well as **Circle Z Ranch** in the nearby Sonoita Valley, include *Duel in the Sun* (1946), *The Furies* (1950), *Winchester '73* (1950), *Broken*

Lance (1954), *Backlash* (1956), *Gunfight at the O.K. Corral* (1957) and *Last Train from Gun Hill* (1959).

East of Elgin is the legendary town of **Tombstone**. None of the famous Hollywood depictions of Wyatt Earp and his gunfight at the O.K. Corral have been filmed here, but no western fan should miss the opportunity to visit the town that was too tough to die, where the Wild West is still celebrated daily on dusty streets.

Canyon de Chelly National Monument is another authentic historical site that has been used only rarely as a filming location. Among the first films shot there were a series of early Zane Grey adaptations, beginning with *To the Last Man* in 1923. *Massacre River* (1949) features the canyon floor of this old Navajo stronghold, while the Gregory Peck vehicle *Mackenna's Gold* (1969) features Spider Rock. No film could do full justice to the majesty of this setting.

New Mexico

New Mexico was especially popular with Hollywood filmmakers during the 1940s. As Tinsley Yarbrough points out, the city of Gallup served as a gateway to the reel West of nearby **Red Rock State Park**, where portions of *Rocky Mountain* (1950), *Fort Defiance* (1950), *Red Mountain* (1951), *Escape from Fort Bravo* (1953), *Fort Massacre* (1957), *A Distant Trumpet* (1963), and *The Hallelujah Trail* (1965) were filmed. The nearby El Rancho Hotel still serves as a reminder of the area's filmmaking legacy.

Also nearby is **El Morro National Monument**, a rock formation so imposing that pioneers carved hundreds of messages on it for fellow travelers. El Morro, also known as Inscription Rock, provided the inspiration for Eugene Manlove Rhodes's short story "Paso Por Aqui," which was adapted to the screen as *Four Faces West* (1948) starring Joel McCrea. The film used El Morro as a filming location.

The most popular western filming location in New Mexico is a cluster of four large ranches on the outskirts of Santa Fe: Bonanza Creek Ranch (formerly Jarrett Ranch), Cerro Pelon Ranch (formerly Cook Ranch), J.W. Eaves Movie Ranch, and El Rancho de los Golondrinas. The accessibility of these ranches to the public seems to change with the times (and, presumably, the ownership). In 1990 David Rothel gained access to Bonanza, Cook and Eaves, with the help of a liaison at the New Mexico Film Commission, and conducted informative interviews with the "film representatives" of each ranch. Carlo Gaberscek and Kenny Stier's 2014 book *In Search of Western Movie Sites* provides the most comprehensive list of films shot at each ranch.

The first Santa Fe ranch to host a major Hollywood production was **Bonanza Creek Ranch**, which provided a ranch house and plenty of grazing land for James Stewart in *The Man from Laramie* (1955). Hollywood returned a few years later, for Delmar Daves's film *Cowboy* (1957), but film projects at the ranch remained relatively few and far between until filmmakers constructed a western street set (for the Terence Hill vehicle *Lucky Luke*) in 1991.

In the early 1960s, filmmakers arrived on the **J.W. Eaves Ranch**. The first production at the ranch was the TV series *Empire* (1962–1963). A few years later, producer/director Gene Kelly and the ranch owner built a western town set for *The Cheyenne Social Club* (1970), starring Henry Fonda and James Stewart. The set was used in several subsequent westerns, including *Billy Jack* (1971), *A Gunfight* (1971), *The Cowboys* (1972), *The Legend of Nigger Charley* (1972) and *Boss Nigger* (1974). A Mexican village set was also built on the range, and featured in the sci-fi western *Timerider: The Adventures of Lyle Swan* (1983), and the Paul Bartel comedy *Lust in the Dust* (1985).

Filmmakers started using the Santa Fe ranches more frequently in the early 1980s, culminating with the epic production of *Silverado* (1985), which made use of Bonanza Creek and Eaves Ranch but was filmed primarily on the nearby **Cerro Pelon Ranch**. A grand-scale western street built for *Silverado* helped to attract more filmmakers to the Santa Fe area in the following years. Since then, the three movie ranches have routinely provided shooting locations for major film and television productions including *Lonesome Dove* (1989), *Wyatt Earp* (1994), *Wild Bill* (1995), *Last Man Standing* (1996), *John Carpenter's Vampires* (1997), *The Wild, Wild West* (1999), *All the Pretty Horses* (2000), *The Missing* (2003), *Into the West* (2005), *The Astronaut Farmer* (2006), *3:10 to Yuma* (2007), *Appaloosa* (2008), *Cowboys & Aliens* (2011), and *Sweetwater* (2013).

El Rancho de los Golondrinas does not promote itself as a movie ranch, but rather as a "living history museum," an educational reproduction of a working ranch in 18th and 19th century New Mexico. Nonetheless, the ranch's Madrid House was featured in *Butch and Sundance: The Early Years* (1979) and its Sierra Village was featured in *Young Guns* (1988). Other westerns shot partly at the ranch include *Wyatt Earp* (1994), *John Carpenter's Vampires* (1998), *All the Pretty Horses* (2000), *The Missing* (2003), *Into the West* (2005), and *Seraphim Falls* (2007).

North of Santa Fe, closer to Taos, there is another ranch that has been featured onscreen at least a few times, beginning with the Disney TV series *The Nine Lives of Elfego Baca* (1960) and the Universal film *And Now Miguel* (1966). **Ghost Ranch** in Abiquiu is a spiritual education and retreat center, but it was also featured in *Silverado* (1985), *Lonesome Dove* (1989), *City Slickers* (1991), *Wyatt Earp* (1994), *The Wild Wild West* (1999), *All the Pretty Horses* (2000), *The Missing* (2003), *3:10 to Yuma* (2007), *No Country for Old Men* (2007), *Cowboys & Aliens* (2011) and *The Lone Ranger* (2013).

In the southern part of the state, the sprawling **White Sands National Monument** has provided striking desert landscapes for westerns including *Four Faces West* (1949), *Hang 'Em High* (1967), *The Hired Hand* (1971), *My Name Is Nobody* (1973), *Bite the Bullet* (1975) and *Young Guns 2* (1990).

The Wide, Wide West

Filmmakers are forever in search of new filming locations that will capture the exoticism of the Old West, and for that reason many famous westerns have been shot far from the lights of Hollywood (as well as the various Little Hollywoods), some of them in locations that are not often regarded as "the West."

One of the first major westerns to be filmed almost entirely on location was *Jesse James* (1939), which was made in the sleepy town of **Pineville, Missouri**. Director Henry King returned a few years later to make the sequel *Belle Starr* (1941). Every year in August the town still celebrates the epic production with its Jesse James Days festival.

Despite the mythic allure of Texas and the fact that so many screen westerns take place there, relatively few western films have been shot in Texas. The location that looms largest in the popular consciousness is no doubt The Alamo, "the shrine of Texas liberty," but that historic mission in **San Antonio** has rarely been used as a filming location. One notable exception is the lost silent film *The Siege and Fall of the Alamo* (1914). A few other westerns, including *The Rough Riders* (1927) and *The Texans* (1938), were also shot in San Antonio. The 21st century westerns *The Three Burials of Melquiades Estrada* (2005), *No Country for Old Men* (2007) and *There Will Be Blood* (2007) were shot in west Texas.

John Wayne shot his film *The Alamo* (1960) at a replica in Bracketville, Texas. For many years, the **Alamo Village** set (also featured in *Two Rode Together, Bandolero!, Barbarosa, Lonesome Dove* and *Bad Girls*) was open to the public, but the site closed its doors in 2009. Disney's 2004 film *The Alamo* was filmed on a new set on Reimer's Ranch in Dripping Springs, Texas. Part of that set was destroyed by wildfire in 2011.

Before the Alamo Village set was built, John Wayne briefly considered shooting his film in **Mexico**, where he had already made *Hondo* in 1953 (in the district of Chihuahua) and where he would later make *The Sons of Katie Elder* (1965), *The War Wagon* (1967), *The Undefeated* (1969), *Chisum* (1971), *Big Jake* (1972), *The Train Robbers* (1973) and *Cahill: United States Marshal* (1973) in the district of Durango. The Mexican Revolution figures into nearly as many western movie narratives as the Texas Revolution, and many A-list westerns of the 1950s and 1960s—including *Vera Cruz* (1954), *Bandido* (1956), *The Wonderful Country* (1959), *The Magnificent Seven* (1960), *Major Dundee* (1965), and the final act of *Butch Cassidy and the Sundance Kid* (1969)—were shot there.

In the 1950s, Hollywood filmmakers were more likely to shoot in Durango, Colorado, than in Durango, Mexico. In 1992, filmmaker Tony Schweikle made a 30-minute documentary about filming locations in the mountains of **southwestern Colorado**, hosted by western star Jack Elam. In *Travel the Movie Trail*, Elam visits a ranch in Gunnison used for winter scenes in *The Searchers* (1956) and *Cheyenne Autumn* (1964) as well as a ranch in Montrose used in the final scene of *True Grit* (1969) and a ranch in Pagosa Springs used for *The Cowboys* (1972). Elam also explores the city of Durango, where scenes for *Butch Cassidy and the Sundance Kid* (1969) and *City Slickers* (1991) were filmed, and the nearby Southern Ute Indian Reservation, featured in the TV movie *The Tracker* (1998). Fans of *True Grit* will also want to visit the Ouray County Courthouse, featured at the beginning of the film, and the main square in Ridgway, which doubled as Fort Smith. Other filming locations for that classic include Ridgway's Owl Creek Pass and Durango's San Juan National Forest. Fans of *Colorado Territory* (1949) will want to visit that film's "City of the Moon," in Mesa Verde National Park.

The most popular movie location in southwestern Colorado seems to be the **Durango-Silverton Narrow Gauge Railroad**. In operation since 1882, the railroad has been featured in many Hollywood westerns, including *A Ticket to Tomahawk* (1950), *Viva Zapata!* (1952), *Run for Cover* (1955), *Night Passage* (1957), *Butch Cassidy and the Sundance Kid* (1969), *Support Your Local Gunfighter* (1971), and *The Claim* (2001).

The nearby **Cumbres & Toltec Scenic Railroad**, which runs between Antonito, Colorado, and Chama, New Mexico, has also been featured onscreen in *The Good Guys and the Bad Guys* (1969), *Butch Cassidy and the Sundance Kid* (1969), *The Hired Hand* (1971), *Bite the Bullet* (1975), *The White Buffalo* (1977), *Indiana Jones and the Last Crusade* (1989) and *Wyatt Earp* (1994).

Another site in Colorado that's worth mentioning is **Buckskin Joe Frontier Town**. Films shot there include *Cat Ballou* (1965), *True Grit* (1969), *The Cowboys* (1972), *Mr. Majestyk* (1974), *The White Buffalo* (1977), *Comes a Horseman* (1978), and the TV miniseries *The Sacketts* (1991). Built in 1957 by MGM, the frontier town set was originally located in Cañon City, where it operated as an amusement park until 2010. More recently, the set was moved to a private ranch in Gunnison.

Jackson Hole, Wyoming, is famous as the filming location of *Shane* (1953). Walt Farmer has written a most comprehensive study of this and other Wyoming filming locations, including Grand Teton National Park and Bridger-Teton National Forest (where parts of *The Big Sky*, *The Mountain Men*, and *Dances with Wolves* were shot).

Most of *Dances with Wolves* (1990) was filmed in **South Dakota**, near the cities of Pierre and Rapid City, and in Badlands National Park and the Black Hills National Forest. The Fort Hays western town used in the film is still standing in Rapid City. *Thunderheart* (1992) was also filmed in Badlands as well as on the Pine Ridge Indian Reservation. Western film enthusiasts may also want to visit nearby Custer State Park, where *The Last Hunt* (1956) was shot, and the town of Deadwood, featured occasionally in the 21st century TV series of the same name.

In the adjacent state of **Montana**, tourists can visit the famous site of Custer's last stand. The final battle in *Little Big Man* (1970) was filmed in Crow Agency, Montana, just down the road from the Little Bighorn Battlefield and National Monument. Other western films shot in the state include *The Big Trail* (1930), *The Plainsman* (1936), *Cattle Queen of Montana* (1954), and *The Missouri Breaks* (1976), which used locations in Billings, Red Lodge, Nevada City and Virginia City. *Heaven's Gate* (1980) was shot on location in the northwestern corner of the state, near Kalispell.

Some scenes for *Heaven's Gate* were also filmed in **Idaho,** following in the footsteps of classic epics like *Northwest Passage* (1940), *Unconquered* (1947) and *The Wild North* (1951). More recently, Clint Eastwood made two films in Idaho: *Bronco Billy* (1980) and *Pale Rider* (1985). The former was shot in Boise and Meridian; the latter in the Sawtooth Mountains near Ketchum.

Filmmaker Anthony Mann did a particularly good job of showcasing the natural landscape of **Oregon** in his film *Bend of the River* (1952), shot partly in the Mount Hood National Forest near Portland. *The Indian Fighter* (1955) with Kirk Douglas was shot further south, near Bend, and *The Great Northfield Minnesota Raid* (1971) was shot in and around Jacksonville, Oregon, rather than Minnesota. Other westerns filmed in Oregon include *Canyon Passage* (1946), *Day of the Outlaw* (1959), *The Way West* (1967), *Rooster Cogburn* (1975), and *Dead Man* (1995).

The northern wilds of **Washington** state are featured in William A. Wellman's *Track of the Cat* (1954), shot in and around Mount Rainier National Park, and in Delmar Daves's *The Hanging Tree* (1959), shot entirely in and around Yakima.

Some of the most memorable American westerns have actually been filmed in **Canada**—*McCabe and Mrs. Miller* (1971) in Vancouver; *The River of No Return* (1954), *The Far Country* (1955), *Unforgiven* (1992) *Into the West* (2005), *Brokeback Mountain* (2005), and *September Dawn* (2007) in the province of Alberta; *The Assassination of Jesse James by the Coward Robert Ford* (2007) in Winnipeg. It is safe to say that the screen western has outgrown the western United States.

Indeed, the western has outgrown the United States altogether. In the late 1960s, dozens of spaghetti westerns were shot in **Spain**, particularly the southeastern province of Almería, beginning in earnest with Sergio Leone's Man with No Name Trilogy. By the early 1970s, the location had become popular with American and British filmmakers, who went there to produce offbeat westerns including *A Town Called Hell* (1971), *Valdez Is Coming* (1971), *Hannie Caulder* (1971), *Chato's Land* (1972), *Chino* (1973), *Charley One-Eye* (1973), *The Spikes Gang* (1974), *China 9, Liberty 37* (1978), *Straight to Hell* (1986), and many more.

Chapter Notes

Preface
1. Libby 48.

Introduction
1. Hart 48.
2. Hart 50.
3. Hart 182.
4. Hart 38.
5. Clark 29.
6. Mix.
7. Wilstach 15–16.
8. DeMille 349.
9. Oller 94.
10. Bogdanovich: *Hell* 277.
11. Munn 19–20.
12. Tuska: *Filming* 373.

Chapter I
1. Haycox 90.
2. Haycox 40.
3. Haycox Jr. 113.
4. Haycox Jr. 114.
5. Vieira 59, Flynn 290–291.
6. Davis 138.
7. Robertson 49.
8. Davis 138.
9. Custen 140.
10. Yeatman 109.
11. Meyer 74.
12. Meyer 73.
13. Meyer 50.
14. Ford 124.
15. Bogdanovich: *Hell* 258.
16. Munn 58.
17. Libby 50.
18. McBride: *Searching* 52–53.
19. McBride: *Searching* 283.
20. McBride: *Searching* 271.
21. Robert Sherman 51.
22. Vieira 202.
23. Vieira 202.
24. Eliot 134.
25. Everson 208.

Chapter II
1. Lloyd 24.
2. Meyer 100.
3. Stevens Jr. 66, Bogdanovich: *Devil* 195.
4. Burns 57.
5. Stanfield 190.
6. Wallis 70.
7. Benson 71.
8. Schickel: *Men* 226.
9. Custen 273.
10. Schickel: *Men* 226.
11. Henry Fonda 24.
12. Henry Fonda 137–138.
13. Bogdanovich: *Devil* 308.
14. Randy Roberts 250.
15. McBride: *Searching* 362.
16. Barra 348.
17. Lake 134.
18. McBride: *Searching* 430.

Chapter III
1. Koppes 328.
2. Schickel: *Men* 155.
3. Thomson: "Niven" 105.
4. Speck 131.
5. Thomson: "Niven" 108.
6. Server 112.
7. Server 52.
8. Bansak 466–467.
9. De Toth 69.
10. Bogdanovich: *Hell* 313.
11. Collier 71.
12. Todd McCarthy 412.
13. Hawks 112.
14. Bogdanovich: *Devil* 341.
15. Kitses: "Borden" 152.
16. Bogdanovich: *Devil* 338.
17. PR Newswire.
18. Bansak 429.
19. Bansak 496.
20. Wellman 99.

Chapter IV
1. Bazin 51.
2. Dmytryk 63.
3. McBride: *Searching* 271.
4. McBride: *Searching* 477.
5. Bogdanovich: *Hell* 287.
6. McBride: *Searching* 497.
7. Munn 133.
8. McBride: *Searching* 504.
9. Henry Fonda 177, Randy Roberts 180.
10. Wicking 55.
11. Arnold viii.
12. Biskind: *Seeing* 232.
13. Sbardellati 208, Drew 95.
14. Kazan: "Statement" 2409.
15. Young 93.
16. Kazan: "Elia" 22.
17. Meyers 246.
18. Blake: *Code* 10, 16.
19. Cooper 220, Meyers 251.
20. Hawks 130.
21. Blake: *Code* 51.
22. McVeigh 50.
23. Schaefer 2.
24. Hyams 12.
25. Hyams 12.
26. Hyams 11.
27. Sarris 108.
28. McGilligan: "Philip" 353.
29. Peterson 325.
30. Lovell 96.
31. Lovell 106.
32. Lovell 98.
33. Brown 220–240.
34. Michael Walker 133.
35. Randy Roberts 420.
36. Munn 177.
37. Blake: *Code* 197.
38. Hoberman: "How" 318–319.
39. Hoberman: "How" 318.

Chapter V
1. Robert Smith 189.
2. Bogdanovich: *Hell* 255.

3. Speck 13.
4. Kitses: "Borden" 161.
5. Kitses: *Horizons* 31.
6. Missiaen 46.
7. Basinger 90.
8. Missiaen 49.
9. Eliot 283, Missiaen 49.
10. Wallis 116.
11. Wallis 116.
12. Herzberg 73.
13. Kitses: "Borden" 159.
14. Wallis 117.
15. Fishgall 122.
16. Biskind: *Seeing* 245.
17. Wallis 154.
18. Wallis 154.
19. Lovell 147.
20. Lovell 152.
21. Douglas 271.
22. Kitses: "Borden" 156.
23. Lovell 153.
24. Wallis 118.
25. Raymond 62.
26. Raymond 53.
27. Nott: *Last* 62.
28. McGilligan: *Film* 134.
29. Thomas 156.
30. Crow 62.
31. De Toth 99.
32. De Toth 101.
33. Dixon.
34. Eric Sherman 48, Kunert.
35. Eric Sherman 200.
36. Boetticher 91.
37. Russell 198.
38. Eric Sherman 49.
39. Eric Sherman 51.
40. Eric Sherman 46.
41. Eric Sherman 46.

Chapter VI

1. Bogdanovich: *Hell* 66.
2. Schickel: *Clint* 110.
3. Eisenhower 226.
4. Graham 127.
5. Graham 179.
6. Graham 247.
7. Eric Sherman 111.
8. Eric Sherman 108.
9. Eric Sherman 103.
10. McBride: *Hawks* 113.
11. Daniel 99.
12. Samuel Fuller 334.
13. Samuel Fuller 334.
14. Eric Sherman 363.
15. Eric Sherman 358.
16. Madsen 332.
17. Herman 382.
18. Peck xiii.
19. McVeigh 93.
20. Hawks 130.
21. Willis 14.

Chapter VII

1. Munn 216.
2. Levy 313.
3. Willis 198.
4. Randy Roberts 471.
5. Willis 221.
6. Critchlow 140.
7. Critchlow 140.
8. Randy Roberts 468.
9. Morella 79.
10. Neider xii.
11. Neider xiii.
12. Yergin 90.
13. Callenbach 10.
14. Mitchell 63, Tavernier 107.
15. Randy Roberts 610.
16. Randy Roberts 618.
17. Ford 284.
18. Biskind: *Seeing* 43.
19. Miller 41.
20. Miller 54.
21. Cook 270.
22. Douglas 337.
23. Manfull 564.
24. Meyer 338.
25. McMurtry: "Cowboys" 50.
26. Bogdanovich: "Autumn" 59.
27. Randy Roberts 635.
28. Joyner 73.
29. Heston 326.

Chapter VIII

1. Kracauer 266.
2. Richie 19.
3. Frayling: *Spaghetti* 134.
4. Frayling: *Spaghetti* 120, 65.
5. Frayling: *Sergio* 134.
6. Frayling: *Sergio* 136.
7. Thompson 53.
8. Schickel: *Clint* 146.
9. Horner 52.
10. Horner 51.
11. Frayling: *Spaghetti* 173.
12. Mott 94, Frayling: *Sergio* 181–182.
13. Frayling: *Sergio* 203.
14. Frayling: *Sergio* 205.
15. Maché
16. Maché
17. Sollima.
18. Cox: *10,000* 117.
19. Cox: *10,000* 143.
20. Frayling: *Spaghetti* 256, 252.
21. Frayling: *Spaghetti* 129.
22. Cox: *10,000* 189.
23. Hodgkiss.

Chapter IX

1. Thompson 57.
2. Heston 468.
3. Lovell 259.
4. Lovell 267.
5. Randy Roberts 557.
6. Fagen 173.
7. Wayne 218.
8. Segaloff: "Walon" 143.
9. Farber 40.
10. Medjuck 25.
11. Goldman 460.
12. Goldman 462.
13. Meyer 417.
14. Goldman 285.
15. Goldman 285.
16. Biskind: *Easy* 42.
17. Peter Fonda 241.
18. Biskind: *Easy* 68.
19. Biskind: *Easy* 74.
20. Rodriguez 61.
21. Canham 173.
22. Biskind: *Easy* 124.
23. Maché
24. Hoberman: *Midnight* 95.
25. Jodorowsky 99.
26. Aleiss 127.
27. Bergen 226.
28. Bergen 225.
29. Crowdus.
30. Fogliett 88.
31. Langlois 79.
32. Shapiro 55.
33. Fagan 188.
34. Tuska: *Frontier* 381.
35. Phillips 43.
36. Robinson 33.
37. Jenson 75.
38. Aghed 129.
39. Kitses: "Peckinpah" 236.
40. Hoberman 91.

Chapter X

1. McMurtry: "Cowboys" 48.
2. McMurtry: "Cowboys" 49.
3. Slotkin 634.
4. Sharrett 220.
5. Siegel 306.
6. Schickel: *Clint* 231.
7. Siegel 366.
8. Kael 388.
9. Exshaw 14.
10. Garfield 165–166.
11. Joyner 238.
12. Segaloff: "John" 286.
13. Bogdanovich: *Devil* 764.
14. Wilson 75.
15. Avery 84.
16. Thompson 262.
17. Bergen 224.
18. Kennedy 45.
19. Poitier 332.
20. David Walker 137.
21. McGilligan: *Jack's* 151.
22. McDougal 58.

23. Tuska: *American* 260.
24. McDougal 182.
25. McGilligan: *Jack's* 277.
26. Bosworth 268.
27. Heston 122.
28. Williamson 38.
29. Schickel: *Clint* 325.
30. Wayne 263.
31. Boulanger 93.
32. Pulleine.
33. Sharrett 226.
34. Bach 123.
35. Bach 339.
36. Greco.
37. Greco.

Chapter XI

1. Reagan: *American* 219.
2. Reagan: *American* 266.
3. Reagan: *American* 548.
4. Erisman 180.
5. Bouzreau 27.
6. Brender 48.
7. Brender 48.
8. Maronie.
9. Swires 18.
10. Boulanger 36.
11. Goldman 238.
12. Goldman 241.
13. Thomson: "Ghost" 59.
14. Thomson: "Ghost" 117.
15. Wolfe xii.
16. Glenn 349.
17. Faludi 381.
18. Morrell x.
19. Faludi 394.
20. Faludi 401.
21. Douglas 402.

22. Morrell xiii, Faludi 405.
23. Norris 130.
24. Norris 130.
25. O'Neill 69.
26. Graham Fuller 181.
27. Graham Fuller 149.
28. Cahill 102.
29. Schickel: *Clint* 403.
30. Schickel: *Clint* 403.
31. Boulanger 192.
32. Goldberg 30.
33. Boulanger 44.
34. Cox: "My."
35. Cox: *X Films* 131.
36. Tavernier 108.

Chapter XII

1. Pierson 287.
2. Wheeler.
3. Anonymous.
4. Costner viii.
5. Costner viii.
6. Turan 249.
7. Turan 249.
8. Thompson 217.
9. Jousse 140.
10. Turan 247.
11. Shickel: *Clint* 461.
12. Turan 247.
13. Behar 156.
14. Behar 157.
15. Modleski 360.
16. Modleski 360.
17. Modleski 360.
18. Ryan.
19. Tapley.
20. Marc 239.
21. Tapley.

22. Marc 239.
23. Zelazny.
24. Cotter.
25. Blake: *Hollywood* 205.
26. Blake: *Hollywood* 195.
27. Fuller: "Lawrence" 181.
28. Kasdan vii–viii.
29. Fuller: "Lawrence" 192.
30. Blake: *Hollywood* 205.
31. Muir 176.
32. Macauley 149.
33. Rosenbaum: *Dead* 161.

Chapter XIII

1. Eller.
2. Mayer.
3. Nussbaum.
4. Havrilesky.
5. Zwick 10.
6. Blunt.
7. Hancock 7.
8. Fischer: "Interview."
9. Wilmington.
10. Pomeranz.
11. Simon.
12. McMurtry: "Adapting" 142.
13. Parfitt.
14. Laukhuf.
15. Anderson.
16. Esther.
17. Esther.
18. Murray.
19. Wood 177.
20. McBride: *Searching* 103.
21. Fischer: "Exclusive."
22. Calhoun.
23. Cormac McCarthy 303.
24. Lawrence.

Bibliography

"Actor Rallies to *Young Guns 2*." *The Los Angeles Times*. August 1, 1990.

Aghed, Jan. "Pat Garrett and Billy the Kid." 1973. *Sam Peckinpah: Interviews*. Jackson: University Press of Mississippi, 2008.

Aleiss, Angela. *Making the White Man's Indian: Native Americans and Hollywood Movies*. Westport, CT: Praeger, 2005.

Anderson, John. "With Only God Left as a Witness." *The New York Times*. January 22, 2006.

Arnold, Elliott. *Blood Brother*. New York: Duell, 1947.

Avery, Kevin, ed. *Conversations with Clint: Paul Nelson's Lost Interviews with Clint Eastwood, 1979–1983*. New York: Continuum, 2011.

Bach, Steven. *Final Cut: Dreams and Disaster in the Making of Heaven's Gate*. New York: Quill, 1985.

Bansak, Edmund G. *Fearing the Dark: The Val Lewton Career*. Jefferson: McFarland, 1995.

Barra, Allen. *Inventing Wyatt Earp: His Life and Many Legends*. New York: Carroll & Graf, 1998.

Basinger, Jeanine. *Anthony Mann (New and Expanded Edition)*. Middletown: Wesleyan University Press, 2007.

Bazin, André. "The Evolution of the Western." 1955. *The Western Reader*. Ed. Jim Kitses and Gregg Rickman. New York: Limelight, 1998.

Behar, Henri. "America on the Brink of the Void." 1993. *Clint Eastwood: Interviews (Revised and Updated)*. Ed. Robert E. Kapsis and Kathie Coblentz. Jackson: University Press of Mississippi, 2012.

Benson, Jackson J. *The Ox-Bow Man: A Biography of Walter Van Tilburg Clark*. Reno: University of Nevada Press, 2004.

Bergen, Candice. *Knock Wood*. New York: Simon & Schuster, 1984.

Biskind, Peter. *Easy Riders, Raging Bulls: How the Sex-Drugs-and-Rock N Roll Generation Saved Hollywood*. New York: Simon & Schuster, 2010.

Biskind, Peter. *Seeing Is Believing: How Hollywood Taught Us to Stop Worrying and Love the Fifties*. New York: Holt, 2000.

Blake, Michael F. *Code of Honor: The Making of Three Great American Westerns—High Noon, Shane, and The Searchers*. Lanham: Taylor, 2003.

Blake, Michael F. *Hollywood and the O.K. Corral: Portrayals of the Gunfight and Wyatt Earp*. Jefferson: McFarland, 2007.

Blunt, Emily. "Kevin Costner: At Home on the Range—Kinda." BluntReview.com. 2003. http://www.bluntreview.com/reviews/costner.htm.

Boetticher, Budd. *When in Disgrace*. Santa Barbara: Neville, 1989.

Bogdanovich, Peter. "The Autumn of John Ford." *John Ford: Interviews*. Ed. Gerald Peary. Jackson: University Press of Mississippi, 2001.

Bogdanovich, Peter. *Who the Devil Made It*. New York: Knopf, 1997.

Bogdanovich, Peter. *Who the Hell's In It*. New York: Knopf, 2004.

Bosworth, Patricia. *Marlon Brando*. Farmington Hills: Thorndike, 2001.

Boulanger, Gilles. *John Carpenter: The Prince of Darkness*. Beverly Hills: Silman-James Press, 2001.

Bouzreau, Laurent. *Star Wars: The Annotated Screenplays*. New York: Del Rey, 1997.

Brender, Alan. "Writer & Director Peter Hyams Takes Us Behind-the-Scenes on His Upcoming SF Drama, *Outland*." *Starlog* No. 45/April 1981.

Brown, Dee. *Bury My Heart at Wounded Knee: An Indian History of the American West*. New York: Holt, 1970.

Burns, Walter Noble. *The Saga of Billy the Kid*. New York: Grosset, 1925.

Cahill, Tim. "Clint Eastwood: The *Rolling Stone* Interview." 1985. *Clint Eastwood: Interviews (Revised and Updated)*. Ed. Robert E. Kapsis and Kathie Coblentz. Jackson: University Press of Mississippi, 2012.

Calhoun, Dave. "The Coen Brothers: Interview." *Time Out London*. 2007. http://www.timeout.com/london/film/the-coen-brothers-interview.

Callenbach, Ernest. "A Conversation with Sam

Peckinpah." 1963. *Sam Peckinpah Interviews*. Ed. Kevin J. Hayes. Jackson: University Press of Mississippi, 2008.

Canham, Kingsley. *The Hollywood Professionals, Vol. 1: Michael Curtiz, Raoul Walsh, Henry Hathaway*. New York: A.S. Barnes, 1973.

Clark, J.B.M., ed. *The West of Yesterday*. Los Angeles: The Times-Mirror Press, 1923.

Collier, Peter. *The Fondas: A Hollywood Dynasty*. New York: G.P. Putnam's Sons, 1991.

Cook, Bruce. *Dalton Trumbo*. New York: Scribner, 1977.

Cooper, Gary. "Testimony of Gary Cooper." *Hearings Regarding the Communist Infiltration of the Motion Picture Industry: Hearings Before the Committee on Un-American Activities, House of Representatives, Eightieth Congress, First Session (October 20, 21, 22, 23, 24, 27, 28, 29 and 30, 1947)*. Washington: United States Government Printing Office, 1947.

Costner, Kevin, Michael Blake, and Jim Wilson. *Dances with Wolves: The Illustrated Story of the Epic Film*. New York: Newmarket, 1990.

Cotter, Marianne. "Walter Hill Rides the Western Wave." *MovieMaker* No. 9/September 1994.

Cox, Alex. "My Older Films." Alexcox.com. 2015.

Cox, Alex. *10,000 Ways to Die: A Director's Take on the Spaghetti Western*. Harpenden, Herts, UK: Camera, 2009.

Cox, Alex. *X Films: True Confessions of a Radical Filmmaker*. Brooklyn: Soft Skull, 2008.

Critchlow, Donald T. *When Hollywood Was Right: How Movie Stars, Studio Moguls, and Big Business Remade American Politics*. Cambridge: Cambridge University Press, 2013.

Crow, Jefferson Brim III. *Randolph Scott: The Gentleman from Virginia*. Carrollton: WindRiver, 1987.

Crowdus, Gary, and Richard Porton. "The Importance of a Singular, Guiding Vision: An Interview with Arthur Penn." *Cineaste*, Vol. XX, No. 2/December 1993.

Custen, George F. *Twentieth Century's Fox: Darryl F. Zanuck and the Culture of Hollywood*. New York: BasicBooks, 1997.

Daniel, Douglass K. *Tough as Nails: The Life and Films of Richard Brooks*. Madison: University of Wisconsin Press, 2011.

D'Arc, James V. *When Hollywood Came to Town: A History of Moviemaking in Utah*. Layton: Gibbs Smith, 2010.

Davis, Ronald L. *Words into Images: Screenwriters on the Studio System*. Jackson: University Press of Mississippi, 2007.

De Toth, André. *De Toth on De Toth*. Ed. Anthony Slide. Boston: Faber, 1996.

DeMille, Cecil B. *The Autobiography of Cecil B. DeMille*. Ed. Donald Hayne. Englewood Cliffs: Prentice-Hall, 1959.

Dixon, Wheeler Winston. "Budd Boetticher." *Film Talk: Directors at Work*. New Brunswick: Rutgers University Press, 2007.

Dmytryk, Edward. *It's a Hell of a Life but Not a Bad Living*. New York: Times Books, 1978.

Douglas, Kirk. *The Ragman's Son: An Autobiography*. New York: Simon & Schuster, 1988.

Drew, Bernard. "John Huston: At 74, No Formulas." 1979. *John Huston: Interviews*. Ed. Robert Emmet Long. Jackson: University Press of Mississippi, 2001.

Eisenhower, Dwight D. *Waging Peace: The White House Years, A Personal Account 1956–1961*. New York: Doubleday, 1965.

Eliot, Marc. *Jimmy Stewart: A Biography*. New York: Harmony, 2006.

Eller, Claudie. "Hollywood Executives Rethink What Is Off Limits." *The Los Angeles Times*. September 14, 2001.

Erisman, Fred. "The Enduring Myth and the Modern West." *Researching Western History: Topics in the Twentieth Century*. Ed. Gerald D. Nash and Richard W. Etulain. Albuquerque: University of New Mexico Press, 1997.

Esther, John. "Avoiding Labels and Lullibies: An Interview with James Mangold." *Cineaste*, Vol. 33, No. 1/Winter 2007.

Everson, William K. *The Hollywood Western*. New York: Citadel, 1992.

Exshaw, John. "Back Off, Lawman: Gerry Wilson on Winner, the West and the Wilderness." *Cinema Retro*, Vol. 5, No. 14/2009.

Fagen, Herb. *Duke: We're Glad We Knew You*. New York: Citadel, 1996.

Faludi, Susan. *Stiffed: The Betrayal of the American Man*. New York: William Morrow, 1999.

Farber, Stephen. "Peckinpah's Return." 1969. *Sam Peckinpah: Interviews*. Ed. Kevin J. Hayes. Jackson: University Press of Mississippi, 2008.

Farmer, Walt. *Wyoming: A History of Film and Video in the 20th Century: Shane Edition*. Self-published CDROM, 2013.

Fischer, Paul. "Exclusive Interview: James Mangold for *3:10 to Yuma*." DarkHorizons.com. August 12, 2007. http://www.darkhorizons.com/features/701/james-mangold-for-3-10-to-yuma.

Fischer, Paul. "Interview: Ron Howard for *The Missing*." DarkHorizons.com. November 16, 2003. http://www.darkhorizons.com/features/760/ron-howard-for-the-missing.

Fishgall, Gary. *Against Type: The Biography of Burt Lancaster*. New York: Scribner, 1995.

Fonda, Henry. *Fonda: My Life*. Ed. Howard Teichmann. New York: New American Library, 1981.

Fonda, Peter. *Don't Tell Dad: A Memoir*. New York: Hyperion, 1998.

Ford, Dan. *Pappy: The Life of John Ford*. New York: DaCapo, 1998.

Flynn, Errol. *My Wicked, Wicked Ways*. New York: Putnam, 1959.

Fogliett, Mario. "Conflicts of Conscience." *Arthur Penn: Interviews*. Ed. Michael Chaiken and Paul Cronin. Jackson: University Press of Mississippi, 2008.

Frayling, Christopher. *Sergio Leone: Something to Do with Death*. New York: Faber, 2000.

Frayling, Christopher. *Spaghetti Westerns: Cowboys and Europeans from Karl May to Sergio Leone*. New York: I.B. Tauris, 1998.

Fuller, Graham. "Lawrence Kasdan; A Humanist in Hollywood." *Backstory 4: Interviews with Screenwriters of the 1970s and 1980s*. Ed. Patrick McGilligan. Oakland: University of California Press, 2006.

Fuller, Samuel. *A Third Face: My Tale of Writing, Fighting, and Filmmaking*. New York: Knopf, 2002.

Gaberscek, Carlo, and Kenny Stier. *In Search of Western Movie Sites*. Victorville: CP Entertainment, 2014.

Garfield, Brian. *Death Wish*. New York: Mysterious, 1985.

Glenn, John, with Nick Taylor. *John Glenn: A Memoir*. New York: Bantam, 1999.

Goldberg, Lee. "Big Trouble in Little China." *Starlog* No. 106/May 1986.

Goldman, William. *Adventures in the Screen Trade*. New York: Warner, 1983.

Graham, Don. *No Name on the Bullet: A Biography of Audie Murphy*. New York: Viking, 1989.

Greco, Mike. "Hard Riding." *Film Comment* Vol. 16, No. 3/May-June 1980.

Hancock, John Lee. "Foreword." *The Alamo: The Illustrated Story of the Epic Film*. New York: Newmarket, 2004.

Hart, William S. *My Life East and West*. New York: Benjamin Blom, 1929.

Havrilesky, Heather. "The Man Behind *Deadwood*." Salon.com. March 3, 2005. http://www.salon.com/2005/03/05/milch/.

Hawks, Howard. *Hawks on Hawks*. Ed. Joseph McBride. Los Angeles: University of California Press, 1982.

Haycox, Ernest. *Trouble Shooter*. New York: Popular Library, 1936.

Haycox, Ernest, Jr. *On a Silver Desert: The Life of Ernest Haycox*. Norman: University of Oklahoma Press, 2003.

Herman, Jan. *A Talent for Trouble: The Life of Hollywood's Most Acclaimed Director, William Wyler*. New York: G.P. Putnam's Sons, 1996.

Herzberg, Bob. *Hang 'Em High: Law and Disorder in Western Films and Literature*. Jefferson: McFarland, 2013.

Heston, Charlton. *In the Arena: An Autobiography*. New York: Simon & Schuster, 1995.

Hoberman, J. "How the West Was Lost." 1991. *The Western Reader*. Ed. Jim Kitses and Gregg Rickman. New York: Limelight, 1998.

Hoberman, J., and Jonathan Rosenbaum. *Midnight Movies*. New York: DaCapo, 1991.

Hodgkiss, Clark. "Interview with Sergio Donati." *Blood, Money and Vengeance*, No. 6/1988.

Holland, Dave. *On Location in Lone Pine: A Pictorial Guide to One of Hollywood's Favorite Movie Locations for 85 Years!* Santa Clarita: Holland, 2005.

Horner, William R. *Bad at the Bijou*. Jefferson: McFarland, 1982.

Hyams, Joe. "Making *Shane*." *George Stevens: Interviews*. Ed. Paul Cronin. Jackson: University Press of Mississippi, 2004.

Jenson, Lee. "Sam and Stella." 1970. *Sam Peckinpah: Interviews*. Ed. Kevin J. Hayes. Jackson: University Press of Mississippi, 2008.

Jodorowsky, Alejandro. "Conversations with Jodorowsky." *El Topo: A Book of the Film*. Ed. Ross Firestone. New York: Douglas/Links, 1971.

Jousse, Thierry, and Camille Nevers. "Interview with Clint Eastwood." 1992. *Clint Eastwood: Interviews (Revised and Updated)*. Ed. Robert E. Kapsis and Kathie Coblentz. Jackson: University Press of Mississippi, 2013.

Joyner, C. Courtney. *The Westerners: Interviews with Actors, Directors, Writers and Producers*. Jefferson: McFarland, 2009.

Kael, Pauline. *Deeper Into Movies*. Boston: Atlantic, 1973.

Kasdan, Lawrence, and Jake Kasdan. *Wyatt Earp: The Film and the Filmmakers*. New York: Newmarket, 1994.

Kazan, Elia. "Elia Kazan on *Zapata*." *Saturday Review*. April 5, 1952.

Kazan, Elia. "Testimony of Elia Kazan." *Communist Infiltration of Hollywood Motion-Picture Industry, Part 7: Hearings Before the Committee on Un-American Activities, House of Representatives, Eighty-second Congress, Second Session (January 24, 28, February 5, March 20, and April 10, 30, 1952)*. Washington: United States Government Printing Office, 1952.

Kennedy, Burt. *Hollywood Trail Boss: Behind the Scenes of the Wild, Wild Western*. New York: Boulevard, 1997.

Kitses, Jim. "Borden Chase: An Interview." *The Hollywood Screenwriters: A Film Comment Book*. Ed. Richard Corliss. New York: Avon, 1972.

Kitses, Jim. *Horizons West*. Bloomington: Indiana University Press, 1969.

Kitses, Jim. "Peckinpah Re-visited: Pat Garrett and Billy the Kid." 1998. *The Western Film Reader*. Ed. Jim Kitses and Gregg Rickman. New York: Limelight, 1998.

Koppes, Clayton R., and Gregory D. Black. *Hollywood Goes to War: How Politics, Profits and Propaganda Shaped World War II Movies*. Los Angeles: University of California Press, 1990.

Kracauer, Siegfried. *Theory of Film: The Redemption of Physical Reality*. New York: Oxford University Press, 1960.

Kunert, Arnold, dir. *Boetticher: One on One*. Sabado Film Productions, 1989. Film.

Lake, Stuart N. *Wyatt Earp, Frontier Marshal*. New York: Houghton Mifflin, 1931.

Langlois, Gerard. "*Candide* in the Wild West." 1971. *Arthur Penn: Interviews*. Ed. Michael Chaiken and Paul Cronin. Jackson: University Press of Mississippi, 2008.

Laukhuf, Adam. "Patriot Act: Jon Voight understands that America is under attack. Why don't you?" RadarOnline.com. April 13, 2007. http://radaronline.com/features/2007/04/jon_voight_1.php/.

Lawrence, Will. "Joel and Ethan Coen on *True Grit*: We Completely Ignored the Original." *The Telegraph*. January 28, 2011. http://www.telegraph.co.uk/culture/film/filmmakers onfilm/8287138/Joel-and-Ethan-Coen-on-True-Grit-We-completely-ignored-the-origi nal.html.

Lawton, Paul J. *Images of America: Old Tucson Studios*. Charleston, SC: Arcadia, 2008.

Levy, Emanuel. *John Wayne: Prophet of the American Way of Life*. Metuchen: Scarecrow, 1988.

Libby, Bill. "The Old Wrangler Rides Again." 1964. *John Ford: Interviews*. Ed. Gerald Peary. Jackson: University Press of Mississippi, 2001.

Lloyd, Everett. *Law West of the Pecos: The Story of Roy Bean*. San Antonio: Naylor, 1931.

Lovell, Glenn. *Escape Artist: The Life and Films of John Sturges*. Madison: University of Wisconsin Press, 2008.

Macauley, Scott. "End of the Road." 1996. *Jim Jarmusch: Interviews*. Ed. Ludvig Hertzberg. Jackson: University Press of Mississippi, 2001.

Maché, Eric. "Tomas Milián: Interview—The Westerns." *Westerns ... All'Italiana!* Ed. Tom Betts. No. 25/Spring 1990.

Madsen, Axel. *William Wyler: The Authorized Biography*. New York: Crowell, 1973.

Magers, Boyd. *So You Wanna See Cowboy Stuff? The Western Movie/TV Tour Guide*. Madison: Empire, 2003.

Manfull, Helen, ed. *Additional Dialogue: Letters of Dalton Trumbo, 1942–1962*. New York: M. Evans, 1970.

Marc, David, and Richard J. Thompson, *Prime Time, Prime Movers*. Boston: Little, Brown, 1992.

Maronie, Samuel J. "On the Set with *Escape from New York*." *Starlog* No. 45/April 1981.

McBride, Joseph. *Hawks on Hawks*. Berkeley: University of California Press, 1982.

McBride, Joseph. *Searching for John Ford: A Life*. New York: St. Martin's, 2001.

McCarthy, Cormac. *No Country for Old Men*. New York: Vintage, 2005.

McCarthy, Todd. *Howard Hawks: The Grey Fox of Hollywood*. New York: Grove Press, 1997.

McDougal, Dennis. *Five Easy Decades: How Jack Nicholson Became the Biggest Movie Star in Modern Times*. Hoboken: John Wiley, 2008.

McGilligan, Patrick. *Film Crazy: Interviews with Hollywood Legends*. New York: St. Martin's, 2000.

McGilligan, Patrick. *Jack's Life: A Biography of Jack Nicholson*. New York: Norton, 1994.

McGilligan, Patrick. "Philip Yordan: The Chameleon." *Backstory 2: Interviews with Screenwriters of the 1940s and 1950s*. Ed. Pat McGilligan. Berkeley: University of California Press, 1991.

McMurtry, Larry. "Adapting *Brokeback Mountain*." *Brokeback Mountain: Story to Screenplay*. New York: Scribner, 1997.

McMurtry, Larry. "Cowboys, Movies, Myths, and Cadillacs: Realism in the Western." *Man and the Movies*. Ed. W.R. Robinson. Baton Rouge: Louisiana State University Press, 1967.

McNeill, Joe. *Arizona's Little Hollywood: Sedona and Northern Arizona's Forgotten Film History 1923–1973*. Sedona: Bar 225, 2010.

McVeigh, Stephen. *The American Western*. Edinburgh: Edinburgh University Press, 2007.

Medjuck, Joe. "Sam Peckinpah Lets It All Hang Out." 1969. *Sam Peckinpah: Interviews*. Jackson: University Press of Mississippi, 2008.

Medved, Harry, and Bruce Akiyama. *Hollywood Escapes: The Moviegoer's Guide to Exploring Southern California's Great Outdoors*. New York: St. Martin's, 2006.

Meyer, William R. *The Making of the Great Westerns*. New York: Arlington, 1979.

Meyers, Jeffrey. *Gary Cooper: American Hero*. New York: Cooper, 2001.

Miller, Arthur and Serge Toubiana. *The Misfits: Story of a Shoot*. London: Phaidon, 2000.

Missiaen, Jean-Claude. "A Lesson in Cinema." Trans. Donald Phelps. *Cahiers du Cinema in English* 12 (December 1967).

Mitchell, George J. "Ford on Ford." 1964. *John Ford: Interviews*. Ed. Gerald Peary. Jackson: University Press of Mississippi, 2001.

Mix, Paul E. *The Life and Legend of Tom Mix*. New York: A.S. Barnes, 1972.

Modleski, Tania. "Our Heroes Have Sometimes Been Cowgirls: An Interview with Maggie Greenwald." 1995. *The Western Reader*. Ed. Jim Kitses and Gregg Rickman. New York: Limelight, 1998.

Morella, Joe, and Edward Z. Epstein. *Brando: The Unauthorized Biography*. Edinburgh: Thomas Nelson, 1973.

Morrell, David. "Rambo and Me." *First Blood*. New York: Grand Central, 2000.

Mott, Michele. "The Old John Ford Talks about

Westerns." 1966. *John Ford: Interviews.* Ed. Gerald Peary. Jackson: University Press of Mississippi, 2001.

Muir, John Kenneth. *The Unseen Force: The Films of Sam Raimi.* New York: Applause, 1994.

Munn, Michael. *John Wayne: The Man Behind the Myth.* New York: New American Library, 2004.

Murray, John A. *Cinema Southwest: An Illustrated Guide to the Movies and Their Locations.* Flagstaff: Northland, 2000.

Murray, Rebecca. "Director James Mangold Brings the Wild West to Life in *3:10 to Yuma.*" About.com. 2007. http://movies.about.com/od/310toyuma/a/310yumajm82907.htm.

Neider, Charles. *The Authentic Death of Hendry Jones.* Reno: University of Nevada Press, 1993.

Norris, Chuck, with Ken Abraham. *Against All Odds: My Story.* Nashville: Broadman, 2004.

Nott, Robert. *Last of the Cowboy Heroes: The Westerns of Joel McCrea, Randolph Scott and Audie Murphy.* Jefferson: McFarland, 2000.

Nussbaum, Emily. "Must-See Metaphysics." *The New York Times.* September 22, 2002.

O'Neill, Patrick Daniel. "Scott Glenn: The Fast-Gun Astronaut." *Starlog* No. 97/August 1985.

Oller, John. *Jean Arthur: The Actress Nobody Knew.* New York: Limelight, 1997.

Parfitt, Orlando. "Director Paul Haggis on *In the Valley of Elah*: The RT Interview." RottenTomatoes.com. January 24, 2008. http://www.rottentomatoes.com/m/in_the_valley_of_elah/news/1703203/2/director_paul_haggis_on_in_the_valley_of_elah_the_rt_interview/.

Peck, Gregory. "Foreword." *Henry King's America.* Metuchen: Scarecrow, 1986.

Peterson, Jennifer. "The Competing Tunes of *Johnny Guitar*: Liberalism, Sexuality, Masquerade." 1996. *The Western Film Reader.* Ed. Jim Kitses and Gregg Rickman. New York: Limelight, 1998.

Phillips, Gene D. "Talking with John Huston." *John Huston Interviews.* Ed. Robert Emmet Long. Jackson: University Press of Mississippi, 2001.

Pierson, David. "Turner Network Television's Made-for-TV Western Films and the Social Construction of Authenticity." *Hollywood's West: The American Frontier in Film, Television, and History.* Ed. Peter C. Rollins, John E. O'Connor. Lexington: University Press of Kentucky, 2005.

Poitier, Sidney. *This Life.* New York: Knopf, 1980.

Pomeranz, Margaret. "*Three Burials of Melquiades Estrada* Interviews." *At the Movies with Margaret & David.* 2005. http://www.abc.net.au/atthemovies/txt/s1630902.htm.

PR Newswire. "The Late Gregory Peck's Interview on the *Hour of Power* to Be Broadcast Sunday, June 22, on the Discovery Channel; 'The Good Samaritan' His First Acting Role." June 19, 2003.

Pulleine, Tim. "Fire in the Streets." *Arts Guardian.* March 8, 1978.

Raymond, Emilie. *From My Cold, Dead Hands: Charlton Heston and American Politics.* Lexington: University Press of Kentucky, 2006.

Reagan, Ronald. *An American Life: The Autobiography.* New York: Simon & Schuster, 1990.

Richie, Donald. "A Personal Record: Kurosawa and I." *Akira Kurosawa: Interviews.* Ed. Bert Cardullo. Jackson: University Press of Mississippi, 2008.

Roberts, Randy, and James S. Olson. *John Wayne: American.* New York: Free Press, 1995.

Robertson, James Crighton. *The Casablanca Man: The Cinema of Michael Curtiz.* London: Routledge, 1993.

Robinson, David. "The Innocent Bystander." *John Huston Interviews.* Ed. Robert Emmet Long. Jackson: University Press of Mississippi, 2001.

Rodriguez, Elena. *Dennis Hopper: A Method to His Madness.* New York: St. Martin's, 1988.

Rosenbaum, Jonathan. *Dead Man.* London: BFI, 2000.

Rosenthal, Lee. *Catalina in the Movies.* Sausalito: Windgate, 2003.

Rothel, David. *An Ambush of Ghosts: A Personal Guide to Favorite Western Film Locations.* Madison: Empire, 1990.

Russell, Lee. "Budd Boetticher." 1965. *The Western Reader.* Ed. Jim Kitses and Gregg Rickman. New York: Limelight, 1998.

Ryan, Desmond. "A Pioneering Woman's Way with the Western." *The Philadelphia Inquirer.* September 15, 1993.

Sarris, Andrew. *The American Cinema: Directors and Directions 1929–1968.* New York: DaCapo, 1996.

Sbardellati, John. *J. Edgar Hoover Goes to the Movies: The FBI and the Origins of Hollywood's Cold War.* Ithaca: Cornell University Press, 2012.

Schaefer, Jack. *Shane.* New York: Houghton, 1949.

Schickel, Richard. *Clint Eastwood: A Biography.* New York: Knopf, 1996.

Schickel, Richard. *The Men Who Made the Movies.* New York: Atheneum, 1975.

Schmidt, Richard J. *A Field Guide to Motion Picture Locations at Red Rock Canyon—Mojave Desert, California.* Montrose: Canyon Two, 2002.

Schneider, Jerry L. *Western Movie Making Locations, Vol. I: Southern California.* Victorville: Corriganville Press, 2011.

Schweikle, Tony, dir. *Travel the Movie Trail.* Aspen: New Divisions, 1992. Video.

Segaloff, Nat. "John Milius: The Good Fights." *Backstory 4: Interviews with Screenwriters of the 1970s and 1980s.* Ed. Patrick McGilligan. Berkeley: University of California Press, 2006.

Segalof, Nat. "Walon Green: Fate Will Get You." *Backstory 3: Interviews with Screenwriters of the*

60's. Ed. Patrick McGilligan. Berkeley: University of California Press, 1997.
Server, Lee. *Robert Mitchum: "Baby, I Don't Care."* New York: St. Martin, 2001.
Shapiro, M.J. "Robert Altman: The West as Countermemory." *Cinematic Thinking: Philosophical Approaches to the New Cinema.* Ed. James Phillips. Stanford: Stanford University Press, 2008.
Sharrett, Christopher. "Fairy Tales for the Apocalypse." July 1985. *Conversations with Directors: An Anthology of Interviews from Literature/Film Quarterly.* Ed. Elsie M. Walker and David T. Johnson. Lanham: Scarecrow, 2008.
Sherman, Eric. *The Director's Event: Interviews with Five American Film-Makers.* New York: Atheneum, 1970.
Sherman, Robert G. *Quiet on the Set! Motion Picture History at the Iverson Movie Location Ranch.* Chatsworth: Sherway, 1984.
Siegel, Don. *A Siegel Film: An Autobiography.* London: Faber, 1993.
Simon, Scott. "Tommy Lee Jones, Exploring New Territory." NPR *Weekend Edition.* January 28, 2006. http://www.npr.org/templates/story/story.php?storyId=5176262.
Slotkin, Richard. *Gunfighter Nation: The Myth of the Frontier in Twentieth-Century America.* Norman: University of Oklahoma Press, 1998.
Smith, Robert E. "Mann in the Dark: The *Films Noir* of Anthony Mann." *Film Noir Reader.* Ed. Alain Silver and James Ursini. New York: Limelight, 2003.
Sollima, Sergio. Interview. "Run, Man, Run: 35 Years Running." New York: Blue Underground, 2004. Video.
Speck, Gregory. *Hollywood Royalty.* New York: Birch Lane, 1992.
Stanfield, Peter. *Hollywood, Westerns and the 1930s: The Lost Trail.* Exeter, UK: University of Exeter Press, 2001.
Stanton, Bette L. *Where God Put the West: Movie-Making in the Desert.* Moab: Canyonlands, 1994.
Stevens, George, Jr., ed. *Conversations with the Great Moviemakers of Hollywood's Golden Age at the American Film Institute.* New York: New Liberty, 2006.
Swires, Steve. "Kurt Russell & Adrienne Barbeau: Survivors of the Future." *Starlog,* No. 49/August 1981.
Tapley, Kristopher. "Michael Mann Looks Back on *The Last of the Mohicans* 20 Years Later." May 12, 2012. http://www.hitfix.com/blogs/in-contention/posts/michael-mann-looks-back-on-the-last-of-the-mohicans-20-years-later.
Tavernier, Bertrand. "Notes of a Press Attaché: John Ford in Paris." 1966. *John Ford: Interviews.* Ed. Gerald Peary. Jackson: University Press of Mississippi, 2001.

Thomas, Troy. *Joel McCrea: Riding the High Country.* Burbank: Riverwood, 1991.
Thompson, Douglas. *Clint Eastwood: Billion Dollar Man.* London: John Blake, 2005.
Thompson, Frank. *Texas Hollywood: Filmmaking in San Antonio Since 1910.* San Antonio: Maverick, 2010.
Thomson, David. "Ghost Riders in the Sky." *The Movies,* Vol. 1, No. 1/July 1983.
Thomson, David. "Niven Busch: A Doer of Things." *Backstory: Interviews with Screenwriters of Hollywood's Golden Age.* Ed. Pat McGilligan. Berkeley: University of California Press, 1986.
Turan, Kenneth. "A Fistful of Memories: Interview with Clint Eastwood." 1992. *The Western Reader.* Ed. Jim Kitses and Gregg Rickman. New York: Limelight, 1998.
Tuska, Jon. *The American West in Film: Critical Approaches to the Western.* Lincoln: University of Nebraska Press, 1985.
Tuska, Jon. *The Filming of the West.* Garden City: Doubleday, 1976.
Tuska, Jon, Vicki Pierkarski, and Paul J. Blanding. *The Frontier Experience: A Reader's Guide to the Life and Literature of the American West.* Jefferson: McFarland, 1984.
Vieira, Mark A. *Majestic Hollywood: The Greatest Films of 1939.* Philadelphia: Running Press, 2013.
Walker, David, Andrew J. Rausch and Chris Watson. *Reflections on Blaxploitation: Actors and Directors Speak.* Lanham: Scarecrow, 2009.
Walker, Michael. "The Westerns of Delmar Daves." *The Book of Westerns.* Ed. Ian Cameron and Douglas Pye. New York: Continuum, 1996.
Wallis, Hal and Charles Higham. *Starmaker: The Autobiography of Hal Wallis.* New York: Macmillan, 1980.
Wayne, Pilar, and Alex Thorleifson. *John Wayne: My Life with the Duke.* New York: McGraw-Hill, 1987.
Wellman, William A. *A Short Time for Insanity.* New York: Hawthorn, 1974.
Wheeler, Jeremy. "Q&A with John Fusco: A Screenwriter's Thoughts on Writing and Living Your Personal Legend." *Wilderness Collective.* April 12, 2013. http://wildernesscollective.com/q-a-with-john-fusco-pt-1/
Whitington, Paul. "The Big Interview: Andrew Dominick, *The Assassination of Jesse James.*" Independent.ie. November 30, 2007. http://www.independent.ie/entertainment/the-big-interview-andrew-dominik-the-assassination-of-jesse-james-26453507.html.
Wicking, Christopher. "Interview with Delmar Daves." *Screen,* 10, 4–5/1969.
Williamson, Bruce. "Robert Altman." 1976. *Robert Altman: Interviews.* Jackson: University Press of Mississippi, 2000.

Willis, Gary. *John Wayne's America*. New York: Simon & Schuster, 1998.

Wilmington, Michael. "Hot on the Trail with Mr. Jones." *Los Angeles Times*. August 1, 1993.

Wilson, Michael Henry. "'Whether I Succeed or Fail, I Don't Want to Owe It to Anyone But Myself': From *Play Misty for Me* to *Honkytonk Man*." *Clint Eastwood: Interviews (Revised and Updated)*. Jackson: University Press of Mississippi, 2013.

Wilstach, Frank J. *Wild Bill Hickok: The Prince of Pistoleers*. Garden City: Doubleday, 1926.

Wolfe, Tom. "Foreword." 1983. *The Right Stuff*. New York: Picador, 2008.

Wood, Robin. "*Rio Bravo* & Retrospect." 1981. *The Western Reader*. Ed. Jim Kitses and Gregg Rickman. New York: Limelight, 1998.

Will, Wright. *Six Guns and Society: A Structural Study of the Western*. Berkeley: University of California Press, 1975.

Yarbrough, Tinsley E. *Those Great Western Movie Locations*. Greenville: Tumbleweed, 2008.

Yeatman, Ted P. *Frank and Jesse James: The Story Behind the Legend*. Nashville: Cumberland, 2000.

Yergin, Dan. "Peckinpah's Progress: From Blood and Killing in the Old West to Siege and Rape in Rural Cornwall." 1971. *Sam Peckinpah: Interviews*. Jackson: University Press of Mississippi, 2008.

Young, Jeff, ed. *Kazan: The Master Director Discusses His Films*. New York: Newmarket, 1999.

Zelazny, Jon. "Kicking Ass with Walter Hill." *The Hollywood Interview*. December 8, 2012. http://thehollywoodinterview.blogspot.com/2009/09/walter-hill-hollywood-interview.html

Zwick, Edward. "Foreword." *The Last Samurai: The Official Movie Guide*. New York: Time, 2003.

Index

Abilene Town 35
The Alamo (1960) 82–84, 93, 158, 183
The Alamo (2004) 157–158, 183
Aldrich, Robert 63–64
Allegheny Uprising 17
Along the Great Divide 62, 174, 175
Altman, Robert 117, 129
Apache 63–64, 65, 99, 173
Apache Drums 42, 43, 174
Appaloosa 165, 182
The Appaloosa 86, 178
Arizona 20, 180
Arthur, Jean 6, 7, 20, 180
The Assassination of Jesse James by the Coward Robert Ford 160, 162–163, 184
Assault on Precinct 13 130–131
Autry, Gene 8, 27, 169, 171, 172, 174, 177

Back to Bataan 28, 46
Bad Company 118, 127
Bad Day at Black Rock 52–54, 174
The Ballad of Cable Hogue 119, 177
The Ballad of Little Jo 148–149
Belle Starr 21, 22, 182
Bend of the River 60, 61, 184
Bergen, Candice 116, 125–126
The Big Country 77–78, 174
The Big Gundown (La resa dei conti) 100–101, 106
The Big Trail 6, 7, 8, 184
Big Trouble in Little China 141–142
Billy the Kid (1941) 15, 23, 179
Blood on the Moon 35, 42, 179, 180
Boetticher, Budd 1, 67–70, 72, 97, 98, 167, 174
Bogart, Humphrey 13, 40, 41, 64, 138
Borgnine, Ernest 53, 54, 111

Brando, Marlon 48, 71, 86, 127–128, 170, 176, 178
The Bravados 78
Brokeback Mountain 159, 184
Broken Arrow (1950) 46–47, 54–55, 146
Bronson, Charles 54, 84, 96, 103, 105, 122, 124, 125, 127, 131, 140, 141, 173
Brooks, Richard 76, 99, 127
Brynner, Yul 84, 85, 174
Buchanan Rides Alone 69, 180
Buck and the Preacher 126, 127
Buckner, Robert 12, 13
Buffalo Bill and the Indians, or Sitting Bull's History Lesson 129
A Bullet for the General (Quien sabe?) 100
Busch, Niven 21, 32–34
Butch Cassidy and the Sundance Kid 111, 112–114, 116, 170, 178, 183

Cagney, James 13, 64, 72, 73, 74, 170, 172
Canyon Passage 42, 184
Cardinale, Claudia 103–104
Carpenter, John 130–131, 132, 135–136, 141–142, 154, 163, 182
Charley One-Eye 127, 184
Chase, Borden 39, 59–60, 62, 64, 66, 98
Cheyenne Autumn 92, 171, 179, 183
Cimarron (1931) 8
Coburn, James 69–70, 96, 128, 144
Coen, Ethan 160, 163–164, 165
Coen, Joel 160, 163–164, 165
Colorado Territory 37, 38, 170, 183
Comanche Station 70
Compañeros (Vamos a matar, compañeros) 105–106
Coogan's Bluff 122

Cooper, Gary 4, 6–7, 9, 16, 21, 22, 32, 34, 38, 48–49, 64, 79–81, 122, 135, 140, 143, 169, 172, 174, 176, 178
Corbucci, Sergio 96, 97, 99, 102, 103, 105, 156
Coroner Creek 36
Costner, Kevin 146, 147, 148, 150, 151–152, 153, 156, 157
The Cowboys 118, 181, 183
Cox, Alex 142–143
Craven, Wes 122, 131, 176, 177
Crawford, Joan 52, 53
Custer of the West 110

Dances with Wolves 146, 149, 150, 151, 184
Daves, Delmar 46, 54–55, 80, 179, 181, 184
Dead Man 144, 152, 153, 184
Deadwood (TV series) 156, 173, 184
Death Rides a Horse (Da uomo a uomo) 102, 156
Death Wish 122, 123–124, 125, 135, 180
Decision at Sundown 69, 70
DeMille, Cecil B. 4, 6, 7, 9, 11, 21, 140, 169, 178
Destry Rides Again 9, 17–19, 59, 170
De Toth, Andre 37, 62, 67
Devil's Doorway 47, 58, 99
Die Hard 143
Dietrich, Marlene 17–18, 19, 24
Dirty Harry 108, 122–123, 124, 125
A Distant Trumpet 92
Django 102, 105
Django, Kill... If You Live, Shoot! (Se sei vivo spara) 102
Django Unchained 167, 171, 173
Dmytryk, Edward 44, 46, 52, 78
Dodge City 9, 12–13, 16, 22, 23, 64, 170, 176
Douglas, Kirk 57, 62–63, 66, 88, 90, 91, 127, 139, 172, 174, 184

Drum Beat 54, 55, 179
Drums Along the Mohawk 17, 25, 178
Duck, You Sucker! (Giù la testa) 106
Duel in the Sun 32–33, 35, 171, 176, 180

Eastwood, Clint 1, 96, 97, 98, 99, 100, 103, 105, 108, 112, 122, 124–125, 127, 129, 131, 135, 140, 141, 143, 146–148, 154, 159, 165, 175, 176, 184
Easy Rider 111, 114, 115, 116, 127, 179
El Topo 115, 116
Escape from New York 135–136, 141

The Far Country 60, 184
The Fighting Seabees 27–29
Firefly (TV series) 156
First Blood 138–139
A Fistful of Dollars (Per un pugno di dollari) 96, 98, 102, 103, 153, 165
Flying Tigers 27–29
Flynn, Errol 12, 23, 24, 25, 32, 64, 140, 170
Fonda, Henry 14, 21, 25, 26–27, 30–31, 38, 46, 78, 79, 93, 96, 103, 108, 114, 181
Fonda, Peter 38, 114, 115, 116, 180
For a Few Dollars More (Per qualche dollaro in più) 97–98, 103
Ford, Glenn 39, 40, 68, 172
Ford, John 1, 2, 6, 7, 9, 15, 16–17, 25, 27, 28, 29–31, 38, 39, 42, 44–46, 52, 54, 55, 65, 87–88, 92, 96, 97, 98, 103, 114, 134, 140, 143, 157, 159, 167, 170, 171, 172, 175, 176, 177, 178, 179
Foreman, Carl 48–49, 52
Fort Apache 38, 45, 46, 88, 93, 172, 179
Forty Guns 76–77
Four Faces West 37, 38, 174, 181, 182
Four of the Apocalypse (I Quattro dell'apocalisse) 106
Frontier Marshal 13, 30, 174
Fuller, Samuel 76–77, 162, 178
The Furies 58, 180
Fusco, John 145, 157

Gable, Clark 66, 72, 88, 90
Garfield, Brian 123–124, 128
Garner, James 108, 109, 143, 152, 154
Geronimo: An American Legend 149, 150–151
Ghosts of Mars 154

Glenn, Scott 138, 140
The Glory Guys 93
Gold Is Where You Find It 12
Goldman, William 112–113, 136, 138
Good Guys Wear Black 139
The Good, the Bad and the Ugly (Il buono, Il brutto, Il cattivo) 98, 99–100, 103
Gran Torino 165
The Grapes of Wrath 25, 26–27, 131
The Great Northfield Minnesota Raid 118, 136, 176, 184
The Great Silence (Il grande silenzio) 105
The Great Train Robbery 4
The Green Berets 110, 142
Gunfight at the O.K. Corral 64–66, 108, 124, 170, 180, 181
The Gunfighter 44, 57–58, 116, 152, 163

Hang 'Em High 108, 182
The Hanging Tree 79–80, 81, 184
Hannie Caulder 126, 153, 184
Harris, Ed 138, 142, 143, 165
Hart, William S. 4–5, 6, 7, 143, 172
Hawks, Howard 1, 28–29, 38, 39, 49, 75–76, 81, 93, 98, 128, 130–131, 132, 134, 140, 180
Haycox, Ernest 9–10, 15
Heat 153
Heaven's Gate 131–132, 151, 184
Hellman, Monte 127, 153
Heston, Charlton 57, 66, 77, 94, 108, 128–129, 144, 152
Hidalgo 157
High Noon 48–49, 52, 80, 81, 97, 122, 125, 135, 140, 169, 176
High Plains Drifter 108, 124–125, 129, 140, 175
Hill, Walter 132, 141, 149, 150–151, 152, 153, 156
The Hills Have Eyes 122, 131, 176
The Hills Run Red (Un fiume di dollari) 99
The Hired Hand 116, 182, 183
Holden, William 20, 27, 39, 111, 180
Hombre 110, 180
Hondo 52, 55, 183
Hopper, Dennis 65, 93, 114–115, 153
Hour of the Gun 108, 109, 110
Hud 88, 90–92
Huston, John 27, 39–40, 47, 72, 119, 132, 177
Hyams, Peter 134–135

In the Line of Fire 148
In the Valley of Elah 159–160

The Indian Fighter 62, 63, 184
The Iron Horse 6, 15, 172, 177

Jeremiah Johnson 119, 178
Jesse James 9, 13–15, 73, 146, 153, 182
Jodorowsky, Alejandro 115
Johnny Guitar 52, 53, 179
Jones, Tommy Lee 154, 158–159, 167

Kasdan, Lawrence 140, 152
Kaufman, Philip 136
Kazan, Elia 47–48, 52
Kennedy, Burt 68, 93, 107–108, 126
The Kentuckian 64
King, Henry 14, 15, 57, 78, 182
Kurosawa, Akira 84, 96, 100

Ladd, Alan 50, 51, 54, 72
Ladd, Alan, Jr. 134, 136
Lancaster, Burt 57, 63–66, 99, 118, 123
Lang, Fritz 21, 23
The Last Hard Men 128–129, 180
The Last Hunt 76, 184
The Last Movie 114–115, 116
The Last of the Mohicans (1992) 149
Lawman 123
The Left-Handed Gun 74–75, 119, 170, 171
The Legend of Nigger Charley 127, 181
Leonard, Elmore 110, 124, 144
Leone, Sergio 1, 96–98, 99–100, 102, 103–104, 106, 112, 115, 153, 156, 179, 184
Let Freedom Ring 11
Lewton, Val 42, 43, 174
The Life and Times of Judge Roy Bean 119, 180
Little Big Man 117, 184
Lone Star 153, 158
Lonely Are the Brave 88, 90, 91, 139
The Long Riders 132, 176

The Magnificent Seven 64, 84–86, 99, 136, 152, 183
Magnum Force 124
Major Dundee 93–94, 183
The Man from Colorado 39, 40, 172
The Man from Laramie 60–62, 70, 181
Man of Conquest 17
Man of the West 79–80, 172, 174, 176
The Man Who Shot Liberty Valance 88, 89, 97, 110, 117, 171

Index

Man Without a Star 62, 66, 90
Mann, Anthony 1, 58–62, 68, 69, 78, 80, 97, 98, 99, 132, 140, 157, 184
Mann, Michael 149–150, 153
Marvin, Lee 68–69, 96
McCabe and Mrs. Miller 117–118, 184
McCrea, Joel 9, 10, 11, 32, 36, 37, 42, 57, 66–67, 86–87, 111, 170, 171, 172, 174, 178, 181
McLaglen, Andrew V. 93, 128
McMurtry, Larry 91–92, 121
McQueen, Steve 84, 85, 131, 175
Midnight Cowboy 111
Milián, Tomás 100–101, 102, 106, 115
Milius, John 119, 124
Minnesota Clay 96
The Misfits 88–90, 177
The Missing 158, 182
Missing in Action 139–140
The Missouri Breaks 127–128, 129, 184
Mitchum, Robert 34–35, 42, 43, 63, 98, 144, 152
Mix, Tom 4, 5–6, 7, 8, 17, 143, 171, 178, 180
Morrell, David 138–139
Murphy, Audie 55, 72–73, 170, 174, 178, 180
My Darling Clementine 1, 29–31, 38, 51, 59, 65, 88, 164, 165, 179

The Naked Spur 60, 68, 69
Nelson, Ralph 116
Nero, Franco 102, 103, 106
Newman, Paul 66, 74, 75, 88, 90–91, 110, 112, 113, 129, 131, 170, 178
Nicholson, Jack 115, 127–128, 131
No Country for Old Men 160, 163–164, 182, 183
Norris, Chuck 139–140, 141, 143

The Oklahoma Kid 13, 64, 170, 172
Once Upon a Time in the West (C'era una volta il West) 103–105, 154
One-Eyed Jacks 86, 170, 175, 176
One Flew Over the Cuckoo's Nest 127, 129
Only Angels Have Wings 28–29
Open Range 156–157
Outland 134–135, 136
The Outlaw Josey Wales 129, 147, 165, 178, 180
The Ox-Bow Incident 25–27, 44, 108

Palance, Jack 106, 144, 161
Pale Rider 140–141, 176, 184

Pat Garrett and Billy the Kid 119
Peck, Gregory 33, 40–41, 58, 77–78, 140, 173, 174, 181
Peckinpah, Sam 86–87, 93–94, 111–112, 119, 122, 132, 158, 175, 180
Penn, Arthur 74–76, 116–117, 119, 128
A Perfect World 148
A Pistol for Ringo (Una pistola per Ringo) 97
The Plainsman 6–7, 9, 80, 170, 184
The Professionals 64, 99, 127, 175, 177
Pursued 32, 33–34, 35

The Quick and the Dead 152, 153, 180

Rambo: First Blood Part 2 138–139
Ramrod 36, 37, 178
Ray, Nicholas 52, 72
Reagan, Ronald 23, 24, 27, 132, 133–143, 172
Red River 38–39, 60, 154, 180
Redford, Robert 66, 112, 113, 119, 131, 177, 178
The Return of Frank James 21, 175
Ride Lonesome 69–70, 97, 174, 175
Ride the High Country 86–87, 111, 170, 175
Ride the Whirlwind 127, 178
The Right Stuff 136–138, 143
Rio Bravo 81, 93, 124, 130, 154, 180
Rio Grande 38, 45–46, 161, 179
Ritt, Martin 91–92
Robards, Jason 103, 104, 109, 119
Rodriguez, Robert 153, 156
Rogers, Roy 8, 127, 143, 172, 174
Run for Cover 72–73, 74, 183
Run, Man, Run (Corri, uomo, corri) 101
Run of the Arrow 76, 146, 178
Russell, Kurt 135, 141–142, 151, 168
Ryan, Robert 67, 68, 111

Sands of Iwo Jima 45
Santa Fe Trail 23, 24
The Savage 47, 66
The Scalphunters 126
Schaefer, Jack 50–51
Scott, Randolph 9, 13, 15, 22, 23, 24, 35–36, 40, 57, 67–70, 86–87, 111, 143, 149, 170, 172, 174, 178
The Searchers 1, 55–56, 114, 122, 154, 159, 161, 169, 179, 183

Selznick, David O. 32–33
September Dawn 160, 184
Serenity 156
Sergeant Rutledge 87, 179
Seven Men from Now 67–69, 174
Shane 49–52, 91, 99, 140, 153, 161, 165, 184
She Wore a Yellow Ribbon 38, 45
Shenandoah 93
The Shooting 127, 178
The Shootist 129–130, 177
Siegel, Don 72, 122–123, 124
Silverado 140, 146, 182
Skin Game 126, 173
Soldier Blue 116, 117, 125, 160
The Sons of Katie Elder 93, 114, 183
Specialists (Gli specialisti) 105
The Spoilers (1942) 24, 176
The Squaw Man 4, 169
Stagecoach 9, 15–17, 18, 30, 31, 44, 110, 171, 172, 174, 176, 179
Stallone, Sylvester 138–139, 140, 141
Stand Up and Fight 9
Stanwyck, Barbara 10, 11, 18, 58, 76
Star Trek (TV series) 134, 135
Star Trek II: The Wrath of Khan 134
Star Wars 134, 135, 140, 174
Stars in My Crown 42
Stevens, George 51
Stewart, James 17–19, 27, 46–47, 57, 59–62, 68, 69, 78, 88, 89, 92, 93, 99, 117, 170, 181
Straight to Hell 142, 184
Stranger on Horseback 67, 172
Studi, Wes 149–150
Sturges, John 40, 53–54, 65, 66, 84, 86, 88, 108–110, 175
Sunset 143
Sutherland, Kiefer 145, 155, 168

Tall in the Saddle 29, 179
The Tall Men 72
The Tall T 69, 70, 174
Tarantino, Quentin 154, 156, 167, 176
Taylor, Robert 11, 23, 58
Tepepa 101–102
Tessari, Duccio 96–97
There Will Be Blood 160, 164, 183
They Came to Cordura 79–81, 178
They Died with Their Boots On 24, 25, 110, 171
They Were Expendable 28, 29, 93
The Three Burials of Melquiades Estrada 158–159, 183
3:10 to Yuma (1958) 81, 161, 174, 180

Index

3:10 to Yuma (2007) 160–162, 182
The Tin Star 78, 79, 97, 138
Tombstone 1, 144, 151–152, 180
El Topo 115, 116
Tourneur, Jacques 42, 43, 67
Track of the Cat 42, 43, 184
The Tramplers (Gli uomini dal passo pesante) 98–99
The Treasure of the Sierra Madre 39–40, 41, 47
True Grit (1969) 110, 114, 175, 183
True Grit (2010) 165–166
The True Story of Jesse James 73, 170
Trumbo, Dalton 90
24 (TV series) 155–156, 167
Two Flags West 42–43
Two Road Together 87, 183

Ulzana's Raid 118, 177
Unforgiven 1, 146–148, 156, 165, 176, 184
Union Pacific 9, 10–11, 18, 178

Vampires 154, 182
Van Cleef, Lee 97, 98, 99, 100, 101, 103, 135

Vera Cruz 64, 86, 88, 128, 183
Vidor, King 23, 32
Virginia City 22, 23, 64, 179
The Virginian (1929) 6, 9, 80, 170
Viva Zapata! 48, 71, 86, 170, 183

Wagon Master 45, 179
Walker 142–143
Wallis, Hal B. 12, 23, 62, 63, 64, 66
Walsh, Raoul 6, 7, 34, 35, 37, 72, 92, 132, 140, 174
Warlock 78–79, 138, 179
Wayne, John 4, 6, 7, 8, 16, 17, 18, 19, 24, 25, 27–29, 34, 38–39, 42, 44, 45–46, 49, 52, 55–56, 57, 60, 67, 81, 82–84, 87, 88, 89, 93, 94, 110, 111, 114, 115, 116, 118, 122, 125, 127, 128, 129–130, 131, 132, 136, 142, 143, 158, 159, 161, 165, 169, 172, 174, 175, 177, 178, 183
Welch, Raquel 126
Welcome to Hard Times 107–108, 171
Wellman, William A. 25, 26, 40, 43, 184
Wells Fargo 9, 170

Western Union 22, 178
The Westerner 21, 22, 32, 44
White Feather 54–55
Wichita 67, 172
Widmark, Richard 79, 83, 92
The Wild Angels 114
Wild Bill 152–153, 156, 173
The Wild Bunch 64, 94, 111, 112, 119, 136, 153, 154
The Wild One 55, 71
Will Penny 108, 112, 175
Willis, Bruce 143
Winchester '73 59–60, 61, 68, 124, 170, 180
Wise, Robert 35, 42
Wolfe, Tom 136–138
Wurlitzer, Rudy 119, 142, 153
Wyatt Earp 1, 151–152, 182, 183
Wyler, William 27, 77–78

Yellow Sky 40–41, 174
Yordan, Philip 52
Young Guns 144–145, 146, 149, 155, 182
Young Guns 2 144–146, 180, 182
Young Mr. Lincoln 25, 27

Zanuck, Darryl F. 13, 14, 15, 26, 27, 31

www.ingramcontent.com/pod-product-compliance
Ingram Content Group UK Ltd.
Pitfield, Milton Keynes, MK11 3LW, UK
UKHW050525150426
5217IPUK00026B/1800